D1548469

Sewing Women

COLUMBIA UNIVERSITY PRESS   NEW YORK

Sewing Women

Immigrants and the New York City Garment Industry

MARGARET M. CHIN

COLUMBIA UNIVERSITY PRESS

Publishers Since 1893

NEW YORK   CHICHESTER, WEST SUSSEX

Library of Congress Cataloging-in-Publication Data

Chin, Margaret May, 1962–

   Sewing women : immigrants and the New York City garment industry / Margaret Chin.

      p. cm. —

   Thesis (Ph. D.)—Columbia University, 1998.

   ISBN 0–231–13308–1 (alk. paper)

    1. Women clothing workers—New York (State)—New York—History. 2. Clothing

trade—New York (State)—New York—History. 3. Alien labor, Asian—New York

(State)—New York—History. 4. Alien labor, Latin American—New York (State)—New

York—History. I. Title.

   HD6073.C62U5365 2005

   331.4'887'097471—dc22

                                  2005043232

Columbia University Press books are printed on permanent and durable acid-free paper.

Printed in the United States of America

Designed by Chang Jae Lee

c 10 9 8 7 6 5 4 3 2 1

CONTENTS

This book came into being because the men and women who sew shared their experiences and thoughts with me. I am thankful for their willingness to discuss their lives. There were also many others, including representatives of the Union of Needletrades, Industrial, and Textile Employees (formerly, the International Ladies' Garment Workers' Union), the Greater Blouse and Sportswear Association, and the Korean Contractors' Association, who were also generous with their time and ideas.

Financial support came in many forms. I was supported as a graduate student by the American Sociological Association's Minority Fellows Program and the National Science Foundation provided additional research funds with a Dissertation Improvement Grant (grant no. SBR-94–00710). The Social Science Research Council provided money for further research with a Post-Doctoral Fellowship in International Migration, and the Woodrow Wilson National Fellowship Foundation Career Enhancement Award allowed me a year off to write. In addition, I received support from the Russell Sage Foundation, and the City University of New York through the Professional Staff Congress, the Diversity Projects Development Fund, and the Asian American/Asian Research Institute.

Support of another kind came from good teachers and colleagues. I would especially like to thank Herbert Gans, not only for his insightful and thoughtful comments but also for all of his wisdom, inspiration, and encouragement, which helped sustain this project. I am grateful to Katherine Newman, Kathryn Neckerman, Robert Smith, Hiroshi Ishida, Vivian Louie, Nancy Foner, Phil Kasinitz, and Gary Okihiro for giving me many useful comments and suggestions. Hunter College's Gender Equity Project and the Sociology Department both allowed me to have ample time to write. Individuals in both programs offered kind words when I needed them most.

Many others have shared their enthusiasm and interest in garment workers and ethnicity. I want to thank Shirley Hune for her continual support and advice. To two long-time friends, Melanie Hildebrandt and Kathy Kaufman, I thank them for their willingness to listen and to read. I am particularly indebted to them for their generosity.

I am grateful to my family for their loving support and encouragement. My parents, Lung and Faye, and sisters, Jade and Annette, shared their excitement in this project. My children, Alexander and Meredith, always provided much-needed distractions and diversions. And to my husband, Perry Pong, my thanks for his help, encouragement, and perspective on life.

Sewing Women

Since the mid-1800s garment work in New York City has been associated with immigration. Immigrants, from Eastern Europeans to today's Asians, have always been in the industry. In the mid-1990s, while doing fieldwork in the Chinese garment shops, I discovered, to my surprise, that the Chinese were not the only ones left in this industry. Korean immigrants operated a sector almost as large. Although the Chinese hired unionized, immigrant coethnic women, the Koreans did not—they hired mostly undocumented Mexican and Ecuadorian men and women. The two sectors are structured very differently, not only in terms of who is working but in terms of pay and even in terms of how the work floor is organized. However, these two sectors coexist in the very competitive New York City environment. How can both sectors be viable?

In this book I examine the role that garment work has played in these contemporary immigrants' lives. In particular, I consider the relationships between the owners and workers and ask when ethnic relationships are helpful and when they are not and how immigration status and gender condition workers' lives. By examining the processes that Mexican, Ecuadorian, and Chinese immigrants use to get jobs, I explore the tensions between coethnic obligation and economic necessity and try to understand how they result in coethnic exploitation or cooperation. Gender and immigration are important factors in the work opportunities that the Chinese employers and workers have. In turn, their opportunities are very different from those available to Korean employers and their Mexican and Ecuadorian workers.

For most immigrants work is central to survival in the United States; thus few would envision emigrating unless they were aware of work opportunities. Work is not just a means to earn money to survive: it plays a large role in the societal status of Chinese, Koreans, Mexicans, and Ecuadorians. Many intermediary factors determine how and where immigrants get jobs. Immigration status and the long-term goals of the individuals (to become U.S. citizens or to return to their home country) affect the kinds of jobs that they strive for and are willing to take. Wages, work hours, and benefits are important considerations if an individual has family and children in the United States. Given a choice, immigrants favor jobs that complement their household roles as parents, providers, or supporters of relatives overseas. Only in this context should we examine how ethnicity and coethnic ties matter. These bonds can be used to advance work prospects—that is, to gain access to jobs and higher wages. They can be positive when members reap benefits from ethnic ties. The ties can also be constraining when they are used to limit access to jobs or other economic opportunities.

The differences between the sectors suggest that the employment market does not operate solely on the basis of free market assumptions—that is, that immigrants will work wherever they can get the highest wages. These immigrants mostly end up in the narrowest settings, which suggests that a number of forces are channeling these immigrants into the garment industry. Are these forces connected to ethnicity and ethnic bonds? How important are structural factors, including route of emigration, neighborhoods, or the way the industry is organized? And to what degree does gender role dictate where an immigrant works? What I found was that immigration status, ethnicity, and gender are intertwined and cannot be totally disaggregated. Examining immigration status and gender provides insight into the specific mechanisms and conditions that alternately turn ethnic ties into resources or barriers in the pursuit of employment.

WHY GARMENT WORKERS?

Garment workers and garment work have always intrigued me. I often wondered why the clothing manufacturing process has remained the same for more than one hundred years. I am the daughter of a former garment worker, and the factories that I remember visiting as a young child looked very similar to the ones I visited for this study. While I was doing my research, most of my aunts were still working in factories in Chinatown. They all worked for the Chinese, and the majority of their own coworkers were also Chinese. Chinatown seemed to be filled with coethnic enterprises that brought money and jobs into the community. Garment work was only one of these enterprises. Although no one would dispute the benefits of the jobs and money that the garment industry provides for the community, many workers wished that their employers were white and not coethnic Chinese. Some felt that they were being exploited. Others thought that conditions might be better uptown in the factories owned by the older Jewish and Italian employers. I wondered why such a sharp gendered division of labor exists among the Chinese, with the majority of the women working in the garment industry and most of the men working in restaurants. I realized that the majority of studies were written with data collected only from the employers and that Chinese workers might have something very different to say.

While doing fieldwork with the Chinese, I discovered that Korean immigrants also worked in the garment sewing shops, not as workers but as employers. They hired undocumented Ecuadorians and Mexicans, both men and women. I initially thought that these two ethnic groups—Chinese and Hispanics[1]—working in the garment industry were more similar, in general, than different, and it turned out that my data supports this conclusion. Coethnicity may have little to do with how work is organized; in fact, how people get hired, trained, and paid may be a result of the route of emigration taken by the worker, the role that the worker plays in the family, the neighborhood where the factories are located, and the structural conditions in the industry.

For example, I found that some aspects of the Chinese sector, like low wages, could be overlooked and dismissed as industry standards, while an informal training program could be overidealized into a version of coethnic harmony and benefit. How do we know this if we do not compare this to the non-coethnic sector? This study is not meant to discount the advantages that accrue from coethnic relationships, but potential disadvantages should also be analyzed. Thus I needed to examine exactly when these coethnic resources are used and why, how they differ from resources in noncoethnic relationships, what kind of benefits can be derived from them, how those benefits differ among the minority groups, and how they lead to different outcomes among the different minority groups.

IMMIGRATION STATUS, GENDER, AND ETHNICITY

Immigrants often face barriers to full inclusion in the economic activities of the host society. They often lack access to network ties that are necessary to succeed

---

1. In this book I use the terms *Hispanic* and *Latino interchangeably,* following the guidelines issued by the Office of Management and Budget (OMB), dated October 30, 1997, which was applied to the 2000 U.S. Census.

in certain kinds of activities. Licensing requirements often prevent immigrants from entering professional or internal labor markets. Moreover, immigrants' skills may not be the skills that employers in the host society seek. The immigrant work sector may exhibit many features of the larger economy. But an immigrant's family may not resemble the families of citizens. Immigrant families may include both documented and undocumented residents in the United States, as well as relatives still in the home country. Legal circumstances often constrain their relationships and their ability to assist each other. I also examine worker-employer relationships, the workers' relationships with work organizations, and how ethnicity relates to these two factors.

I also examine gender differences, the supply of workers, training, and the organization of the shop floor. The process of immigration and resettlement funnels immigrants into different jobs, which sometimes redefine gender roles. Immigration status affects the workers' lives and the degree of family support that they need or acquire here in New York City. In particular, many emigrants must decide whether to bring their children or leave them in their home country. These factors affect men and women differently, including how they organize their work lives.

Hispanic men and women with few family responsibilities here in New York City have more freedom from their usual gender roles, if those roles involve being a caretaker or a homemaker. Because they often are here illegally, they leave their children in their home country. The absence of dependents allows them to pursue jobs that they might not take otherwise. Men and women can both take on the role of economic breadwinner and take whatever jobs are available in the garment industry. In this particular case, illegal immigration places Hispanic men and women in roles that are less gendered than usual in their society (at least temporarily), until they have to care for children here in New York City. Hispanic men find employment in the Korean sector of the garment as easily as Hispanic women do. Chinese men and women tend to emigrate with their children and bring with them their traditional gender roles. The Chinese sector of the garment industry is dominated by women.

Work, which includes hiring, training, pay schedules, and the organization of day-to-day production, is organized to give the owners control over their workers. This includes control of the workers' use of their own social contacts. Chinese employers encourage workers to recruit others, especially friends and kin. Employers treat their workers paternalistically. Korean employers tend to eschew nepotism among their employees. The different patterns of coethnic social relations in each sector offer both advantages or disadvantages to the workers.

By comparing these two immigrant populations in the garment industry, I hope to highlight how immigrants can or cannot influence the work situations into which they are channeled. But focusing on how social networks lead to employment downplays the cultural explanations of why immigrant women enter the garment industry. I hope to illuminate how historic, economic, and social contexts influence women to take jobs in the garment industry.

THE STUDY

I chose to do a comparative study in order to get a closer look at how immigration status, ethnicity, and gender are interrelated. I used ethnographic fieldwork, consisting of observations and interviews, to explore two sectors of the New York City garment industry—Korean factory owners whose workforce is dominated by Mexican and Ecuadorians, and Chinese factory owners, who hire Chinese almost exclusively. I draw data from almost three years of fieldwork, in 1994 to 1996 and 1999 to 2000.

My fieldwork included observing four garment shops, two owned by Chinese and two owned by Koreans. I used these observations to get a sense of the daily lives of the workers and owners. The Chinese shops were unionized and located in lower Manhattan's Chinatown; the Korean-owned shops were not unionized and were located in the West 30s and 40s in midtown Manhattan. I interviewed fifteen Chinese and fifteen Korean owners about their perspectives on hiring, work, and ethnicity. I found these thirty owners in a variety of ways, including seeking referrals from the shops where I observed and from the Chinese and Korean business associations.

I interviewed 112 workers—57 Chinese (2 men and 55 women), and 55 Hispanics (19 men and 36 women) of whom 27 were Mexican and 24 were Ecuadorian. The rest were women from Central America or the Dominican Republic. I found most of the workers in union-sponsored English-as-a-Second-Language classes, at the Garment Workers' Justice Center or at the Garment Industry Development Corporation. The latter, established in 1984, is a consortium of labor, business, and government groups that offer an array of services to maintain the competitiveness of local apparel manufacturers and contractors and to increase workers' skills (Bowles 2000).

In addition to learning about the workers and owners, I tried to understand the background and history of the garment industry. I interviewed union officials, the leaders of the Chinese and Korean contractor associations, officials from the New York State Department of Labor's Apparel Industry Task Force, and former garment workers.

ORGANIZATION OF THE BOOK

In the first chapter I review the history of the New York City garment industry. In chapter 2, I review the literature on ethnic businesses in the United States. I discuss emigration and immigration strategies used by the Chinese, Korean, and Hispanic immigrants in chapter 3, where I also introduce how gender and children affect emigration and immigrant work roles. Chapter 4 is about the people in the garment industry. In chapter 5, I discuss how the employers choose their workers. In chapter 6, I discuss the assets and liabilities associated with ethnic resources, in terms of getting a job and getting paid, and I analyze the organization of the workforce in relation to how workers are hired in chapter 7. In chapter 8, I discuss the significance of immigrant status, gender, and ethnic resources in relation to work. And in the epilogue I briefly discuss the status of the garment industry in 2004.[2]

2. "Sewing Woman" is also the name of an interesting documentary made by Arthur Dong in 1982. It is based on oral histories of his mother who was an immigrant garment worker in San Francisco.

CHAPTER I

Legacies

New York City Garment Industry

THE EARLY GARMENT INDUSTRY

At the end of the nineteenth century, urbanization, the development of a national market, and rapid population growth spawned a demand for ready-made women's wear (Kessner 1977; Waldinger 1986; Green 1997; Foner 2000). By 1880 the industry in New York City was producing 40 percent of ready-to-wear clothes, and Russian Jews were replacing Irish and German Jewish workers in manufacturing and production (Pope 1905; Helfgott 1959b). By 1909, the two leading industries in New York City were the manufacture of women's and men's clothing (Odencrantz 1919/77). By 1920 the women's garment industry had 165,000 workers (Waldinger 1986:50, Kessner 1977).

The industry adapted itself to the new Jewish immigrants from Eastern Europe who were both workers and employers. The German Jews and the Irish were in the upper ranks of the industry. They ran sewing factories inside large manufacturing firms that also designed and distributed the clothing (these shops are initially known as "inside shops") (Pope 1905). In those factories women dominated the workforce even before 1840, but as immigration increased, men took jobs as sewing machine operators, and by 1880 the men dominated many of the skilled positions that women once held.[1]

These immigrant Jewish men came mostly from Russia and Poland. They provided the garment industry with poor and industrious workers. Many had been tailors in their home country and adapted to machine production (Pope 1905). While some were experienced sewers, few knew the American work organization. They did not know how many hours of work were appropriate, nor did they know how much to request in wages (Kessner 1977). These men easily accepted whatever wages and hours the employers offered them. The garment industry soon became dominated by Eastern European Jews, employing women and increasing numbers of men. Men went into coats and suits, and young women, who usually worked between the years of adolescence and childbirth, joined the lighter trades, which produced shirtwaists, undergarments, and children's clothing (Lorwin 1924; Waldinger 1986).

The more enterprising of the first Eastern European Jews became contractors during the late 1870s and 1880s. They developed a system in which the more recent hires, usually members of their families and acquaintances from the old country, reported to work at small factories that were housed in tenements on the Lower East Side, where they also lived (Seidman 1942; Howe 1976). Kessner (1977:62) reports that the Russian Jews' ability to recruit and keep workers from their hometowns often gave them an advantage over German Jewish manufacturers. Because of their old country contacts, the Russian Jews were able to recruit workers efficiently. They also broke production into tasks that required fewer skills. For example, a job that required a skilled tailor in 1880 was performed by a semiskilled machine operator in 1905 (Kessner 1977:65). Training decreased as shops developed the task-oriented sewing process to accommodate the increasing numbers of untrained workers. This, according to Howe (1976), allowed the Russian Jews to push their workers far harder and thus produce more than the German Jewish manufacturers could.

The pay and wage system also changed during the 1870s. Pope (1905) found that the earlier, more skilled workers preferred to be paid according to the task, known as the piecework system, rather than according to the amount of time that they worked. Experienced workers found that they earned more money with the piecework system—because they could sew fast and could complete many more pieces—than if they were paid at a straight rate for whatever they produced in a given amount of time. However, the less skilled preferred the time-based system. The Eastern European employers implemented a task-based pay system, requiring workers to produce a certain number of pieces in a set amount of time. The workers received a certain base wage only if they met their quota. This system benefited the less skilled workers because they could get a more even rate of earnings over time, especially during slow seasons (Pope 1905).

The ease of recruiting coethnics did not allow employers to screen for the most capable workers. Personal connections and assurances do not guarantee skilled workers, but they may ensure loyal workers. Therefore, to ensure productivity, employers had to develop a dual pay system: one that was based on the amount of work completed (piecework), the other on number of hours worked. Thus they were able to absorb the massive numbers of newcomers without having to implement intensive training programs. At the same time, employers retained the system of homework, which was especially desirable for the Jewish women workers. Jewish women were very receptive to taking work home and to working in the smaller shops. Jewish women preferred the flexibility of working at home (Kessner 1977).[2]

During this early period, unionization became increasingly important. As Pope (1905) noted, before 1880, except for the cutters—the most skilled workers—garment workers evinced little interest in unionizing. Organizing workers was difficult because of the many nationalities, the large number of workers, homework, and the great numbers of small garment shops. However, as the workforce came to be dominated by Eastern European Jews, and as more and more factories came under the contract system, union membership increased because information about the benefits of joining passed easily among the employees. Also, the Jewish workers were willing to attend Yiddish-language meetings to discuss job conditions and ways to improve them.

Women were important in the development of the garment industry. They participated in mass manufacturing, unlike the male tailors who worked in the early custom trade (before 1840). In this early period women were also employed as cutters and were hired to manufacture pants, vests, and cloaks. By the end of the 1880s, however, women had virtually disappeared from the ranks of the cutters, and women became confined to machine operating and the less-skilled tailoring work such as buttonhole making, felling, and basting (Pope 1905; Gamber 1997). Men were considered more skilled and capable of doing the heavier work. However, this pattern changed with the entry of the less-skilled Eastern European men. These men went to work side by side with many of their coethnic women.

The dominance of Jewish workers in the garment shops started to change shortly after 1892 when homework, which was popular with Jewish women, was outlawed.[3] After this change, fewer Jewish women were willing to work in the industry. However, immigration brought many Italian women into the business. Even though Italian women liked to work at home, many new workers were willing to work in the factories because of economic necessity (Odencrantz 1919/77). The availability of a willing workforce made employers amenable to giving up homework.

Moreover, employers liked to hire Italian women because they were less sympathetic to unionization and accepted less than the standard union wage (Pope 1905). With a multiethnic workforce easily available and a diminishing supply of Jewish women workers, Jewish contractors made a decisive change in work organization and production that would increase their profits. Contractors turned from recruiting coethnics to advertising extensively in the Italian newspapers to attract women to replace Jewish workers (Odencrantz 1919/ 77:43), and the number of Italian women in the industry grew.

The task-based work system and the division of labor made the employment of some of the less-skilled Italian women possible and profitable, as had the employment of Jewish men before them (Pope 1905). Thus by 1908, despite the tendency for the "employees to be recruited from the same race as the foreman," the clothing industry became an exception, with Italians working for Jewish employers alongside other Jewish workers (Kessner 1977:77).

Italian women quickly became the second largest group in the industry. They had few alternatives, especially those who lived in the Italian district.[4] Italians, both first and second generation, dominated the industry because of its image of being clean and feminine (Kessner 1977:75). The needle trades were appealing because they evoked housewifery (Odencrantz 1919/77:39). Many Italian women had been trained in fine needlework and regarded it as similar to the individualized custom work that they had done in Italy. For those women who were not trained, the notion that they might one day make their own garments appealed to them. However, they rarely learned how to make a whole garment (Odencrantz 1919/77). For workers in New York City the emphasis was on speed and completing tasks for mass marketing, not quality and one-of-a-kind pieces (Odencrantz 1919/77). The Italian women found adaptation to task-based work and, later, section work[5] to be difficult because they were virtually untrained in machine skills. Italian men, unlike Jewish men, often took jobs that required heavy labor, positions that were often unstable and low paying; thus Italian women, unlike most Jewish women, were often compelled to work into their childbearing years.[6] The majority worked in the garment industry.

The hiring of thousands of Italian women drastically altered the character of the industry, again creating a female-dominated industry of mixed ethnicities. With homework outlawed, work organization moved into larger factories that used an even greater division of labor.

By 1910 fashion buyers congregated regularly in New York City, attracted by many factors. Textiles were available in a greater variety and at better prices. New York was a leading port city with textiles entering both domestically and internationally. Buyers were also close to sources of textile production (Rischin 1962). Moreover, New York was a cultural capital and hub for travel to Europe. Thus the city was particularly sensitive to fashion change (Waldinger 1986).

Immigration slowed drastically after the passage of the Immigration and Naturalization Act of 1924. However, the garment industry did not immediately feel a labor shortage. The immigrant population was still large, even after

Jews and their children started to move up and out of the garment industry in the 1910s and 1920s (Helfgott 1959a, 1959b). Both first- and second-generation Italians, whose mobility was slower, remained in the industry (Kessner 1977; Helfgott 1959a, 1959b). This was confirmed in 1911 when the Dillingham Commission Report on Immigration noted the importance of the garment industry, even for second-generation Italians (Kessner 1977).

The task-based work system, and later an even more elaborate division of labor called section work, and larger factories were standard in the industry until the advent of large-scale Chinese coethnic employment and ownership during the late 1960s and 1970s. The major changes between World War I and the 1960s included formalizing hiring, the growth and development of unionization, and the entrance of black and Puerto Rican workers.

Union Relationships with Workers

The International Ladies' Garment Workers' Union (ILGWU), chartered on June 23, 1900 (Lorwin 1924), was influential in organizing Jewish workers against their Jewish employers. The first significant test of this relationship occurred during the ILGWU strike in 1909–10. Known as the Uprising of the 20,000, the strike was a telling sign of the union's increasingly multiethnic membership. In all, nearly 30,000 workers struck, including 21,000 Jewish women, 2,000 Italian women, 1,000 American women, and 6,000 men (Green 1997:54).[7] The impromptu strike, to protest the women's poor working conditions, began in November and lasted until February 1910, when the women won a fifty-two-hour workweek and provisions for work in off-seasons, among other concessions. This strike was especially significant for the Jewish workers in the union, because only 55 percent of the women were Jewish in this particular branch of the union, which was 80 percent female (Lorwin 1924:149).[8]

But why did so many Italian women stay at their machines? Only after the strike did the union turn to organizing Italian women, many of whom had stayed on the job because they feared being fired. At the ILGWU convention in 1910, a resolution that asked for the formation of an Italian local was presented and rejected. The ILGWU leadership, which was mostly Jewish, decided that representation should be by craft and locals rather than by nationality. Moreover, if Italian workers had their way, all the other immigrant groups would want separate locals as well (Green 1997). Resolutions to charter Jewish, non-Jewish, and non-Italian locals were struck down. The ILGWU maintained that worker unity was paramount.[9]

However, by 1922 Italian locals were an integral part of the union.[10] Although Italian and Jewish workers had their differences during this period, many members believed in uniting workers in fraternal bonds regardless of national or religious origins. Although sanctioning Italian locals brought closer relations between the Jewish and Italian workers, this cooperation was also a "sign of the newcomers becoming old-timers and consolidating their joint power within the union" (Green 1997:226). Even so, many thought the ILGWU remained basically a Jewish union with mostly Jewish leadership (Green 1997).

On the factory floor the increase in Italian representation in the union meant easier access to union benefits for Italian workers but did not necessarily mean better treatment and different work organizations in the Jewish-owned shops. In the 1930s, even when the workforce industry-wide was fairly evenly divided between Italians and Jews, the bosses were five times more likely to be Jewish. In contrast, Italians were almost twice as likely to be workers (Kessner 1977).

According to Waldinger (1996), New York's garment industry grew in the 1920s and 1930s, although its market share diminished. Work opportunities spread outside New York City. The increasing costs of labor in New York City and improvements in technologies allowed firms to aggressively seek out less expensive labor elsewhere and helped garment factories flourish beyond the New York City limits. A brief downturn occurred in the industry during the Depression and 1930s; however, the demand for clothing increased once again during World War II and beyond.

Section work, which was even more differentiated than task-based work, gained acceptance among the newer workers and garment shop owners, although older skilled workers were greatly opposed to it. Because these workers dominated the union, they were able to prevent large-scale introduction of section work until World War II (Hall 1959).

World War II—1965

A few black workers gained access to the garment industry during a World War I labor shortage (Wrong 1974). During the war and for the next twenty to thirty years, a small number of African Americans were employed to make less expensive and less complicated clothing in shops that accommodated workers with fewer skills (Spero and Harris 1931:178, 337). Then, during World War II, African Americans made significant strides in the industry.

The period from World War II to 1965 was a time when shortages of Jewish and Italian workers created opportunities for members of nonwhite ethnic groups. Until 1965, when its demographics changed significantly, New York City's population remained at just under eight million people. The changes in the ethnic composition of the city, which would come to be reflected in the garment industry, were followed by a restructuring of the clothing business. The majority of the employers continued to be mixed white ethnics, but nonwhite ethnic workers began entering section production jobs.

Since the turn of the century the industry had evolved along with the city's ethnic composition, changing from a business dominated by coethnics to non-coethnics and from male to female workers. The industry also stepped further from its informal hiring techniques. Shortly after World War II, in the 1950s, as employers grew more distant socially from their workers' networks and as they experienced a shortage of labor, garment employers turned to formalized union hiring halls and the local offices of the New York state employment service (Laurentz 1980; Waldinger 1986). Section work and formalized hiring from agencies were just two ways in which the industry maintained itself before the arrival of large numbers of Chinese coethnic employers and workers.

Throughout the 1960s the garment industry declined in New York City, especially because owners were moving factories elsewhere to escape the union. However, New York City never lost all its garment production work because of the availability of labor willing to do the work, the erosion of the union, and the convenience of being close to suppliers and designers. According to Waldinger (1986), New York–based manufacturers needed both proximity and speed during this postwar period.[11] Contractors in New York City were able to keep lead times short because they had few transportation and communication costs. Local contractors were more flexible and could handle small orders and style changes quickly, unlike larger factories that were located in the South or a foreign country. Thus the more stylish manufacturers or those who needed to keep inventory low relied on these contractors or garment factories. Sewing factories provided just one source of the multitude of external economies that have kept manufacturers and all ancillary services, such as button sellers, trim makers, and pleaters, in New York City.

Between the end of World War II and the late 1960s, the garment industry attracted American-born members of racial minority groups, including blacks, Puerto Ricans, and some Chinese Americans. The apparel industry was unionized, secure, well paying, and often the only industry that would hire these groups (Wrong 1974; Bao 2001; Ortiz 1996).

While there is some literature on African Americans in the garment industry, I found little discussion of their relationship with the Jewish employers, other than a brief mention in Wrong's 1974 survey of employer preferences for nonblack minority workers. More has been written about the relationship of African American workers to the industry as a whole and to the union. Union membership gave black workers some mobility in the industry, despite a period in the 1950s when garment owners were interested only in decreasing the skill level required to produce garments, thus keeping wages low in the industry (Hall 1959). However, that was when blacks and Puerto Ricans entered the industry in great numbers.

Other Minorities Move into the Industry

While African Americans and Puerto Ricans were replacing white ethnic workers who were leaving the industry, Chinese immigrants entered the clothing business both as workers and garment shop owners and used the industry as a vehicle for upward mobility, just as the Eastern European Jews had before them.

AFRICAN AMERICANS

During and right after World War II the garment industry saw a general increase in the demand for workers (Waldinger 1996). Improved economic conditions and wartime growth and demand supported whatever quantities manufacturers could produce with whatever facilities and labor they could find (Waldinger 1986). Employers suffered acute labor shortages and could no longer fill even their least-skilled jobs (Wrong 1973; Waldinger 1986, 1996). As the war continued, openings were filled by newcomers who were willing to accept minimum wage. As a result, by 1950 more than 20,000 black workers were employed in the industry, which had fewer than 3,000 African American workers in 1940 (Waldinger 1996) Likewise, in 1950 the garment industry had nearly 13,000 native-born Hispanic workers, where only 1,400 were employed in 1940 (Waldinger 1996:142). By 1950, 7.1 percent of all apparel workers and 7.6 percent of female apparel workers were black (Wrong 1974:34).

The Great Migration increased the number of black New York City residents before and during World War II. White workers left the city to take jobs in the war industries, and apparel industry employers turned to blacks to fill their vacancies and meet wartime orders (Helfgott 1959b; Northrup 1944; Wrong 1974). The garment industry added nearly sixty thousand jobs between 1940 and 1950. These opportunities during the war and postwar periods favored blacks, especially women. During this period African Americans reached their all-time employment high in the industry but rarely reached management (Waldinger 1996). Increased competition between older immigrant workers and blacks, coupled with the downward pressure on wages from contractors outside New York City, helped keep African Americans in the lowest-paying garment industry jobs (Helfgott 1959b).

Although white migration from the garment industry created openings for blacks in the 1960s, factories continued to leave the city in search of a less-expensive, nonunionized labor force. Moreover, African Americans were seeing competition for garment industry jobs from other minority groups, especially Puerto Ricans and Chinese. For example, by the 1960s New York City employers preferred to hire Puerto Ricans over blacks because many employers believed that Puerto Rican women had a tradition of needlework in their upbringing and therefore brought that skill with them to the job. Many employers believed that African Americans did not make good needle workers, whereas owners favored Puerto Ricans because they were more willing to put up with inferior working conditions and to accept direction without question (Wrong 1974). The other minority group in competition with African Americans was the Chinese, who did not compete directly with blacks for jobs. Nonetheless, the Chinese may have reduced the number of jobs available to African Americans. Approximately seventy-five hundred Chinese workers were employed in 250 Chinese-owned shops in New York's Chinatown in the late 1960s and 1970s (Wrong 1974:103). Thus although the actual number of garment industry jobs available in New York City decreased, African Americans were unable to increase their share of apparel work in the 1960s.

Puerto Ricans

In the 1950s emigration from the island of Puerto Rico greatly increased the numbers of Puerto Ricans in New York and established their presence in the city. Like blacks, Puerto Ricans, especially women, replaced the garment industry's retiring white ethnics, whose sons and daughters were not interested in the garment industry (Waldinger 1996). From a low of only 1,400 native-born and 1,900 foreign-born Hispanic workers in 1940, the garment industry saw 13,500 native-born workers and 20,700 foreign-born Hispanic workers holding needle trades jobs by 1980. By 1990, however, the garment industry saw a significant decline in the numbers of native-born and foreign-born Hispanic workers, to 5,029 and 14,547, respectively, because of a decline in the industry and because foreign-born Asian women had replaced many Puerto Ricans (Waldinger 1996:142).

Puerto Ricans faced many of the same conditions that blacks did. While Puerto Rican representation on the shop floor increased, very few were able to break into the leadership of the ILGWU. Thus they had little influence to improve wages and shop floor conditions. They were also conspicuously absent from the better-paid shops and the men's coat and suit industry. Puerto Ricans were more heavily represented among workers in children's apparel, rainwear, and women's clothing (Ortiz 1996). By the 1960s Puerto Ricans too were beginning to feel the changes in the industry. However, they did not turn away from the industry in the large numbers the way blacks did. Between 1950 and

1970, the proportion of blacks employed in the garment industry remained the same, while the percentage of Hispanics tripled.[12]

Black and Puerto Rican workers have always worked in the lowest-paid sectors. The exodus of garment industry jobs from the city in the two decades after World War II coincided with trends toward globalization and decentralization, thus decreasing the amount of work that was available to local New York City contractors (Waldinger 1986). Lower wages in the South and in foreign countries served to depress wages within New York City as contractors sought to remain competitive (Helfgott 1959b).

Waldinger (1986, 1996), Wrong (1974), and Ortiz (1996) suggest that other factors convinced African Americans and Puerto Ricans to search for jobs elsewhere. Waldinger (1996) suggests that after passage of the Civil Rights Act of 1964 and the implementation of affirmative action, minorities found better opportunities elsewhere and left the industry as soon as they could. Elaine Wrong (1974), who conducted fieldwork in the garment industry in the 1960s, also found a scarcity of black "job applicants during periods when welfare rolls were climbing" (63), suggesting that the unemployed had calculated that welfare checks were often more generous than what they could expect to earn on the shop floor. Employers also reported that fewer young African Americans were seeking jobs in the garment industry (Waldinger 1996). With better opportunities elsewhere, blacks and Puerto Ricans no longer looked for jobs in the garment industry.

Many blacks believed that the union played a role in limiting their opportunities in the industry. Although black membership and participation in ILGWU activities expanded after World War II, there were signs of dissatisfaction. Despite their presence and importance in the garment industry, no African Americans were represented among the top union leadership as late as 1960 (Northrup 1944; Wrong 1974). Black workers also believed that the Yiddish- and Italian-language locals were holding jobs for members of their own groups (Wrong 1974:53).[13] For example, many black men were overlooked for training as cutters.[14] The rules set up by the union to prevent nonunion members from assuming union jobs were profoundly discriminatory against the black workers.[15] Many black and Puerto Rican workers believed that the union was impeding their progress in the industry (Laurentz 1980).[16]

Wage competition from outside New York City kept wages depressed and discouraged black and Puerto Rican participation. Between 1964 and 1980, the New York garment industry lost hundreds of thousands of jobs. The contraction of the industry, and the lack of opportunity and training to move into better positions, explains why blacks and Puerto Ricans remained on the lower rungs and why they ceased to enter the industry in significant numbers (Laurentz 1980; Ortiz 1996).

Changes in Work Organization

Little has been written about changes in work organization after World War II. From what has been written, it appears that employers did very little reorganizing, except to move out of New York City to search for less-expensive labor (Waldinger 1986; Wrong 1974). We can infer a gradual change in hiring practices. Although the union was losing membership because contractors were moving to nonunion states or out of the country, by the 1960s the ILGWU and New York State Department of Labor had arranged for hiring halls to help employers find workers. Employers had few connections in the African American and Puerto Rican communities and could no longer recruit through word of mouth (Wrong 1974; Waldinger 1986).

According to Wrong (1974), few blacks were able to network within the industry, which meant that few African American workers were recruited through personal social contacts. On the other hand, some Puerto Rican workers who came into the industry in the 1960s seemed to be able to recruit co-ethnic workers (Wrong 1974). Such social support on the job may be one reason why Puerto Ricans stayed in the industry longer.

CHINESE AMERICANS

Native-born Chinese made their first entrance into the garment industry during the 1940s and 1950s. They entered as both sewers and garment shop owners. Few Chinese women quoted in the literature said that they worked or knew others who worked in the Jewish- or Italian-owned garment factories. In fact, New York City had very few Chinese women before World War II. In 1940 there were six Chinese men for every Chinese woman (Zhou 1992:34). However, after World War II many Chinese women entered the United States as a result of the War Brides Act of 1945, which permitted wives of members of the U.S. armed forces to enter the United States.[17] From 1944 to 1953 women comprised 82 percent of Chinese immigrants to the United States (Bao 2001).

The Chinese who owned garment factories on the Lower East Side of Manhattan in the 1950s were ambitious. According to Bao (2001) and Kwong (1987), Chinese owned three or four shops in 1950. By the mid- to late 1950s, they owned about fifteen shops on the Lower East Side and in Chinatown. According to three informants who worked in these shops, the owners were American-born sons and daughters of Chinese parents who were shopkeepers or laundry owners. The parents provided the capital to invest in these garment shops, or the owners used their GI benefits to buy the shops. Kwong (1986) and Bao (2001) also mention the entrance of World War II veterans into the industry as garment shop proprietors.

These early factories were created in an effort to duplicate the success of their Jewish neighbors on the Lower East Side and to provide opportunities for the second-generation Chinese. Thus while much of the literature assumes that the garment industry has always been an immigrant industry (in fact, after World War II the industry was dominated by nonimmigrants), second-generation Chinese who were looking for upward mobility entered the garment industry as entrepreneurs. These were the pioneers who countered tradition by not opening a laundry, a business that was in decline after the introduction of washing machines (Zhou 1992).[18]

THE CHINESE AND THE UNION

From the start, the relationship of the Chinese and the union was different from black and Puerto Rican workers' relationship with the ILGWU. New York City's Local 23 of the ILGWU began to gain Chinese members as early as 1957 (Bao 2001). However, the drive for unionization of Chinese workers started at the top, with the manufacturers who distributed work to the Chinese garment shop proprietors (Bao 2001). According to a former ILGWU organizer, few union organizers spoke Chinese or had access to the female workers in Chinatown. He acknowledged that union organizers were uncomfortable going into a closed community. At the time the simplest way to organize was to approach the midtown manufacturers, white men who spoke English, like the ILGWU organizers. These manufacturers wanted steady production by good workers. This was difficult because many garment factories owned by Jewish and Italian proprietors were no longer profitable and were either leaving New York City or closing altogether (Wrong 1974; Waldinger 1986).

The ILGWU, which was losing membership, was willing to offer the midtown manufacturers a deal. These manufacturers agreed to only send their work to unionized garment shops. With this concession in hand, the ILGWU approached the Chinese garment shop owners, who were more than willing to sign their workers up for union membership to guarantee steady production. Moreover, the union benefits would help ensure that these shops had a stable workforce (Bao 2001).

The workers had no objection to being members of the union. Unfortunately, they had little idea of what a union was (Bao 2001). A seventy-year-old Chinese woman, who formerly worked in the garment industry, told me: "Who would complain? We also got vacation pay and health benefits and even money if someone in our family died. Everyone signed up, and we didn't have to pay for membership. Every year, in the early 1960s, the owner would pay for us."

By 1969, 23 percent of Chinatown residents interviewed in a survey conducted by Columbia University students were working in the apparel industry (Chinatown Study Group 1969:52). Throughout the 1960s Chinese membership in the ILGWU grew despite declines in almost all other affiliates in New York. In 1971 Local 23-25, which had greatest number of Chinese members in the nation, became the largest ILGWU affiliate (Bao 2001).

Chinese women were recruited directly into the union by their bosses. Unionization helped both employers and employees. Employers were able to solicit work from the manufacturers who would give work only to unionized shops, while the women automatically received union benefits. This unprecedented organizing move left the union with a membership that understood little of what a union stood for, except health insurance benefits. As a result, Chinese women did not play a significant role in the union until the 1980s (Bao 2001).

The entrance of the Chinese into the garment industry created significant changes in work organization to accommodate coethnic women workers and employers. This work organization remains in place today. In the chapters that follow, I will discuss the impact of these changes as well as the historical role that the Chinese owners played.

1965–PRESENT

Globalization and Immigration

The advent of global production, restructuring of the manufacturing industries, and changes in immigration patterns all affected the new immigrants' role in the garment industry. Worldwide competition affected the wage levels of the workers. The erosion of job opportunities seemed not to affect the new immigrants as much as it did the native-born workers who left the business. Although the city had lost large numbers of manufacturing jobs as well as thousands of garment jobs, small garment firms emerged to fill a niche in mid- to high-priced goods (Waldinger 1986).

From 1970 to 1987 the garment industry in New York lost an average of 2.8 percent of its jobs annually (Bonacich et al. 1994). However, the continuing presence of garment shops in New York City shows that the industry was still evolving within the context of larger global economic changes (Friedman 1992; Foderaro 1998). Even with increased competition from foreign imports, the garment industry has been resilient in the United States and in New York City in particular.[19]

Having a local garment production center allowed manufacturers the quick turnaround time that they needed for women's fashions (Waldinger 1986). This production center was located in New York, because the city had long been the fashion design capital of the United States (Abeles et al. 1983; Kwong 1987; Waldinger 1986). Moreover, advances in computer technology allowed manufacturers to analyze product sales and to quickly and locally produce more of any product that they needed. This matters to producers' bottom line (Foderaro 1998).

But the resilience and growth of the garment industry have much to do with the economic restructuring of New York City as well. As Sassen (1983) argues, New York City had to restructure its economy by attracting service businesses that create high-wage jobs, those in finance, insurance, and real estate. To serve the needs of these new high-wage employees, immigrants and minorities often take low-wage jobs.

As city officials concentrated on reviving the city's economy in the 1980s, immigrants were once more flocking to New York City. Among the investors attracted to the city were prominent fashion design houses. New York City had the communications and finance connections that facilitated the marketing of fashion products globally and locally, a sizable local population willing to buy such products, and plenty of immigrants who could produce them.

During the 1980s Donna Karan, Liz Claiborne, Anne Klein, Eileen Fisher, and many other notable designers and manufacturers decided to open design houses in New York City (Kurt Salmon Associates 1992). Moreover, other designers and manufacturers, like Bill Blass, Geoffrey Beene, Oscar de la Renta, and Nicole Miller continued to make most of their apparel in New York City. More recently, Jones New York, J. Crew, Eddie Bauer, and Victoria's Secret have also started to make swimwear in New York City (Foderaro 1998). At the same time, the number of Asian and Hispanic immigrants increased. By the 1980s, at its peak, the Chinese garment industry counted more than five hundred sewing shops with more than twenty thousand Chinese workers (Abeles et al. 1983; Kwong 1987; Bao 2001; Park 1997). And the Koreans added four hundred garment shops, with nearly fourteen thousand Hispanic workers (according to IL-GWU officials and officers of the Korean contractors' association). Fueled by the increase in demand for designer and high-priced clothes and the availability of workers to produce garments, the New York City garment industry was the second-largest apparel producer in the United States after Los Angeles (Bonacich et al. 1994).

Thus in the 1990s New York City still had a significant garment industry, albeit one that was smaller than in decades past. Immigrants such as Chinese, Koreans, Mexicans, and Ecuadorians are vital in this industry. New York City no longer concentrates on large orders, but new technologies in communications have made small refill orders very profitable.

In 1995 the ILGWU merged with the Amalgamated Clothing and Textile Workers' Union to become the Union of Needletrades, Industrial and Textile Employees (UNITE). The union's hope was to become stronger so as to withstand labor abuses. But the proliferation of small garment shops producing nonunion clothing further weakened the union's influence. The importance of the ILGWU, and subsequently UNITE, to some workers diminished, especially for those members who branched out to work in unionized hotels and other industries. The union took a new tack, by educating new immigrant Chinese and Hispanic workers in the early 1990s. According to union organizers, to strengthen its ties to its members, the union opened Garment Workers' Justice Centers in key neighborhoods—midtown Manhattan, Sunset Park, Brooklyn, and Chinatown. These centers offered English classes, naturalization information, and worker's rights information, to make the union more attractive to Hispanic and Chinese workers, both members and nonmembers, even those who were undocumented, and to inform them about what a union could do for them. While the workers were pleased with the availability of classes, it was unclear how successful they were in strengthening the position of the union among those who did not understand the union's role.

The confluence of global conditions and the entrance of undocumented workers have made union organizing all the more difficult. The union stands at a crossroad. It can either advocate for all workers—so that garment jobs remain in the United States—because even the most exploitative garment shop will remain so long as it can hire workers willing to put up with the conditions. Or the union can advocate for the elimination of sweatshops altogether, which would drive many of the garment jobs away—taking with them union fees and dues paid by members and, of course, the jobs that these workers need so desperately.

CHAPTER 2

Doing Ethnic Business

In 1950 New York City was a major center of U.S. manufacturing. Apparel manufacturing was its anchor, accounting for 32.8 percent of manufacturing employment. However, by 1996 apparel had slipped to only 7.9 percent of manufacturing employment, and apparel accounted for only 2.2 percent of employment citywide (Levitan 1998). Even with this drastic decline, women's outerwear production became a larger proportion of all clothing produced. In fact, women's outerwear grew from 46.5 percent of garment industry employment in 1974 to 69.9 percent in 1996 (Levitan 1998). Most of my fieldwork involved workers who make women's apparel.

The ability of the garment industry to hang on by a thread in New York City is part of a much broader phenomenon of global restructuring that is characterized by flexibility. Specialty designers and retailers no longer needed to send their sewing overseas. This is especially true for those who want a small order to test the market or a quick run of a particular piece that is selling far above expectations. Such jobs are not worth the planning that overseas production requires. Moreover, the cost of the small run in New York City is usually not much greater than overseas production would be. New York City–based designers or retailers can send their runner the few blocks to a small Korean-operated shop to request that the work be done. Or they can take their product to a contractor in Chinatown. Whichever contractor in New York City who can produce the items for the least cost will get the production job. The garment industry in New York City is uniquely structured with a clear division of labor. At the top of the business hierarchy are the retailers and designers who sell and design clothing for the public. The next step below are the jobbers, who coordinate the actual production of the garment—including acquiring the materials such as cut cloth, buttons and zippers, thread and tags. And on the bottom are the contractors, who actually produce the garment for the jobbers.[1]

This hierarchy is also stratified by profits and racial differences. For each dress that the retailer sells for $100, $50 is profit. The other $50 is split between the jobber and the contractor. Ultimately, on average the jobber will spend 22.5 percent, or $22.50, on fabric and notions and keep $12.50 as profit. The remaining 15 percent, or $15, goes to the contractor to pay for labor and other expenses. In the end the worker who actually sews the dress will probably get only $6 (Bonacich and Appelbaum 2000).

In New York City, Asians and Hispanics share the bottom in the contractor sector, as both workers and employers. They are in the lowest tier and earn the least. Data from a 1998 report on the New York City garment industry show that 83.5 percent of operators, fabricators, and laborers (who make the garments) were of either Hispanic or Asian descent. On the other hand, at the very top, with the best-paying positions are whites, who hold 54 percent of the executive, administrative, and managerial positions, 67.2 percent of the professional specialty jobs, and 68.8 percent of marketing and sales positions (see table 2.1).

In New York City the ethnic division of labor is very specific, although the data in table 2.1 do not capture it. Asians in particular are employers in many contractor shops. Typically, they are educated, English-speaking Koreans and Chinese who hire either Hispanic or Chinese immigrants. Many Koreans, and some Chinese, had professional jobs in their home country but are not able to obtain the same kind of employment in the United States because of their inability to meet licensing requirements and their lack of contacts in the mainstream economy. Korean and Chinese employers receive just a small portion of the profits earned from the sale of garments. Both the Chinese and Korean employers serve as contractors, and their work is full of risk because they have no guarantee of long-term contracts; they hire Chinese and Latino workers who do the lowest-paid work of all.

The modern garment industry is a very different industry from that of the midtwentieth century. No longer is large-scale, overseas mass production appropriate for assembling all garments. The smaller, more flexible local contractor is in high demand. However, if demand falls short for particular garments, the small contractor is also expendable. Asians and Hispanics feel the brunt of the economic fluctuations in the industry. If Chinese and Korean contractors cannot get job orders, they cannot provide work for their Chinese and Hispanic employees.

In 1996 nearly 70 percent of all manufactured clothing in New York City was produced in these Chinese- and Korean-owned garment factories, accord-

TABLE 2.1   *Racial/Ethnic Group Share by Percentage of Occupations in New York City Garment Industry*

Occupation/Group	White	Black	Hispanic	Asian	Percentage of total
Executive, administrative, managerial	54.0	5.5	25.4	15.0	9.1
Professional specialists	67.2	7.9	16.6	8.3	4.3
Technicians	18.8	0.0	51.9	29.3	0.2
Marketing and sales	68.8	10.8	13.4	7.0	5.2
Administrative support, clerical	36.3	20.7	32.3	10.7	9.6
Service	18.1	2.6	66.3	13.0	0.9
Precision production	30.9	15.0	37.9	16.3	10.2
Operators, fabricators, and laborers	12.1	5.4	43.5	40.0	55.1
Race/Ethnic Group Share of Total	25.3	9.3	38.1	26.8	100.0

Source: Mark Levitan, *Opportunity at Work: The New York City Garment Industry* (New York: Community Service Society, 1998), table 4, p. 31.

ing to garment union officials and other people I interviewed. Most residents of New York City did not even realize that Manhattan is home to hundreds of small garment factories. The Chinese garment shops employed twenty thousand workers and the Korean shops, twelve thousand, making this industry one of the largest employers of Asian and Hispanic immigrants (see tables 2.2 and 2.3 for summaries of their similarities and differences).

The Chinese and Korean factories have a very different look and feel about them. The Chinese contractors hire only other Chinese to work in their shops. The Manhattan shops are situated in Chinatown and are a part of the ethnic community and economy.[2] The Chinese workers and their employers share a native language. In fact, some contractors were former employees. Chinese workers develop relationships with the owner-employers that offer mutual benefits—often their children attend public schools on similar schedules, which means that both employer and employee bring their children to work on weekends and holidays, and class divisions are muted because of their common eth-

TABLE 2.2   *The Chinese- and Korean-owned Shops in the New York Garment Industry: Similarities*

Both

1. produce moderately priced women's clothing

2. attract producers who want a "made in USA" label

3. are flexible, able to produce short runs of fashionable items

4. are competitive

5. have been in business for less than ten years

TABLE 2.3   *The Chinese- and Korean-owned Shops in the New York Garment Industry: Differences*

	Chinese	*Korean*
Unionized	Yes	No
Coethnic workers/employer	Yes	No
Documented workers	Yes	Few
Training	Yes	No
Work organization/pay	Piecework	Section work at hourly rate
Wages	Lower/changes with work	Higher/hourly wage
Location	Chinatown	Midtown
Gender of workers	95 percent female	65 percent female

nic/racial background. Moreover, Chinese women workers develop close relationships with each other; their shared culture and language attract a steady stream of new Chinese women workers and underpin an informal training system for newcomers.

Shared ethnicity, however, does not eliminate worker grievances. Chinese workers often feel exploited by their Chinese employers because they are paid by piece rates, which often mean wages even lower than those paid to undocumented Hispanics.[3] Chinese employees believe that working for white-owned garment shops would be an improvement because they would be paid hourly wages instead of piecework rates.

The Koreans hire mostly undocumented Hispanics who work on small assembly lines. Few Korean coethnics want these jobs; most are interested in going into business for themselves. Korean employers have little trouble communicating in Spanish. While they are not of the same ethnicity, Korean employers and their Hispanic workers have shared similar experiences as recent immigrants. Both Koreans and Hispanics consider themselves hard-working immigrant Americans, whether they have proper documentation or not. The Hispanics feel that Koreans understand their economic situation better than whites would. Koreans, they feel, at least give Hispanics an opportunity to work for minimum wage. The best workers are highly sought after by Korean employers and can shop around for the best pay. The newest immigrants, however, are often taken advantage of and offered rates for their work way below the minimum wage.

The workers are not completely exploited. Some are at the bottom of the pay scale and receive health benefits, whereas others receive a higher wage but no benefits.

CHINESE IN CHINATOWN, HISPANICS AND KOREANS IN MIDTOWN

9 A.M. CANAL STREET #6 AND N SUBWAY STATION

At the subway stop I watch the throng of Chinese women heading for work at the garment shops. They fan out north, south, east, and west toward the garment shops in and around the Chinatown area. Many go to the large shops just north of Chinatown—toward SOHO and little Italy. Others head toward shops on the west side of Broadway off Canal Street, and some even go farther, to the tiny shops in the tenement buildings on East Broadway. On their way they pass the still-closed Chinese gift stores and specialty shops. Some bakeries and grocery stores are open.

Women shop as they go to work—sometimes buying vegetables and fruits and sometimes breakfast or lunch. Street vendors and stores are just preparing the cooked foods and fresh fruits that they will sell during the lunch hour. It looks as though all these women were just shopping and not actually on their way to work. On the street level I see no indications that factories are nearby. However, when I look up through the large windows of the century-old loft buildings, I can see the tubes of fluorescent lights, the steam billowing from windows, and the piles of cloth. Occasionally, I can also see clothing hanging on racks just inside the windows and even garment workers sitting at their machines.

Uptown, about two miles away, a similar scene takes place. But the ethnicity of the workers and the feel of the neighborhood are different.

8 A.M., 42ND STREET AND 8TH AVENUE SUBWAY STATION

Mexicans, Ecuadorians, and Dominicans come pouring out onto the streets to go to work in the shops in the Garment District. They walk south along Eighth Avenue and fan out into the numbered side streets. The majority of these shops are located between 35th and 41st streets between Seventh and Ninth Avenues. This neighborhood has an industrial feel as trucks are double parked to load and unload clothing and other materials. I can tell right away that clothing is being produced in these buildings. Within thirty minutes men are pulling dollies with cloth or racks of just-made clothing. The buildings are large industrial buildings. The stores cater to all the needs of garment manufacturing: sewing machine stores, sewing machine repair shops, button stores, fabric stores, zipper stores, and stores that carry other sewing notions. This is not an ethnic neighborhood. But by 10 A.M. women with little carts that sell hot tamales and other ethnic foods are at their stations. By the end of the day these ethnic food carts have disappeared.

These two examples from my fieldnotes give a sense of how garment workers are differentiated by location and ethnicity. Most Chinese coethnic shops are located in Chinatown—in an area with only about fifty thousand Chinese residents[4]—so the presence of about twenty thousand Chinese garment workers at four hundred garment shops has a huge economic and social impact on the Chinatown community. Garment workers make up nearly a third of the ethnic Chinese consumers who purchase goods in Chinatown. Many services in Chinatown, such as banks, hair salons, and travel agencies, depend on these garment worker–consumers. Many, perhaps most, of the Chinese garment workers do not live in Chinatown—they come to Chinatown from Brooklyn and Queens because the jobs in Manhattan are unionized and provide much-needed health insurance benefits. These are extremely important to Chinese women because their husbands often do not have coverage in the Chinese restaurants where they work. Moreover, factories in Manhattan often pay wages by check. This is especially important for workers who want to establish their yearly income and credit records to that they can buy homes and arrange for relatives to emigrate.

The garment shops are concentrated in an area just north of Canal Street, which is also known as Little Italy. The large buildings in this area have big lofts that suit garment production well. At one time the lofts might have held other kinds of manufacturing; however, the majority house garment shops now. Most are walk-ups with a freight elevator. On the street level most stores or storefronts are Chinese ethnic stores. Occasionally, one will find an Italian storefront. Trucks of all kinds—food delivery trucks, garment delivery trucks, and pickup trucks—are parked in the narrow streets. Although the area is in Little Italy, its character is distinctly Chinese and houses a "garment production sector" (see figure 2.1).

The twelve thousand Mexicans, Ecuadorians, and Dominicans who work for Koreans do so in about three hundred garment shops in midtown Manhattan in the West 30s—where they are just one part of the large garment district. Just about all the jobs that support garment manufacturing—including designing, pattern making, sample making, pleating, marketing, and sales—can be found in midtown Manhattan. However, the garment industry is just a small part of a midtown area that is bustling with many different kinds of businesses. Many diverse groups hold jobs in this area, and the effect of the Hispanics' presence in midtown is not as great as that of the Chinese in Chinatown.

The Sites

Chinatown Shop Floor

When I climb up the dark and dusty stairways to the garment shops, I cannot help noticing that these buildings have been around for at least one hundred years. The ornamental molding and the ironwork on the railings are clues to the former grandeur of the building. The windows are huge, allowing for plenty of natural light. On all the landings, doors are thrown open.

When I peek in, I see rows and rows of sewing machines, set three or four feet apart. On one side of the shop by the windows are two pressing machines used for ironing. In another little area is a family altar with offerings. And in yet another area are about a half-dozen large rice cookers, which are steaming rice for lunch. I also spot jugs of boiled water.

Each little area is personalized. Each woman has placed a back cushion on her chair. Each woman has brought snacks, ranging from crackers to candy to dried plums arranged in a tin on her sewing table. They are listening to Hong Kong pop music that the owner has piped through the shop floor. Some women are discussing their children. Some have already started working. Some are getting ready to work—gathering threads and opening up their bundles. The forewoman has already distributed the bundles to each spot. Other women are filling their jars with drinking

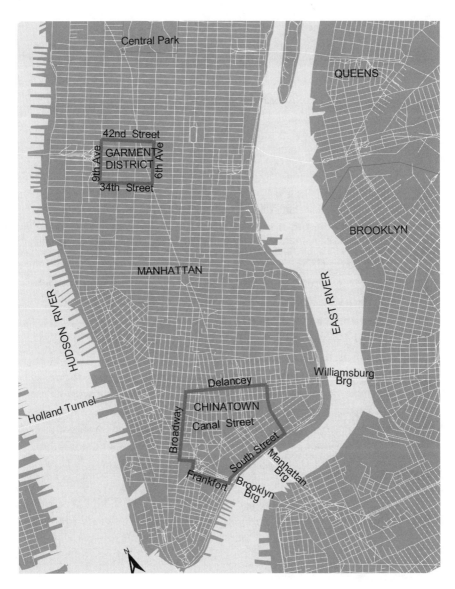

Central Park

QUEENS

42nd Street

GARMENT DISTRICT

9th Ave

6th Ave

34th Street

MANHATTAN

BROOKLYN

HUDSON RIVER

EAST RIVER

Williamsburg Brg

Delancey

Holland Tunnel

CHINATOWN

Broadway

Canal Street

South Street

Manhattan Brg

Frankfort

Brooklyn Brg

N

FIGURE 2.1 *Map by Merih Anil, Center for Urban Research CUNY Graduate Center.*

water and settling their lunch by the heater. Some are still coming in, ignoring the punch clock on the wall. No one uses the punch clock. It is 9:15 A.M.

Over by the pressers is a finishing area where the garments are hung, bagged, and tagged. An African American man is collecting garments for pickup.

Bundles of cloth are all over. The space seems tight for forty workers and materials.

The owner's office is close to the entranceway—no one is there yet—but I notice that the office is small and cramped, dominated by a huge calendar that lists orders and due dates. On the office door are Chinese posters depicting " fortunate sayings," such as " Prosperity."

KOREAN SHOP FLOOR

Many workers wait to ride up in the freight elevators. Workers seem to get off at almost every floor. As in the buildings downtown, there are large open loft spaces, but these buildings are not as old. The elevators are more modern, and the spaces appear to have been renovated. There are tiles on the floor and on the ceiling.

The workers file in, line up to punch their time clock, and sit down at their machine. Each worker's space is larger than the space given to the Chinese workers but less personalized. The work has already been distributed. A bell rings at 8:30 and all the machines begin. At the sound of the bell all chit-chat suddenly ends, and all one can hear is the loud whir of the machines. Like the Chinese shops, this shop has a finishing area and an area with pressers.

The Korean owner's office is near the entrance. He and his wife are there—walking the floor and monitoring the work. The office is large with a big desk and a rack with samples of the clothes that the factory is producing.

As these two descriptions from my fieldnotes suggest, garment production is very different in the Korean and Chinese sectors. The differences stem not only from the way the garment shops' owners see their work and role but also from the way the garment workers do their work.

The Chinese owners see themselves as a capable group that has good communications with Chinese workers. The workers and owners share many values. Workers can come and go to run errands during their workday so long as they complete the work that is expected of them. Garment production in the

Chinese factories can be quite relaxed and informal. At the extremes, one person might make three bundles of clothing, while another makes only three pieces in the same amount of time. Often one sees a woman informally training another. These women will be paid piecework rates for each whole garment they complete.[5] Each woman can sew as slowly or as fast as she needs to, giving the workplace a casual atmosphere. Every now and then children of the garment workers or the owner can be found at the shop, usually doing homework in the evenings. If school is closed, they may spend all day in the shop.

The Korean owners, in contrast, see themselves as professional business owners who need to take their work seriously. Thus they have large offices that announce their importance to the designers and the inspectors from the New York State Department of Labor. Rarely are children on the shop floor. Video cameras survey areas of the shop. The owners know Spanish, and those who have lived or worked in Central or South America know it well. Thus they can communicate with the workers on the shop floor. The Mexican, Ecuadorian, and Dominican workers value their boss's ability to communicate with them. At the same time the work is highly regimented. Each group of workers sews a certain number of seams on pieces of cut cloth (a section of the garment), and those partially sewn pieces are passed to another group of sewers to sew another group of seams. Together, after all the seams are sewn, the assembled cloth resembles a garment. Thus in the Korean shops work is passed from person to person. They cannot delay, and workers have to keep up their production, because garment assembly in these factories depends on a closely controlled order for sewing seams and sections of the garment. These workers are paid hourly wages in cash.

The Union

The International Ladies' Garment Workers' Union (ILGWU), which later became the Union of Needletrades, Industrial and Textile Employees (UNITE), was represented only in the Chinatown garment shops. Put another way, the Chinese workers were the only ones in my study population who were unionized. As I mentioned earlier, Chinese workers were attracted to this industry because it was unionized and offered health insurance (Bao 2001).

The union was trying to address the problem of its lack of representation in other shops around the city; during the periods when I conducted interviews (1994–96 and 1999–2000), the ILGWU had a community-organizing component that brought the union, English classes, and workers' rights education into the workers' communities. In Chinatown, midtown Manhattan, and Sunset Park in Brooklyn, workers' centers welcomed both unionized and nonunionized workers. More Chinese workers began to avail themselves of the training, citizenship, and English classes that the union offered. The union card, for some, became more than just a health insurance card.

The workers' centers helped build the loyalty of union members by offering them valuable and convenient services near their homes. Furthermore, these centers encouraged the participation of workers who were nonunion members or undocumented. The information provided helped to mitigate the exploitation of workers, which benefits union members because it blunts the power of owners to undercut them. While union officials could only hope that these centers would eventually increase union membership, in the short run they at least educated workers about their rights in the garment shops.[6]

SIMILARITIES AND DIFFERENCES AND THE LITERATURE

The Chinese coethnic and Korean-Hispanic garment-contracting sectors produce similar items under similar market conditions. But underlying these similarities are a multitude of differences. The two sectors manufacture similar women's outerwear (dresses, blouses, pants, skirts) that sell for similar prices, even though the workers' characteristics, work organization, and pay are different (see tables 2.2 and 2.3).

Of the workers I studied, the Chinese were approximately 95 percent unionized and the Mexican, Ecuadorian, and Dominican workers were not unionized at all. The majority of all Hispanic workers were newcomers who arrived in the United States within the previous five years. Nearly a third (38 percent) of the Chinese had arrived within the previous five years. The Hispanics were mostly undocumented, whereas the Chinese were almost all permanent residents or citizens. The Chinese received lower wages than the Hispanics. However, the two sets of owners were similar in that the majority had opened their shops within the previous ten years, and close to half (43 percent) had some previous experience in the garment industry. Although the Chinese-owned garment shops were supposed to only sew union work, they also competed for work from the nonunion manufacturers that also supplied the Korean-owned shops. Thus the two sectors encountered similar conditions in the economy and had a similar relationship with many manufacturers in the industry. These two sectors competed with each other and existed side by side. How was this possible?

Guided by the larger literature and my own research, I emphasize two sets of relationships in answering these questions: the relationships between immigration, family circumstances, and gender, and the relationships on the job floor between owners and workers, and among the workers themselves.

Immigration and Family Circumstances

This study extends previous work on immigration by emphasizing the importance of such factors as the social organization of emigration, for both documented and undocumented workers, and the family relationships and obligations that immigrants have to others here and in their homeland. By comparing the Korean and Chinese sectors and examining the social relationships among the workers and owners, I can see the influence of gender, immigration status, and family circumstances, and the relationship of these factors to ethnic job-finding networks.

Studies of immigrants have long shown that the emigration process itself organizes networks of individuals entering particular industries (I. Kim 1981; Portes and Bach 1985; Gold 1992; Smith 1994). Many earlier studies have also addressed the power that women gain after they emigrate and find a job (Grasmuck and Pessar 1991). What is often missing, however, is attention to changing gender status and roles among both documented and undocumented immigrants as they organize their lives in New York City. Immigrants' lives are arranged according to particular circumstances surrounding their migration status and the extent of family support required or acquired in New York City. In particular, many immigrants have had to make a choice about their children, whether to bring them or to leave them in their home country. These factors affect men and women differently and shape their work lives accordingly. Researchers rarely discuss the balance of work and family among immigrants.

Hispanic women and men in the garment industry often enter the United States without their children. Couples that come together also leave their children in their home country with relatives. Thus they have relatively few family responsibilities in New York City. Both men and women assume the role of breadwinner when they arrive. Circumstances of illegal immigration often complicate the ability to bring children to the United States and thus place Hispanic men and women in roles that are less gendered than in the traditional family.

Simultaneously, the immigration process has made garment industry jobs more gender neutral. Hispanic men from poor farming communities see any job in a " factoria," including work in a garment factory, as a move upward. The Korean-owned sector of the garment industry, which hires Hispanics, reflects these dynamics. In my sample, 35 percent of workers in this sector were male. Both male and female undocumented workers did not have children living with them in the United States. Some of the women, especially the Dominican women (a minority in this sector), were citizens or permanent residents. For them, the family balancing act was extremely difficult because of the need for child care during work hours and the pull that they felt when their children needed them. Although the sector was gender neutral in hiring, the women who had to care for children had more traditional gender roles.

Immigration plays a different role for the Chinese workers. Most Chinese emigrate legally and bring children and other family members with them to New York City. The ethnic Chinese sector of the Manhattan garment industry changed over time throughout the 1960s and 1970s, as did women workers and their roles in the Chinese community. The garment sector provided an economic and social role for women that allowed Chinese working-class families to survive and even thrive in New York City. The women in the industry have much more independence and influence than any study has recognized so far. The Chinese women have used their ethnic embeddedness in the community to strengthen their ability to perform their work for pay and for their family—in other words, because employers share their workers' ethnicity, workers take advantage of the owners' sympathy and of their proximity to the services available in the ethnic community.

The Chinese sector of the industry has both the formal union benefits that provide health insurance and many informal benefits as well. These informal provisions give women the flexibility that allows them to cope with their long working hours—often from 9:30 A.M. to 7:30 P.M. They often come to work after dropping their children off at school, do their grocery shopping during their lunch hour, frequently take their children and groceries home after school ends, and return to work in the early evening. This flexibility, rarely seen in other manufacturing or professional industries, allows the women to balance their work-family load. While the Chinese women work very long hours for low wages, they are able to take care of their household needs by shopping and shuttling children during their breaks. Although the women are extremely tired and strained, they can maintain their role as the primary caretaker of their children and of the house.

Their husbands, who have little access to jobs with health benefits, also seek jobs that pay good wages—usually in cash. For the most part, men have been able to remain in those industries like food service—which are run informally, without benefits—so long as the men are paid well and in cash. The Chinatown community businesses benefit, but there is a down side for the men. Because women in these families have health insurance, the men have been reluctant to organize for benefits and to demand much more of their employers. At the same time the women feel pressured to stay in their garment jobs longer than they may wish. However, the work of these women has helped sustain at least one generation, perhaps two generations, of Chinese immigrant families in the United States.

Ethnic Business

Most of the many studies of ethnic businesses (Light 1972; Bonacich and Modell 1980, Portes and Bach 1985; Waldinger 1986; Light and Bonacich 1988; Waldinger et al. 1990) focus on the association between immigrants and business, and business and the ethnic community, and less on the coethnic relationships themselves and how factors such as gender and immigration status might affect these relationships.

Most of the literature has stressed the positive uses of ethnic bonds, that is, the use of networks, and the obligations or responsibility of entrepreneurs to help other coethnics in the community (Portes and Bach 1985; Bailey and Waldinger 1991; Zhou 1992). Waldinger (1986, 1996), for example, emphasizes that ethnic networks are conduits for information, allowing immigrant employers to learn about the salient characteristics of their workers, thereby reducing uncertainty when hiring and training. Ethnic networks also provide a basis for the construction of a set of shared understandings about the obligations and responsibilities that bind employers and workers. These relationships are maintained to advance the goals of the firm.

At the same time a number of authors acknowledge that ethnic bonds can hide exploitation, especially when entrepreneurs capitalize on coethnic relationships (Portes and Bach 1985; Sanders and Nee 1987, 1992; Light Bonacich 1988; Zhou 1992). Exploitation of coethnics generally does occur in immigrant businesses, even in immigrant businesses that are located outside the immigrant enclave (Light and Bonacich 1988; Yoon 1997). The exploitation is most likely to involve cash labor, unlimited work hours, and undocumented status. Kwong (1997) specifically refers to working for coethnics in the enclave as a trap. Once immigrants take such a job, they have little opportunity to move up and out of the enclave.

Entrepreneurship is an option for many Korean immigrants because they have access to a high level of ethnic and economic resources, such as money, education, and connections (Light 1972; Bonacich and Modell 1980). The ethnic business literature also discusses the role of ethnic businesses in the larger society, with much written about Koreans, who tend to open shops in neighborhoods populated by other ethnic groups (Light and Bonacich 1988; Yoon 1997; Min 1996). As such they interact with both their customers and their employees, both of whom often mistakenly identify the entrepreneur as someone who is oppressing them by extracting large profits and wielding power over the employees and the neighborhood. The customers and employees seldom speak the same language as the entrepreneur (Bonacich and Appelbaum 2000). Thus when a crisis occurs, the community blames the entrepreneur. Koreans' solidarity can be galvanized when they are criticized (Min 1996). Other scholars, like Abelman and Lie (1995) and Yoon (1997), emphasize that not all Korean entrepreneurs find themselves in this predicament. In my study Hispanic workers would not consider Korean garment shop owners to be a middleman minority. The relationship between these two groups is based on both class antagonism and the conditions in the New York City garment industry. Hispanics search for Korean employers because they can get jobs with them. Hispanics know that Koreans in New York City pay much better than Koreans in Los Angeles. Hispanics and the Korean shop owners share a common emigration experience and a common language (Spanish). While New York has no shortage of undocumented workers, it does have a shortage of experienced and skilled garment workers. Thus some undocumented workers make more than minimum wage, and on average they make more than the Chinese workers who have documents. By the same token, Koreans have their shop floor under strict control. And Korean owners can prevent workers from helping their friends to get jobs because the Koreans prefer to hire outside the worker networks.

The enclave itself is a concentration of ethnic firms that hire a significant proportion of workers from the same minority group, and the term *enclave* aptly describes Chinatown as a whole (K. Wilson and Portes 1980; Portes and Bach 1985; Zhou 1992). Some researchers have argued that the existence of the enclave allows immigrants to find jobs that pay more than the low-wage they could find outside the enclave. Enclaves act as havens for immigrants, shielding many who do not speak English and lack other skills from dead-end jobs in the wider labor market while channeling them into jobs (both good and not so good) in the enclave. Employment in the enclave, the argument goes, is better than outside the enclave, for both the employers and the workers. Implicit in this argument is that immigrants who stay at jobs within the enclave do better than those who leave it. Proponents of the enclave economy would argue that ethnic solidarity involves reciprocal favors, which explain why enclave workers experience returns from their investment in education and work experience similar to those gained by workers in better, nonenclave jobs. The Chinese garment workers are embedded in their communities and as a whole have benefits that are not included in their wages. They also have more liabilities than the various enclave studies (Zhou 1992) have mentioned. This is especially true in regard to gender and family roles. Women tend to have lower wages than men. The women take on the training of new workers whom they bring in. In the end, the women become embedded in a web of obligations from which they often cannot disentangle themselves. As workers and women, they become indebted to their male employers, who hire these women's relatives, although the senior women benefit by getting easier work from their employer.

CHAPTER 3

Getting from There to Here

I left very quickly because my husband told me that I should be ready as soon as he had the money and place for me. I knew I would come but did not want to discuss it much and plan for it too much because I knew I would have to leave my baby (eighteen months). I cried every night for three months because I missed her so much. My husband thinks we did it right by leaving her because now my mother and her have so much more than we all had when we were together.   —*Mexican woman in her twenties*

We waited a long time to come to New York. Just about everyone else in the village had left already. We were just waiting for our papers to clear, and once it did, everyone, my husband and my two children, just packed up all of our belongings. Our relatives in New York asked us to bring their things for them because we were the last of our family in the village. On the day we left, we padlocked the door to our house.

—Chinese woman in her thirties

When people emigrate, it is a very serious decision. Many families put years of planning into the process. Immigrants often arrive with other people, and these other people, whether they work or not, affect both short- and long-term plans of the family in the United States and in the home country. This is especially true when immigrants bring children. Men and women take different roles when they arrive with children. In turn, the family structure affects gender roles. Gender roles can limit the types of jobs that one can accept. Or they might add incentive to seek employment in an area that one might not have considered.

IMMIGRATION AND FAMILY STRUCTURE

How does family structure influence the settlement and work patterns of garment workers in the United States? Many immigration studies mention the influence of family structure on plans to remain in the United States or to return
to home (Massey et. al. 1987; Pessar 1989). Looking at historical patterns, Kessner notes that flows of permanent immigrants in early twentieth-century New
York were characterized by the emigration of whole families that intended to
remake their lives and homes in the new country, whereas temporary immigrants, often Italian, were usually young men who intended to make money
and return home (1977).

In my study all the workers and factory owners whom I interviewed were
economic immigrants who came permanently or temporarily, with some leaving families in their homeland. Some Chinese immigrants initially came on
their own for economic reasons and stayed because they could earn more in the
United States. They hoped to provide their children with better opportunities.
These immigrants usually ended up bringing the whole family over and tried
to become permanent residents. Some Mexican immigrants came as undocumented couples and decided to stay even though their offspring remained in
Mexico with their grandparents. These Mexican immigrants explained how
their family situation affected the jobs that they were able to get or how the
jobs they did take influenced the ability of their children or other family members to come to New York.

This study problematizes the notion of "male only" and "family" immigration as primary indicators for temporary or permanent immigration. Whereas
the common wisdom is that men on their own are sojourners, many in fact intend to bring their families. And those who come with wives think of the move
as a temporary, quick way to earn money rather than as a permanent strategy.
Who emigrates has changed dramatically in recent years, with increases in female and family emigration, and with these changes have come particular outcomes. Women are emigrating in higher numbers because of the job opportunities. And they are emigrating regardless of documentation status. However,
women rarely come alone. They are also unlikely to travel on foot across the
desert to get to New York. Women enter New York by plane, car, or bus and
usually overstay their visas, thus becoming undocumented.

As earlier studies suggest, a woman's presence influences family formation
among immigrants and their future plans. For example, undocumented couples
who emigrate together consider themselves family but are reluctant to see
themselves as permanent immigrants. Interviewees stated that they emigrated as

a couple to work together for their future, either here or in their homeland. If they subsequently have children here, they may become permanent immigrants. Not surprisingly, I found that initial emigration patterns, family structure in the United States, and probable family reunification are better indicators of who will become permanent immigrants than the gender of the immigrant (see also Massey et. al. 1987; Grasmuck and Pessar 1991; Hondagneu-Sotelo 1994). Indeed, as I will show, emigration patterns and family structure influence entry into the garment industry. There is also the question of how emigration to New York and working in New York influences an immigrant woman's sense that her status has risen now that she works and earns more money. At the same time men also challenge gender norms because they too come from poor countries and because jobs that are thought of as women's work in the United States now may be coveted by certain groups of men.

A comparative analysis of emigration among two groups—one with the legal means to emigrate and the other without—highlights some fundamental differences that distinguish emigration with children and emigration without them. In turn, this comparison brings out how gender roles may facilitate or constrain both women's and men's emigration, settlement, and the ability to attain and maintain a garment job.

In analyzing the data from the interviews, I found four distinct types of emigration patterns: family, staged, transnational, and single. The most important distinguishing factor among immigrants was whether they were legal or illegal. And among both the documented and the undocumented, I found distinctions based on gender, marital status, and whether they had children.[1]

Immigration Routes

What is legal immigration? How does it differ from the type of immigration used by most Mexicans and Ecuadorians I interviewed? The majority of the Chinese enter as permanent residents on immigration visas. Mexican and Ecuadorians most often enter with a short-term visa for visiting and tourism and overstay their visa limits, or they enter without any type of documentation at all.

Mexicans and Ecuadorians use emigration as a safety valve to escape poor economic conditions at home. In these cases, They rarely regard emigration as permanent. They use the wages that they earn in the United States to support family members in their homeland. The Chinese practice is one of long-term immigration, with whole families legally emigrating to pursue a new life, one that they hope offers social and economic mobility. Chinese often spend several years in China or Hong Kong waiting for their immigration papers to come through. Of the three undocumented Chinese (Fujianese) whom I interviewed, two intended to stay, have their status legalized, and apply for reunification of their family. Although these Chinese used illegal means to get onto U.S soil, they were still planning for eventual permanent legal immigration.

Immigration laws heavily influence the process of emigration. The 1965 immigration law was written to favor family reunification, especially for groups with large numbers already here, because the law specifies preference allocations for family-sponsored immigrants as well as individuals with special skills. Only those with legal residency, either permanent residency or citizenship, are allowed to petition for immigration papers for family members. Permanent residents may seek immigration visas only for their spouses and unmarried children. However, U.S. citizens can petition for visas for their spouses, unmarried or married children, brothers, sisters, and parents. Although those with special skills can also apply for an immigration visa, the need for workers with specialized skills has decreased since the early 1990s.[2]

Since the mid-1970s Asians in particular have benefited from these laws. In New York City the large Chinese population continues to bring family members to the United States under the Immigration Act of 1965. Thus new legal immigrants became permanent residents or citizens who then petition for visas to bring over other family members. Furthermore, the small number of Chinese who initially entered illegally, from Fujian Province, as documented by Peter Kwong (1997), are now using the family preferences in the 1965 Immigration Act to bring their own family members over. Some undocumented Chinese who want to emigrate permanently and gain legal status are able to apply for political asylum in the United States because of the Tiananmen Square massacre in 1989 and the U.S. stance against China's one-child policy. Thus illegal Chinese immigrants may in fact have a long-term plan to legalize their immigration status and to bring family members to the United States.

However, many fewer Mexicans and Ecuadorians are here legally. The quotas for immigrants from those countries are too small to meet the demand of all those who want to come to the United States. And not enough family members are already here legally to petition for relatives to join them. Perhaps more important, many who are here are undocumented and have not legalized their status. The immigration and asylum laws do not provide exceptions that Mexicans and other Hispanics can use like the Chinese do.

About one-third of my Hispanic interviewees (mostly women) overstayed their visas , and the rest (mostly men) entered illegally. Ecuadorians said that it cost them $6,000 to $7,000 to come to the United States, whereas Mexicans reported spending at most $2,000 per person (the average was $1,000) to get here. According to my informants, this was fairly typical. The majority of the Mexican and Ecuadorian workers did not have a family history of permanent emigration to the United States. In planning their trip, few thought of emigrating permanently. Although several told me that they had relatives who could have applied for legal immigration visas for their entry, they chose to enter with their "visiting" visas because it required less effort.

Nearly all the Hispanics with whom I spoke, except for the few Domincans with documents, wanted to work for a few years to earn money to better their lives in their home country. Although the undocumented Hispanics did not have official work visas, they were correct in asserting that plenty of employers were willing to hire them.

Current immigration strategies conform to the legal processes and structures that these groups have used in the past. The Chinese have a much longer-term family-centered approach, especially in how they save, plan, and approach their permanent emigration to the United States. On the other hand, the majority of the Hispanics see emigration as a safety valve—and therefore approach emigration as a short-term solution. They do some planning and pool their savings to help individuals leaving for a short-term stay in the United States.[3]

MIGRATION PATTERNS

My interviews yielded four types of emigration patterns: family, staged, transnational, and single. As table 3.1 shows, these patterns vary by group, with the Chinese much more likely than Hispanics to emigrate in a family unit (thirty-one families versus five) and Hispanics more likely to follow what I call a transnational family pattern.

Family
Family is defined as all members of a nuclear family emigrating together as a single unit at the same time. In this definition I also include childless couples. I do this because Hispanic couples define themselves as a family unit to distinguish themselves from others who emigrate in stages over time or who leave family members, especially spouses, behind in their home country. In general, family emigrants are more affluent than those who emigrate alone because they have enough money to come over together.[4] According to my interviewees, the emigration of a family unit requires that the family have enough money to pay for the passage of everyone traveling and higher levels of personal commitment by the adults to make life work in New York City. Chinese couples who emigrate this way also label themselves as a family unit.

I found that Hispanic families with children did not emigrate as a family unit. The lack of documents or visas, and the consequently arduous trip and expenses, precluded bringing the children. Hispanic couples who came together

TABLE 3.1   *Migration Patterns of the Chinese and Hispanic Interviewees*

	Cantonese	Fujianese	All Chinese
Family	31	0	31
Staged	10	0	10
Transnational	0	2	2★
Single	0	1	1★
		44	

	Mex	Ecu	Dom	CA	All Hispanics
Family	4★★	0	1★★	0	5
Staged	3	3ᴸ	1ᴸ	0	7
Transnational	8★★★ᴸ	9★★★	1	1	19
Single	4	10	0	0	14
					45

Note: Eighty-nine of the interviewees discussed this topic with me.
Mex = Mexican, Ecu = Ecuadorian, Dom = Dominican, CA = Central American
L—Legal Hispanic immigrants
★Undocumented Chinese from Fujian Province, China
★★Family = spouses only, no children
★★★One member of a couple who leaves children and spouse behind

tended to be no older than twenty-five and physically healthy (according to their own descriptions). Four of the five couples who came as a "family of two" were from Mexico and one was from the Dominican Republic.[5]

Thirty-one of the forty-four Chinese informants emigrated with their family. This is the typical Chinese pattern for emigration. The U.S. State Department often takes as long as ten years to process applications from documented family members in the United States for their relatives to emigrate. Often, relatives—usually siblings or parents already living in the United States—apply for family visas for single individuals. As the single people wait for their name and number to come up, they often marry and have children. As their family grows, they put more money away for the trip, and their relatives in the United States save more money for them too. In summary, the

Chinese I interviewed were legal immigrants who planned to keep the family intact. The long waiting period allowed them, as well as their relatives, to save money for their resettlement.

Hispanic couples who come together as a family unit cite three reasons for emigrating this way. One is companionship and fear of losing their partner. Women, especially those who emigrated with a partner, said that they believed that it was better to stay with their husbands lest they lose them. Stories abound in Mexico and Ecuador of husbands who find new lovers in the United States and abandon their wives at home. However, both women and men mentioned that they wanted to be with each other for companionship. Another reason to emigrate together is that they can earn more to support their future life back home. Interviewees explained that two able-bodied individuals can make more money faster than one; having two earners allows them to return to their homeland faster and with more money. Third, all said that they had no important responsibility for children (someone else could care for them) or elderly parents that tied them to their homeland. Given their decision to emigrate together, these couples often gathered sufficient resources and information far in advance to make the trip. This meant arranging for enough money to pay their passage to the United States, and gathering information about where to go, where to live, and what jobs to get in the United States.

Staged Migration

In this emigration pattern different members of the nuclear family unit emigrate sequentially in a staged manner. In other words, individual members of the family emigrate over a period of time. This is the only emigration pattern in which Hispanics and Chinese have almost equivalent numbers; ten Chinese and seven Hispanic families emigrated in this manner.

Both Chinese and Hispanics reported similar reasons for undertaking this type of emigration pattern. Critical was the desire to stretch limited funds. This type of timed emigration also allows immigrants in the United States to save money for the second person's journey, to send remittances home, and to set up a household in New York before other members follow. For example, husbands often emigrate first, before their wives and children. However, once things are arranged, the second person or even the rest of the family emigrates. (A staged emigration often includes an additional worker, who comes to New York at a later time to earn money for the whole family.)

The Chinese often carefully plan their staged emigration. Circumstances in China often prevent the emigration of any additional family members. One parent comes first, leaving the other parent to care for the children. Most often the husband comes first to prepare a household. Of the ten Chinese families who emigrated with a staged emigration plan, only one woman came before her husband. This woman had applied for a visa under the special careers quota from Hong Kong and was given a high priority for emigration. However, the family did not have enough money for everyone to emigrate together. While she worked as a garment worker in New York, she earned enough to bring family members here. Although she had been given special immigration consideration as a pastry–dim sum chef, she found working in the factories more lucrative. In another example, the one documented Dominican woman who emigrated in this staged pattern did so as a result of her parents' petitioning the State Department for a visa for their daughter. None of the Hispanic staged emigration cases involved children. Four of the seven Hispanic families planned staged emigration as part of the economic survival strategy of the extended family. Spouses and/or other family members joined each other in the United States when they had enough money to get here.

Several Hispanics whom I interviewed had not anticipated staged emigration. The emigrant intended to support a transnational family and did not plan to bring over other family members. However, conditions in New York turned out to be better than expected; the Hispanics found openings for jobs that their spouses could easily fill. The Hispanic spouse who arrived first worked hard to earn enough money to pay off old debts back home as well as to support family at home. After a short time in the United States the husband would ask his wife to join him in New York because finding work was easier than expected and he had come to feel safe even without documentation.

Transnational Family

There is a fine line between a planned and staged emigration and supporting a transnational family. For Hispanics the question is whether they will be able to support a family in the United States. Many workers who initially support a transnational household hold onto the idea of returning and building a better life back home with the money earned in New York.

Transnational families maintain households in two places; the one in the United States primarily consists of an individual or couple, and the family back home is the extended family: spouse, children, parents, siblings. The immigrants are engaged in paid work in the United States. The household in the homeland is maintained by remittances (E. Glenn 1983).

In my sample the undocumented—the Chinese from Fujian Province and the Hispanics from Mexico and Ecuador—were the immigrants who maintained transnational households.[6] Sometimes immigration laws, lack of family or kinship support, and/or financial hardships prevent members of the family from reuniting. However, in the majority of cases the family in the United States needs to make a deliberate decision to support two households. For them, this is the only economic solution that is feasible. Those working in New York City usually send money to their spouse or parents to support children or other family members in the homeland.

Most interviewees who maintained families in their homeland were here by themselves. Surprisingly, half the transnational Hispanic families involved women in the United States who were in their forties or older. The seven women who were alone here told me that they were married, widowed, or divorced and that their husband or mother was caring for the children back home.[7] Other Hispanics in the transnational category were eight men who were working to support wives and young children back home. On average, these men were younger than the women who were supporting their families back home. The men were similar to those described by Massey and colleagues (1987)—newlyweds whose household resources were stretched thin. Many were fathers who left children in the care of their spouses. The only exception was one Mexican couple who explained that they intended to send money back home as long as they could. They never intend to bring their child or any other family members to the United States.

Singles

Single men were the only ones who emigrated on their own. In my sample only three young women in their late teens emigrated alone, but they came as part of a staged migration pattern, to be united with a parent or grandparent, and so were not included in this category. One Mexican male came as a student and overstayed his visa.

Most single men who emigrate come to New York solely to find work and save money to use when they return home. Three of the Mexicans, the Fujianese man, and four of the Ecuadorians came as "sojourners" to make their fortune here in the United States and then return home.

The other emigrants in this category were men who came to experience living in the United States and to learn English as well as to make money. Often they arrived with friends or were invited by friends. They were in their twenties or thirties. They usually had a set idea of when they planned to return home, usually within three years. These men usually had jobs in their homeland and were not that poor, but they were interested in earning what they could in New York. They tended not to want to settle in the United States and generally saw living here as a premarriage adventure.[8]

MIGRATION AND SETTLEMENT PATTERNS AND LONG-TERM PLANNING

Social Connections and Resources

It is important to have acquaintances in the United States because they are important sources of information about settlement. All the immigrants were efficient at gathering information from friends and especially from family members who had already made the trip (Grieco 1987). Their contacts in the United States provided information about specific places to live, available jobs, and the logistics of emigrating and living with spouses and children in New York City. Listen to one Chinese woman in her thirties: "My sister told me everything we had to do. Before we immigrated, she described what the subway ride was like, how long it took to get to work, the garment factory, Chinatown, and what living in an apartment building would be like. We lived with them while we slowly looked for a place nearby. I've always been a farmer and never saw a factory. The biggest city I've been to is Guangzhou. Everything she told me was true, and I am lucky that she helps me so much."

Or to an Ecuadorian woman in her fifties: "I've been here two years. I live close by to my brother. He had friends with space for me when I came. My brother told me that I should come to New York. He told me that I could get finishing work here. It was the only work he said I could do. I didn't know what he was talking about—*finishing work* was not a term that they used in Ecuador. He described it to me as cutting threads, putting bags on clothes, and other little things. Well, that sounded simple enough that I could do it. It sounded very easy. I thought that I could do those things, so I came to do work here."

Friends and relatives in New York City send back reports on life in the city, and they are regularly called upon for emigration information. It is not surprising that most emigrants rely on friends and relatives to find out how to get to New York City and find a job there. Those already here may influence the type of emigration pattern that the individual chooses. As my sample indicates, the Chinese and Hispanics prefer different strategies. These differences are partially the result of documentation status, but they also are a result of new emigrants' following the proven methods of earlier emigrants.

Settlement and Family

As table 3.1 shows, the Chinese families most often emigrated as a unit, either as a couple or with children. While it may seem much easier for one spouse to come first to settle and later make arrangements in a staged emigration process, the Chinese whom I interviewed disagreed. They stressed that when parents and children come together, settlement is faster. While it may be more daunting to arrange all the logistics for family emigration, my informants said this orients family members toward settlement, while separation and staged emigration do not.

The Chinese also said that while having children and a spouse in New York may be more complicated than just having to take care of oneself, a spouse is a wage earner as well as a caretaker for the children. When both members of a couple are wage earners, setting up a livable household is easier. In effect, having more adult members in New York City generates more resources for adjustment and settlement. Two parents here also allow for some flexibility in caring for children. Said one Chinese woman in her forties who had two children, "It would be very hard for my husband to have come alone here. Even when I first got here, I had to work right away to help pay for our rent. I paid a lady next door to watch our kids. She was '*hoe pien*' [very cheap]. Without I or the children here, I don't think we would have saved enough to buy our home. I would have stayed with them [in China], and life there was not worth staying. Here the children are learning English and I am making good money. It's better for them to be here, and see how much we have been able to get together."

Moreover, immigration laws support bringing over additional members of the extended family, which can also provide more resources. In particular, immigration laws allow the Chinese to plan for their parents' emigration, and a number of Chinese immigrants have brought parents to New York to be babysitters. If they are fortunate, their parents are already in New York because of an application submitted much earlier by another family member. One Chinese woman in her thirties explained, "Even while I worked at my first job in Brooklyn, I had my mother-in-law, who was already here, to . . . take care of my two small children. Most of the time my children would live in Chinatown with my mother-in-law, while I and my husband lived in Brooklyn. My children would go to school in Chinatown and come to Brooklyn on the weekends."

In contrast, very few children emigrated with their Hispanic parents. Mexican and Ecuadorian emigration to New York City is still relatively low compared to emigration of the Chinese.[9] The social support network for child care is not as extensive for Hispanics as it is for the Chinese. Moreover, legal immigration is less accessible because there are fewer legal Mexican and Ecuadorian immigrants who can apply for visas for new family members. Legal immigration would guarantee a less arduous trip for all involved. Legal immigration would hasten the emigration of Hispanic grandparents to watch over children, thereby increasing the growth of Mexican and Ecuadorian communities in New York City. Thus planning a trip with children, not to mention planning for their care in New York City, is difficult for many Hispanic emigrants. Because relatives who could care for children are few and far between, Hispanic children often are left behind. A Honduran woman in her thirties told me, "My son is back in Honduras. I haven't seen him for three years. I hope to go back next year. Sometimes you just have to leave the children. Many people do this. You can't make enough money without doing this. I send money home for my son." A Mexican woman of about the same age confided, "Yes, there are many like me who leave their children home. Sometimes, it just costs too much to raise the children here and go to work. You end up not making much money. Plus it is difficult to find a babysitter and good care for him [her child]" in New York City.

The pattern of leaving children back home applied to both older women and some couples who were working in the garment industry (see Foner 1986 on a similar pattern among West Indians). Few Hispanics consider emigrating with children. Traveling illegally with children is difficult. Undocumented status, combined with the need to earn money, makes it hard to earn enough to bring children here and care for them in New York City. It is less expensive to have relatives care for the children back home. Hispanic workers do not see a future here without their family, and they lack the social support available in their home country. Absent a more lenient immigration policy, they cannot bring over grandparents or other close relatives who could take care of their children while they work. It should be noted, however, that only one Hispanic couple had a child born in New York City, and these parents extended their plans to stay indefinitely; other couples who emigrated together were well positioned to stay if their situation in New York turned out to be more promising than the one they left behind.

Gendering in the Two Sectors

Family emigration and the entry of women in the Chinese garment sector influence work organization and create jobs known as women's work. By the same token, when almost no children emigrate, which was the situation among the Hispanics working in the Korean sector, women and men are not confined to gendered roles as caregiver and earner. Instead both are primary wage earners. And because both men and women worked in the garment sector, a set of gendered images of workers did not exist in the Korean-owned sector.

The majority of the Chinese women I interviewed did not speak English and knew very little about jobs outside the Chinese community. According to them, they had few choices. The majority of jobs in Chinatown are either in the garment industry, which is mostly female, or in the restaurant industry, which is mostly male.

In the Chinese garment sector the gender division is clear. Everyone with whom I spoke said that more than 97 percent of the workers are women. Moreover, the sector is organized around the women and their needs, especially those concerning children. The Chinese women are almost all permanent immigrants, they are settled, and they have or plan to have children.

Sewing is recognized as a gendered occupation in the Chinese community. Chinese men told me that they do not enter the garment industry because it is a woman's job. The two Chinese men I interviewed in the garment industry complained that the restaurant business was too physically strenuous and the only place for them to work was in garments. Both were men in their late forties. For them, working in a female-dominated industry was better than not working at all.

The Chinese women agree with the men that the restaurant business is too strenuous for women, and they will not enter the restaurant industry because it is known as men's work. Waiting tables is seen as too physically strenuous and unfeminine. Moreover, according to these women, few server jobs were available to them. The only time women serve food in Chinese restaurants is during dim sum hours, when they can push carts around. On the other hand, the garment industry is seen as a women's industry and jobs are plentiful. Except for the two or three presser jobs that are available in every garment shop, all sewing and finishing jobs are usually held by Chinese women. A Chinese woman in her forties told me, "I used to work for the longest time in the restaurants. I used to waitress and push a dim sum cart around. That was just part-time work. I also used to work in a 'cleaning clothes establishment'; I used to check the laundry. But when I got pregnant, I could not do that kind of work anymore. It was too heavy for my body. I need to sit down and do less strenuous work. So I went to look for a job in the sewing factory. Here, we sit and sew all day."

Another Chinese woman of the same age told me, "I used to work in a factory fixing things [in China]. I really worked fixing wheels and different kinds of mechanical things. I would rather work in a factory like that. It's pretty big, much bigger than the garment factories. I worked there for twenty years. And now I am a garment worker. Everyone told me that I would be working in the garment factory. There isn't much else, especially not like what I was doing, everything here needs English. When I arrived someone took me to a garment shop."

Two other factors, flexibility of hours and the availability of health insurance, attract Chinese women with children to the industry. Flexibility of hours is especially important for them beause it allows them to arrange their schedules around child care and household and work responsibilities. For example, if their children are school age, the women can save on child care expenses if they can drop their children off at school and pick them up in the afternoon. Women can shop or accomplish other household errands during the course of the day, as a Chinese woman in her fifties told me: "When my kids were young—my youngest was five and my oldest was twelve when I started working. I have three kids, an older daughter and two younger sons. When I first got here, we lived in Chinatown and sent the kids to school. I would leave work early to pick them up and didn't come to work until I dropped them off at school. It worked fine. When my mother-in-law came, she took care of them." Another woman, in her forties, reported, "When I first moved here, we lived with my mother-in-law in Chinatown. We did everything down here. My kids could even just come up to visit me after school. I could always go home to see them." Child care was critical for these women because the majority had children or were planning to have children. Chinatown had comparatively few day care opportunities. However, grandparents, friends, and others were willing to be paid babysitters. As one woman in her forties explained:

> I have a son who is six. My husband's sister took care of him when we first came. Now my husband's mother takes care of him. She came here last year. He goes to first grade now. I could only work when I first got here because my sister helped take him. We don't live close by. We live in Queens, and I save a lot of money with my mother-in-law.
>
> I live in Queens, it's not bad—taking the train isn't so far. This factory is very convenient to the trains. And you saw, I went out at lunch to buy groceries for home. We all do that.

Flexible time is not as important to the Hispanics. As I noted earlier, Hispanics usually did not come to New York with children. Generally, the only other family member to emigrate with the Hispanic garment worker was a spouse. Thus family responsibilities, such as caring for children, were minimal compared to the family responsibilities of the Chinese. The Hispanics could work in the Korean-owned sector, which had set hours everyday, six days a week.[10]

A few Chinese men do enter the garment industry, but they have not changed the gender images of the Chinatown factories. One man in his forties explained why he took up garment work:

> I used to teach kindergarten in Gong Hoi before coming here. Kindergarten was much better than working in the factories. I press clothes in

the factories in Chinatown and Queens now. But the work is very hard. No, I'm not interested in a restaurant job either, that work is just as hard on your body. I can't do that.

I much prefer working as a teacher than as a presser. The presser's life is very hard. You have to use the heavy machinery and you inhale all the chemicals from the cloth when they get pressed. It is extremely unhealthy. I really don't like it. That is why I want to try sewing. I think the job is much more flexible.

As a presser, you usually have to work in the evenings and on weekends. I don't like doing that. I'd rather sew on these machines and try to have some evenings free.

There were still too few men, however, to have an effect on the work organization that the Chinese women require. And few Chinese women were willing to give up their places for new men wanting to enter the business. Another reason that Chinese men were beginning to show up in small numbers in the garment industry was that the restaurant industry was facing a downturn. As a Chinese man in his forties reported, "The economy is bad, people go out less and so there are fewer restaurants. Plus in each restaurant, there are fewer people working than in each shop. There may be only a couple of cooks, two to three waiters, a few busboys, dishwasher, and a cook's helper. In a garment shop you may have forty people working from sewers to finishing people. Many shops have more people than that. Some men have decided it may just be easier to find a job in the garment industry. But most men will just start looking for restaurant jobs outside of the city. Men can still make more in restaurants." Still, there was no flood of male workers trying to enter the garment industry. Chinese male workers seemed to avoid the industry because of its gendered nature and because garment work paid less than work in the restaurants.

In contrast, in the Korean garment sector, one-third of the Hispanic workers were men. While it is not as well known, garment industry jobs were a significant source of jobs for Latinos outside the restaurant, grocery, and delicatessen sectors. Hispanic men who could not or who did not want to find jobs in those areas looked for garment work. Usually, they were able to find jobs. Hispanic men told me that working in a garment factory was like working in a "factoria,"[11] and wages were very good. Men who worked in many industries told me that they could earn higher wages in the long term in the garment industry than in other industries.

Like Chinese women, Latinas who worked in the needle trades also said that this was the only industry where they could find work. They told me that jobs in grocery stores and restaurants were for men and most did not hire women because of the physical labor required. Only two Latinas mentioned the availability of work in sectors such as housecleaning or babysitting (I can only speculate that the networks of the workers I interviewed did not connect them to housecleaning or babysitting jobs). Moreover, many women had experience in the garment industry from jobs in the *maquilas* (internationally owned factories located in Mexico and South America that employ the local population) in their homelands. Thus garment sewing was the job of choice for Latinas.

A Honduran woman in her twenties told me, "I've always worked; ever since I was fifteen, I've always sewed. I worked in many places in Honduras. When I first started sewing, the sewing shops were very small. Now they are very large. I last worked for an American company. There were six hundred people. I last worked training new women workers who never ever worked the machines. They didn't even know how to thread the machine . . . so when I came here, I wanted to look for a sewing job." And a Mexican woman in her twenties told me, "I worked for a little while as a babysitter—I can make $150 if I find five children to take care [of] in a week. But I can make more sewing."[12]

Hispanic men are not stigmatized by doing garment work, which they do not view as female work. They joined the industry easily because they could find jobs. Because Latinos come to the United States to find work and earn money, they are willing to work in any industry that offers jobs. Garment work was appealing because it paid relatively well, as a Mexican man in his thirties reported:

> It's not that hard to find work—you can find work anywhere if you're undocumented. People work in restaurants, delis, grocery stores, and you can always find a job. So we are not afraid of leaving our jobs. But the garment factory gives you more of an opportunity to do better. In a deli, there may only be two levels [of seniority or experience]. In a garment shop you can always improve yourself and learn to make more by learning new skills or by sewing faster.
>
> Here there is no real difference between men and women. There is an equal chance where they both can get jobs.

And an Ecuadorian man in his thirties reported, "Men come work sewing because there are jobs. If you can work a machine, you can make more money. My first job already I got paid four dollars an hour. And my last job I got paid $5.50."

Hispanic men were less likely than their Chinese counterparts to think of gendered reasons to avoid the garment industry. The Korean garment sector, moreover, was not structured specifically to accommodate women and thus may also have felt less threatening to the men who entered. Many men had experience with or knew of others who worked in garment factories in their homeland.[13] In addition, because the immigrant couples were usually alone or without children, the husbands and wives did not need to assume traditional roles. Here in the United States they were both money earners. Thus the sector seemed welcoming to both men and women.

Documentation, Migration, and Gender

As Massey and his colleagues (1987) note, the immigrants' ability to settle permanently and find a better job is directly related to their support system here. Latinos, I found, were more likely to extend their stays in the United States when their spouses were with them. And that is why we see shifts in the emigration plan among many Hispanics, from a transnational/household pattern to a staged emigration pattern. As one or the other spouse becomes adjusted to life in New York, more opportunities arise and the likelihood of staying increases. Moreover, when children are born in New York, parents are more likely to stay. As one twenty-six-year-old Mexican woman told me:

> I've been here three years and my husband has been here for five years. He was nineteen when I got pregnant. He was very drunk when it happened and he felt very responsible. He came to New York because he had to support us.
>
> He chose to come to New York because it was the capital of the world. And because it was the capital of the world, it couldn't be so bad. He came in through Texas as an undocumented. He was very lucky. The border people told him that if he could find someone who would support him, then he could come through. He was lucky that he had an ex-brother in law in Connecticut who helped him out. He flew right to New York.
>
> I came when I started hearing rumors of him finding a new wife. I called him immediately and told him that I was coming and that our child will stay with his mother. His brother-in-law and he had enough money to pay for my trip. I was sewing in Mexico before I came and easily found a job. I repaid him very quickly.
>
> We have one son now who is ten months old, born here. We are doing well here, making enough to send home to take care of our daughter and to live here. I found a Mexican woman with a young child to babysit my baby. We miss our daughter, but we have no plans right now to go back.

Legal status has an effect on who comes with the migrant, especially children. In turn, children affect the gender roles of men and women in the garment industry. When parents are unaccompanied by children, men and women have fewer gender expectations both at home and at work. Fewer gendered expectations create more open-mindedness about the type of work that one is willing to do. Thus more Latinos enter the Korean-owned garment sector, and in turn the sector is not segregated by gender. The data from the Chinese workers indicate that having children in New York puts tremendous pressure on them to conform to gender roles.

CHAPTER 4

The Attractions of Cloth

Here in New York, almost all the shops are owned by Koreans. They are everywhere in this neighborhood. The buildings on the East Side from Seventh to Eighth [Avenues] are newer and nicer and those from Eighth to Ninth [Avenues, which] are older and more rundown. No, there isn't really a difference in terms of the quality of clothing that they make. And no real difference in how people would choose where to work. Some of the shops over there [on the West Side] paid really well.   —*Mexican man in his thirties*

If you're working, you have to be working for the Chinese garment shops in Chinatown. Every block you can find a garment shop. You can't tell from here. You have to look up, see them through the windows. See the clothing.   —*Chinese woman in her thirties*

Emigration patterns and past experience in the garment industry help to shed light on both the long- and short-term motivations of the individuals who enter the New York City garment industry. Garment production is a worldwide industry, helping to modernize many countries in Asia, Latin America, and the Caribbean (see Bonacich and Appelbaum 2000). Not surprisingly, experienced garment workers and managers emigrate from these countries to the United States. Some go work in the New York City apparel industry.

At the same time some people in the industry never saw the inside of a garment factory before they got a job there, nor had they ever used a sewing machine. How can some of these individuals coexist with the experienced ones?

Who are the Korean and Chinese owners, and who are the Chinese and Hispanic workers? What motivates them to enter the industry? In this chapter, I describe the backgrounds of people who enter the industry and compare the individuals in the two sectors.

Overall, among my interviewees both sectors had a corps of workers with sewing or garment industry experience. I found that Chinese owners as a group had the most experience in the garment industry, more than Hispanic workers, Korean owners, and Chinese workers. Fifty-three percent of the Chinese owners and 33 percent of the Korean owners had some experience in the industry, whereas 47 percent of the Hispanic workers and 25 percent of the Chinese workers had prior experience in the garment industry. The owners' previous experience and the number of people they know in the industry are intimately connected to why they chose this line of work and how they organize their work. Similarly, the workers who know how to sew would rather be in a profession in which they can use their skills. They may lack English proficiency and documentation, but their skills are valuable.

It is more surprising to learn why and how others with no experience end up in the industry. For example, owners who were born in the United States or belong to the "1.5 generation" (those who emigrated as children, usually before the age of ten), see more opportunity in the garment industry than in their former professions.[1] Some workers view garment work as one of the few options open to them. They lack English proficiency and sometimes documentation. In their minds, at least, the needle trade factories give them an opportunity to work.

CHINESE AND KOREAN GARMENT SHOP OWNERS

The backgrounds of the garment owners whom I interviewed were similar to those of the Chinese and Korean small business owners in New York City studied by Lee (1999), Min (1996), Park (1997), Zhou (1992), and Kim (1999). The owners clearly labeled themselves as hard-working immigrants who were trying to secure their families' future. Most believed that they could do no better than their garment job—but that their American-born or American-raised children would have more opportunities. On the whole, they did not describe themselves as minorities, people of color, or as belonging to a racial group. They saw themselves as immigrants first and foremost. Those who were brought up in New York and had better English skills saw limited mobility in other professions and therefore returned to the factories, where they thought they had a slight advantage over recent immigrants.

The Backgrounds of the Owners

The garment shop owners whom I interviewed were all from Korea, China, or Hong Kong. The Chinese owners were conversant in English, although two wanted to be interviewed in Chinese. I interviewed them in a combination of English and Chinese. The Korean owners spoke English very well, and I conducted their interviews in English.[2] Garment contractors need to speak English to bid for jobs from garment manufacturers in midtown Manhattan. The Korean garment shop owners, on the whole, were more educated than the Chinese, although both the Korean and Chinese immigrants mentioned economic mobility and education for their children as the primary reasons for leaving their home country (see table 4.1). I spoke to a total of thirty garment shop owners, fifteen Chinese and fifteen Korean, all but four of whom were male.

All the owners came to the United States legally with their families. Thirteen of the Korean owners came with wives and children to New York, and two came with their parents when they were teenagers. I would classify these two as part of the 1.5 generation. Three of the Chinese owners are also members of the 1.5 or second generation, and the rest emigrated with their wives, husbands, and children.[3]

One major difference between the Chinese and Koreans is the level of experience each group attained in the garment industry. While some Chinese moved up into ownership after being workers in the New York garment industry, five of the Koreans (one-third of those interviewed) actually had been part of the management teams of large Korean sewing shops in Korea and in Latin America and so were highly trained in the production and management of garment factories (see table 4.2).

Status and Downward Mobility After Arrival

More than half of the Korean shop owners (eight) were professionals in Korea before they emigrated to the United States (see table 4.2). Moreover, fourteen

TABLE 4.1 *Educational Experience of Garment Shop Owners Interviewed*

	Educational Level*			
	< HS	HS	Col	> Col
Korean (N = 15)		1	10	4
Chinese (N = 15)	4	8	3	

*< HS—less than high school, HS—high school, Col—College, > Col—more than college

TABLE 4.2   *Work Experience of Garment Shop Owners Interviewed*

	Previous Jobs				
	Gar Ind mgmt	*Gar Ind worker*	*Retail/Sales*	*Prof*	*Other*
Korean	5	0	1	8	1
Chinese	4	4	4	3	

Gar Ind—Garment industry; Prof—Professional; Other—usually, laborer.

of the fifteen Korean employers interviewed had at least a college degree (see table 4.1). These employers experienced downward mobility in terms of occupation, although five of the eight believed that their current living standards were better than they would have been if they had stayed in Korea (even though they no longer held professional jobs). According to what they told me, they were living well in New Jersey or on Long Island, and they believed that the United States offers their children more opportunity than Korea does. Their children went to high-quality elementary and high schools and might apply to Ivy League colleges. Upward mobility for these Korean families is a combination of doing well professionally for themselves and educational achievement for their children (Park 1997). One Korean owner in his forties told me about his career:

> I have been doing this for fifteen years. I started in 1980. I live in Long Island in New Hyde Park; when I started out, my wife worked with me and we lived in Queens. Yes, I was an engineer, I came because my sister was already here as a nurse. I came in 1979. I tried to learn English to get a job. It was too hard. . . .
>
> We knew friends and family who ran small shops in Queens giving homework out to Korean women. I worked there, and one of the owners and I got together to open a shop in Manhattan. He knew of places to sew for and had experience, and I had money. It only cost $80,000 to get our first shop. We leased space and bought equipment and hired some Korean women and Hispanic women.
>
> When we got enough money, we moved to New Hyde Park. My children go to good schools for free. They are in junior high and high school.
>
> I can never make enough money to send them to good schools like that in Korea. Now I have enough to send them to good colleges here. It's

hard work to own a sewing factory, and we don't make as much as we used to, but my family has done well here.

Most owners express the sentiment that one can be successful in the United States, if one works hard. In contrast, personal contacts in politics and business spell success in Korea. Even though they earned a high income and were educated businessmen, the Korean shop owners believed that they did not have enough clout to ensure their children's success. Overall, the criteria that they used to assess their own achievements were their children's accomplishments in school. These owners believed that their children would have had fewer opportunities (especially for getting into one of the better universities) to excel in Korea. Emigrating to the United States would give the entire family a bigger boost up the mobility ladder. Both parents and children would benefit.[4]

A Korean owner in his forties told me,

> I came in 1980. . . .
>
> Their education is much better than I could have given to them in Korea. Our neighbors and friends tell us that the high school they are going to now will get them into excellent colleges, maybe even Harvard. I would have never been able to send them to any Ivy League school in the United States had I stayed in Korea. Their education will give them much more, and that kind of education can be used in Korea too. They will be able to do what they want anywhere, which is something that we could not do in Korea.
>
> Here I work very hard in my factory but I make enough, and now my children are doing well in school. . . .

Another Korean owner, also in his forties, reported:

> Back then [1978] I owned a factory and was exporting things made in the United States to my brother in Korea, who was selling them in Korea. That's how I got in the business to start with. My brother, he wanted me to do this. When I first started, I just had a few machines. It was a real small operation. You can't make much. Now this is the biggest I've ever been, and I can make about two thousand pieces a week.
>
> Yes, I plan to stay in America. This is my country. I've been here for fourteen, fifteen years now. My children are here, and they like it fine and are doing well. A while ago, someone said to me that Asians are going to take over the country. But I don't think so. Maybe it's the first generation like me [who work so hard] but not like my children. They don't want to do it. They don't need to do it.

Only one of the Korean garment shop owners believed that he would have done better if he had stayed in Korea. He was one of the more recent immigrants who came when Korea's economy was growing at a much faster rate than that of the United States. He spoke critically of how the garment industry in New York had become saturated with others like himself.[5] Even though he believed the economy was better in Korea, he did not want to return because he would not be able regain his old job and status. His friends and classmates were now doing much better in Korea than he was here in the United States. He explained:

I've been doing this since 1987 . . . and I don't think business is that good. Everyone told me the United States is good, and you can make much money. But I haven't seen that. I work hard here, but I'm not getting rich from this. There is not enough work for my factory to do. There are too many shops.

My wife and I are trying to design our own clothes to sell at flea markets. We just started doing that at RF [Roosevelt Field Mall] and sold some to small stores, and we are beginning to make some money. Sewing for other people is too competitive. I have a big factory here. I had much money to start and put most into this, but there is not enough work. Too many Koreans are doing this.

I was a chemist in Korea. I can't do that now. I can't remember anything to do with chemistry. My wife works here with me. She didn't work in Korea. In Korea, she would be taking care of the children. . . .

I don't know if it will be better for the children. They are six and three. If they are good children, it will be all right. But here the kids are too crazy. Yes, there is a lot of opportunity, but the children are spoiled.

No, I don't think about going back to Korea. I can't get my old job back. What can I do there? I am better [off] staying here even though I don't like it. My friends in Korea are doing better than me.

All the Chinese employers wanted to emigrate to the United States. Even the garment factory owner from Hong Kong wanted to emigrate. When I interviewed the Chinese owners, none expressed regrets, even though business was not as profitable as they had expected or as profitable as it had been ten years before. All the Chinese owners considered the move into garment shop ownership in the United States as either a lateral or upward move on both the career and status ladders. Two Chinese owners had been partners in the garment businesses before, but most of the rest had no prior experience in the industry and had only the most minimal management skills before opening their own shops. Two had been foremen or forewomen in the shops, and four others had been garment workers. Listen to the two who did have previous experience in the needle trades. The first is a Chinese woman who was in her forties:

> I've always worked in the garment industry. In Hong Kong my parents owned a big factory with hundreds of workers. I came here because my husband got to emigrate. In 1983, we came, and I thought I would try a shop. It didn't cost very much money. And my parents helped out over the telephone.
>
> I made the right decision to come to the U.S. My family was doing well there, but I am also doing fine here. My son goes to a good school, and he will get a good education here and get a good job. In Hong Kong, my son may not get as good of an education as here. Now if my son wants, he can get a great job in Hong Kong with a U.S. education. It wasn't like that before, but now it is. I think it is better.
>
> My husband, he helps when he can in the factory. He mostly does all the paperwork that is necessary. He likes it here, but he's having trouble learning English. I already learned some, and my son speaks it well.

A Chinese owner in his forties told me,

> I came over in 1985 with my family. There was no question that I would be in the garment industry. This is what I know how to do, and I will still do it. I know that Hong Kong was very popular, but even when I was leaving, they told me that many of them were looking for other places to manufacture that were less expensive.
>
> When we got here, I really did not have a choice at what I wanted to do. I didn't want to work in the restaurants.
>
> It's better here than in Hong Kong. We live in a nice house in Queens. Our children are doing well. My wife and I knew a little English, so it wasn't that hard to learn more. I think we made the right decision to come here. My wife and I are used to New York. We lived in a city that was more crowded than here.
>
> The only problem now is that work is not that good. It was better before. We may start changing our business. If there is more demand for nonunion work, we may move out of Chinatown to be able to do that. Here in Chinatown, every factory is unionized, and all the business agents know everyone else. It's hard not to be unionized. We may move uptown

or to Brooklyn. We have friends that just did that to avoid the union. If business is bad, we have to take a risk, we either lose money here, and we may be able to do better there.

I suppose we may be able to find other jobs. We don't know, but we don't want to go back to Hong Kong.

Two old-timers, who had been in the New York garment business for many years, had no doubts that emigrating had been the right thing to do. According to these men, both of whom had been farmers in China, anyone who had the chance left China. The Chinese, like the Koreans, believe there is more opportunity in New York for their children; however, the Chinese also thought that emigrating would give them a better standard of living and offer a simple way to improve their own status immediately. One of the former farmers told me,

I came over from Hong Kong in 1970, and I've been doing this since then. I used to work in the shops in Chinatown as a presser. I learned by watching and thought I could manage a shop. I got my wife (she was a garment worker) and another friend to help me, and we opened one factory to try. . . .

We came to the U.S. because everyone was coming over, and I got a chance through my brother. Everyone wanted to come. No one wanted to stay in Hong Kong or China. Everyone thought the U.S. was the best country with the highest standard of living.

We all came, when anyone got the chance they came. Everyone did better in the U.S. I don't know of anyone who would have wanted to stay back then. Maybe now, people are beginning not to be afraid of Hong Kong. If they are making money now, they will stay. But when I left, the U.S. is where everyone made money, not anywhere else. No one gave up the chance to come.

The 1.5- and second-generation owners were the most critical of the garment industry and of their chances for upward mobility in the United States. While they had less experience with garments than the older immigrants did, they spoke English better and were trained in the American school system. Although they had trained to be engineers or computer technicians, these young men had a difficult time getting jobs in their fields or believed that they were being underpaid. While they did not say that race was an obstacle, they did recognize that being nonwhite has disadvantages. As one Chinese man in his thirties said:

I went to Baruch College in business and thought it would be simple to get a job in accounting. I'm good at math. It wasn't bad, but when I worked there for five years and didn't get much of a chance to be promoted, I started looking for some other things to do. I did not think the company liked me and really thought that I should just stay at my desk all the time just doing paperwork. I didn't think that was fair; they never even let me try to get new clients or work at different locations. Others would be able to go to clients and get work, but I was just given all paperwork to check and enter the data.

Opportunities seemed much brighter to the immigrant garment owners and their families. These owners were educated and saw the endless possibilities that were also available to their children. Those who were brought up in the United States saw fewer opportunities, especially in the jobs that they were trained in. The garment industry was a natural choice, but the job did not hold the prestige that they had aspired to.

Getting into the Garment Industry

Not one of the garment shop owners in my study ventured into the industry without the encouragement of friends or relatives who gave them tips and leads about how to start. As a group, the Korean owners were more experienced than the Chinese, especially in the management of large overseas garment shops. Five Korean owners had previously managed garment shops in Latin America or Korea. However, they were new to the industry in the United States. On average the Koreans owned or worked in the U.S. industry for eight years versus thirteen years for the Chinese. A little more than half of all the owners were never directly involved with the garment industry before owning a factory in New York. They became interested in the industry only through friends or relatives in the business. Some, like the Chinese 1.5 generationer, were exposed to the industry through the work of a parent.

Eight of the fifteen Chinese owners I interviewed had previous experience in the garment industry (see table 4.2). The other seven were employed in a different line of work before running a garment shop. The three owners from Hong Kong, and the one from the Guangdong area of China, actually knew manufacturers and had contacts with others who needed sewing done in the United States. Through those contacts and friends in the industry in New York's Chinatown, they easily got contracts and work for their factories. They brought with them money as well as experience. One Chinese man worked in a garment shop for more than five years, first as a presser and then helping the owners check finished items. He, his wife, and another male friend, also with similar experience, later became owners themselves. The three other Chinese owners were women who once worked as sewers in factories owned by other Chinese.

A Chinese man who had been in the business for more than twenty years told me:

> In 1975, I opened my first factory. We made lots of money and had lots of business. Five years later I opened my second factory. I only closed that one four years ago [in 1992].
>
> We always got our work from this company called Coinpart.[6] Before, they just used to give us work and we would make it. All the clothing would be shipped out all over the U.S. Now the stores have to order [from the manufacturers] before they give us work. Things have changed very much. Our clothing just used to be shipped to Macy's, Gimbel's, everywhere. Now we only make enough for JC Penney. . . . we only have one sewing shop now.
>
> We have always been a unionized shop. We always do everything that ought to be correct. We try to follow the rules. We pay by check always—we're not like those other businesses that come and go.

A Chinese woman in her forties, who worked and owned a factory in Hong Kong, told me: "I've always worked in the garment industry. In Hong Kong my parents owned a big factory with hundreds of workers. . . . I thought I would try a shop. They spoke to the manufacturers they worked with in Hong Kong and set up meetings with me for their lines who needed U.S. production. I met them and made contacts. That is how I started this. The manufacturers are good, but they are always rushing you."

All the Korean shop owners I interviewed got involved in the garment industry through personal connections. One Korean owner's brother had been in retailing and suggested that clothing made in the United States would sell well in Korea. All the others had family members or friends in the industry. A Korean man in his forties said, "I used to be a mechanic, but I had a sister here who is a nurse. She did very well and told me that I could too. She had lots of friends here who told her that I could work with them in their garment factories. And when I first got here, that's what I did. I worked with them in Queens. Only seven years ago did I get enough money to open my own shop."

Another Korean owner, a man in his thirties, told me that going into the garment industry required more business knowledge than the grocery or delicatessen business. To him, garment work was higher in status and a step up from running grocery stores because you had to manage many more people and deadlines, whereas in a grocery all you needed to know was how to buy and sell. As he explained: "You see, this business is not like the grocery business. It really is a business; the ones who don't have an education can't do it. They fail. They don't understand all the complexities. This is not a grocery business. There it's easy. They buy, you sell. You know how much you spent on everything and then you sell. Here, you have people to manage, and workers to work and manufacturers that want certain things and deadlines."

In contrast, another Korean owner, a man in his forties, thought that it was much easier to start and manage a garment business than a grocery store. It was less expensive and required only some capital investment in machines and space and not a huge outlay for stock:

> I myself have had my shop for twelve years. When we started moving to Manhattan, I was one of the first to move a factory here. We were the risk takers, and it was profitable.
>
> Rent is cheap and the location is good. When they [Korean garment shop owners] first started over fourteen years ago, most shops were in Queens and then gradually moved to Manhattan.
>
> It was much cheaper to open a garment shop than to open a store. For grocery stores, you need key money [a nonrefundable payment to the leaseholder or building owner]. Here in midtown [Manhattan], you don't. People just moved out, and you could just spend $100,000 to open a shop. Just need to get machines, it's the only overhead—nothing else—and you can always find workers. People come looking all the time.

For the five Koreans who had worked in garment shops before, the transition to working in the factories in New York City was relatively easy. They had already heard about the shops and expected to open a shop once they emigrated. They even knew that they were going to hire Spanish speakers because friends and family who had emigrated previously had told them about Hispanic workers. Moreover, three of these five were conversant in Spanish (or at least a Romance language) because they had worked in Korean-owned factories in Mexico, Guatemala, or Brazil. In fact, they mentioned that the smaller shops that they had here were easier to manage than the shops they worked in before. A Korean owner in his forties reported:

> Before I got married, I was sent to manage a very large factory in Guatemala. There were 150 workers at least. I worked there for three years, first doing work on the line—making sure that the workers were all sewing properly and making sure that they were all working at their top

speed. I also had to move people around to make sure that each section was working at a good speed. We didn't want any one section to move too much ahead of another because then you have parts of clothing that are lying around, waiting to get sewed. After I did that for a year, my company moved me up to the office, and there I was in charge of hiring and quality control. I had to check the garments to make sure that they were sewn properly. When I went back to Korea, I got married and had two children. I continued to work for them as a manager until I came to New York. I never thought about doing anything else other than garment. For me, I thought it would be easy to do this. I only thought that I would make much more money here. I didn't know there was so much competition to get work here.

Whereas most Chinese and Korean immigrants were drawn to the industry by the prospects of a good career, members of the Chinese and Korean 1.5 generation turned to the industry because they felt blocked in the careers that they had trained for.[7] They were frustrated by the lack of rewards in fields such as engineering, marketing, and sales, and they saw friends and relatives in the garment industry who were earning more money or had more independence than they did. Moreover, they were convinced that because of their command of English and their ability to deal with "Americans," they would be more successful in an immigrant-dominated sector. Thus they turned to the garment industry. However, they, like the others, used the social ties they had with family and friends in the industry and invested money that they had saved, borrowed, or brought with them from their homeland. A Korean man in his thirties, who considers himself a member of the 1.5 generation, told me:

I came to the U.S. when I was sixteen years old with my parents. I'm only thirty-four. I went to some high school here and then went to the New Jersey Technical School and got a degree in mechanical engineering. I'm a part of the knee-high generation. I worked for a couple of years in marketing and did not like it. I make more money now than when I was in sales.

I knew seven families, all distant relatives, all working in the garment industry, and I thought I would try too. I didn't know anything when I first started here eight years ago. I just got fifteen machines, set them up, and started to get work. After a year, I could expand to forty machines. . . . I have three shops now. My brother helps me manage a shop upstairs on the sixteenth floor, and I just opened another shop across the street. It is really nice. I put tile on the floors. Manufacturers like it clean and like tiles on the floors. I know much about the manufacturers now. They talk to me because I speak English well.

Similarly, a Chinese man in his twenties, also a member of the 1.5 generation, related:

My mother used to sew and be a forelady. I used to help her out. I know something about assembly and quality. My partners are like me, they wanted to try. My partner is from China, and only five years older than me. He couldn't find a good job either. He didn't want to be a bank teller.

No. I'm not born here, came from Hong Kong. One of my partners is from China and the other is from Hong Kong, and we invested together. All of us speak English and Chinese and thought we could do better than some of the older owners. It only cost us $50,000 to open the shop.[8] We have only been in business for five years and we are doing fine.

The garment shop owners used a variety of means to finance their shops. A survey of the thirty owners found that starting a garment factory can cost anywhere from $50,000 to $100,000, depending on the kinds of machinery that the owners want to purchase or lease, the cost of renting loft space, and utilities. These loft spaces usually require little work because they are often already garment factories. Therefore furnishings like tables are usually in place. Owners may only need to buy or lease the machinery they want their workers to use. Owners can also easily estimate the cost of electricity based on the previous owner's usage. What is variable are the employees' wages and the payments that the owners receive for the work done.

The majority of the Chinese owners pooled their money with partners or gathered short-term loans from friends or family to open their shops. For example, the two owners who had relatives in the garment business in Hong Kong had enough money or savings from their parents to open a shop without borrowing from others. The young Chinese partners pooled their savings to start the business. These Chinese partners had worked in white-collar industries and saved enough money for the new venture. One of the old-timers pooled his money with a partner, and the other old-timer had saved enough money to start a business. One borrowed money from a bank, and the rest borrowed money from friends or other relatives—whom the owners called "partners."[9]

The Korean owners were less likely to pool their savings with other Koreans to start a business. Ten owners had brought enough money with them from Korea to start a business, which was their intention. The rest of the owners had help from family and friends. For example, the former mechanic said he borrowed from family or friends. And the youngest owner had help from family members who were already in the business. None of the Korean or Chinese owners mentioned using a rotating credit association.[10]

Chinese and Hispanic Garment Shop Workers

Compared with the garment shop owners, the workers had much less education but were but much more likely to have experience in garment or manufacturing work. Thirteen percent of the owners had less than a high school education compared with 88 percent of the workers.[11] Only 6 percent of workers had a college degree, whereas 23 percent of the owners I interviewed had a college degree or better. Among the Chinese, this educational disparity is less apparent. Eighty percent of the Chinese owners had less than twelve years of education, which is surprisingly close to the education levels of the Chinese workers (88 percent had less than twelve years of education). Only 12 percent of the Chinese workers had completed some college or finished college, whereas 20 percent of the Chinese owners had finished college. The educational disparity between the Korean owners and Hispanic workers is huge. Eighty-eight percent of the Hispanic workers had less than twelve years of education. None of the Korean owners had less than twelve years of education and only one (6 percent) acknowledged having only a high school diploma (see tables 4.1 and 4.3). When the workers are compared in terms of educational experience, Chinese and Hispanics had similar characteristics, even though 35 percent (nineteen of fifty-five) of the Hispanics interviewed were male.

TABLE 4.3   *Years of Education—Garment Workers*

	< 8 yrs	< HS	< Col	Col*
Chinese (N = 49)				
Men				1
Women	28	15	3	2
Latino (N = 49)				
Men	13	2	1	3
Women	12	16	2	

*< 8 yrs = less than eight years of education; < HS = some high school; < Col = some college; Col = college degree.

Note: Ninety-eight of 112 interviewees answered the question about education.

TABLE 4.4 *Work Experience of Garment Workers Interviewed**

| | Previous Jobs | | | | | |
	Gar Ind mgmt	Gar Ind worker	Retail	Manu	Agr	Prof
Chinese (N = 55)						
Men						I
Women		14	8	18	12	2
Hispanic (N = 51)						
Men	I	6	2	2	7	I
Women		17	3	11	I	

*One hundred six of 112 interviewees answered the question about work experience in their home country.
Gar Ind mgmt—garment industry management; Gar Ind worker—garment industry worker; Retail—retail and sales; Manu—manufacturing; Agr—agriculture; Prof—professional

Likewise, there are huge disparities in the work backgrounds of the workers and owners. Of the owners, 37 percent had held a professional job back home, while only 4 percent of the workers had done so (see tables 4.2 and 4.4).[12] Surprisingly, only 36 percent of workers had previously worked in the garment industry, whereas 43 percent of owners had experience in a garment shop. None of the owners had been in any other kind of manufacturing, whereas 29 percent of the workers had done other manufacturing work. About one-fifth of the workers and none of the owners had been farmers.

However, differences appear in workers' work experiences. Overall, the Hispanics had more experience in the garment industry. Forty-seven percent of the Hispanics had worked in the garment industry in their previous job in their home country. In contrast, 25 percent of the Chinese had worked in the garment industry back home. Another 24 percent of the Hispanics had been in manufacturing, while 33 percent of the Chinese had been in manufacturing. Twenty-two percent of the Chinese had been in farming compared with only 16 percent of the Hispanics.

The majority of all workers, 88 percent of the Hispanics and 81 percent of the Chinese, had experience in the garment industry, manufacturing, or farming. Among the Hispanics whom I interviewed, nearly 88 percent of the women (28 of 32) had been in the garment industry or manufacturing, in contrast to 37 percent of the men (7 of 19). Interestingly, 37 percent of the men had

TABLE 4.5   *Worker Wage and Garment Shop Experience (Averages)*

	Take-home wages	Age	Years in U.S.	No. places wked	Years in Gar. Ind.
Chinese (N = 42★)	$4.04/hr	40 yrs	10	4	8.8
Hispanics (N = 45)	$5.30/hr	34	5.6	4.4	5
Men (19)	$5.70/hr	32	3.8	5	2.8
Women (26)	$5.16/hr	35	7.3	4.1	6.4

Note: Both Chinese and Hispanic workers average fifty hours a week (Monday through Saturday); eighty-seven of 112 interviewees answered the question about wages.
★All but two were female.

been in farming, whereas less than 1 percent of the women had worked in farming. Thus while the work experience of the Chinese seemed to spread evenly across the three major industries, Latinas seem to come overwhelmingly from the garment industry, and Latinos' job experience is split evenly between the garment industry and farming. Few Latinos have worked in manufacturing.

Table 4.5 summarizes the average wages, years worked in the New York City garment industry, number of places worked, and age and time spent in the United States. Almost all the Hispanics were relatively new workers in the industry with an average of five years of experience; the Chinese averaged 8.8 years of experience. The Hispanics had been in the United States for an average of just 5.6 years, whereas the Chinese averaged ten years in the United States. On average these Hispanic workers were six years younger than the Chinese women. The Latinos were the youngest.

As a group, Latinos were also most likely to have earned the highest wages, at $5.70 an hour, even with the fewest years of experience in garment work (2.8 years). However, as a group, they had switched jobs more often than the Chinese women and Latinas. A sizable group of Chinese immigrants had worked steadily in the industry since 1970.

Worker Categories

Most garment shop owners told me that they entered the garment industry because they knew others in the business who encouraged and supported them. Workers, however, were looking for jobs suited to their family needs and that welcomed documented and undocumented immigrants who knew little English. Workers need jobs that fit their circumstances, that is, the conditions surrounding their immigration status and their family position, particularly as wives and mothers. The workers found jobs when someone brought them into a shop or directed them by giving them the address of the shop (Granovetter 1974; Portes 1995; Holzer 1996).

The Chinese garment sector is an immigrant industry where newcomers find work easily. One reason is that the flexible organization within the Chinese factories meets the workers' needs. The organization—which includes flexible hours and whole-garment piecework[13]—provides the newest, untrained immigrants, and any older woman returning to work, with the ability to work alongside high school and college students working part time as well as women who have made a career in the garment industry.

The Korean sector of the garment industry in many ways fits the needs of the Hispanic workers. Hispanics usually come looking for specific types of jobs that pay wages in cash. Korean employers are willing to hire undocumented Hispanics. And the industry provides higher wages to the more skilled workers.

There are major differences between the Chinese and Hispanic workers. Although workers in both groups had held, on average, four jobs in the industry when I interviewed them, the Chinese had been in the garment industry almost twice as long as the Hispanics. This suggests that either the jobs that the Hispanic workers hold are less stable or that they leave and look for other jobs more frequently. Additionally, the Chinese were older, with an average age of forty; the average age of the Hispanics was thirty-four. This age difference is partially related to immigration policies and to the length of time that each group had been in the New York City area. As I discussed in an earlier chapter, Hispanics who are healthy, do not have children, and can emigrate without documents tend to be younger than the Chinese. The Chinese were more likely to emigrate as families, and because of the paperwork, the process usually takes longer, so that many newer immigrants are middle-aged. In addition, many of the older working Chinese immigrants arrived as early as 1968, the first wave after the immigration law reforms of 1965. The last difference is that Hispanics earn more, making an average of $5.30 an hour compared with $4.04 an hour for the Chinese. I will address this discrepancy in a later chapter.

Chinese Women

The Chinese women I interviewed fell into three categories. First is the group that was new to the industry, including women who had been in the industry for five years or less (eighteen women) as well as new immigrants who were working in the industry for the first time. This group also included long-time immigrant women with older children who had never before worked in New York but had decided to work after their children started school or were old enough to be independent. The second group was made up of students—young women working part time while they went to school (three women). And the third group was comprised of women who had always worked in the garment industry as a career (thirty-four women). The majority of these women (twenty-eight) had worked for ten years or more, although some (six women) had worked as few as six years. It is unusual to see all these types of women in a single industry. However, this can be explained by the organization of the workplace, which can accommodate all of them.

> I don't plan on learning English. If I need a few words, I will learn those. I'm too old to learn another language. My sister-in-law took me to find work in the garment shops. Her garment shop is very nice. In the beginning I would go everyday and not earn any money. I would just spend my time learning how to piece together garments, and just try to turn on the machine. My sister-in-law would show me how to sew the pieces and how to turn on the machine. The machine was so loud it scared me. Now I can sew but still very slow. I make a little money, enough to help buy food. I don't think I could have found another job.

The second group, which I least expected to meet in the industry, was comprised of students. The garment shop's piecework and flexible schedule were important not only to mothers with children but to high school and college students who wanted to work. Young women students in the industry are relatively new immigrants still living at home with their parents. They know some English, but they have not moved on to the other youth-oriented part-time jobs, such as those in fast-food restaurants, clothing, and other retail stores. Two drawbacks that they face are their lack of facility in English and the relative paucity of retail jobs in Chinatown or the Asian communities in Brooklyn or Queens, where they live. The garment industry offers opportunities that fit their school schedules. Two college students told me how garment work fits into their lives. A Chinese woman in her twenties told me, "Well, my older sister used to work in the factory before I got here. She would go there after school. She went to high school here and went to a two-year college. My mother took me to the factory where I learned what my mother did, which was hemming. Then my sister would only work part time after school."

Another Chinese woman in her twenties said, "I go to community college, and I come to work on the weekends and a couple of days a week. If I get busy during finals in April and December, I don't work. Work is slow then. In September there is a lot of work and I work more then. I take some classes during the day, but most of the time I take classes at night. I sew fast, so I make much more here than working any other job. My mother works here and always helps to make sure I can come to work when I need it."

Long-time garment workers, those who averaged ten or more years in the business, make up the third category. By working in the industry, they have saved enough to help buy houses and move their families to the outer boroughs. These workers provide not only income for their families but also low-cost health insurance through their membership in the union. The career workers whom I interviewed had contributed to their own and their children's upward mobility.

Of the three groups, the long-time garment workers are the real backbone of the industry. They sew the majority of the production work and recruit and train new workers, both in skills and in the work culture of each shop. Because they are recognized as such by the owners, they are frequently rewarded with easier jobs that allow them to earn more money, especially in bonuses and favors.[14] Thus these workers help stabilize production levels in the industry. An experienced Chinese worker in her late fifties told me:

> I worked in the garment factory for seventeen years and have been in the U.S. for eighteen years. I came to the U.S. with my husband and two kids. When my kids were young, my youngest was five and my oldest was twelve when I started working. I have three kids, an older daughter and two younger sons. When I first got here, we lived in Chinatown and sent the kids to school. I would leave work early to pick them up and wouldn't come to work until I dropped them off at school. It worked fine. When my mother-in-law came, she took care of them. Back then it was easy to come from Hong Kong. I could never make that much money in Hong Kong. Here, I made enough to send my kids to school and to help buy a house.

Another experienced worker in her late forties told me: "When I first moved here, we lived with my mother-in-law in Chinatown. We did everything down here [Chinatown]. My kids could even just come up to visit me after school. I could always go home to see them. Now we have a big house in Brooklyn; my mother-in-law doesn't like living there because she can't just go outside and buy groceries on the corner. . . . Yes, I helped with the payment from my salary."

The reliability of these experienced workers enables the Chinese garment factory owners to offer other workers part-time work or a flexible schedule. As one woman said: "The boss likes me to work full time. I sew fast and neat.

When a sample comes, I just have to look at it once over, then I can make it. Many others can't do that."

Other workers are valued for their recruiting and training abilities, like this Chinese woman in her forties: "I don't need to ask friends to come work here. They always ask me if there is a job. The reputation of the factory is very good. And when I can bring someone in, I always do. It's easy, when I see a seat open, I ask the boss if my friend can come. He almost always says yes, unless he already promised the seat to another worker. And when my friend is here, I just tell them what the boss and forelady likes. They just have to do it. Most of the time, they learn how to sew by themselves. And the boss treats me nice, especially if the worker I bring in is good or is trying hard to learn." Another Chinese woman in her forties told me, "Whenever I bring someone to work at this shop, I always teach them what to do. I'm in charge of them, and I want them to be good workers. The boss knows how well I teach them. If he sees that I'm teaching them well, sometimes I get a bonus."

Hispanic Workers

Hispanic workers fall into only two categories: men and women. They were almost all the same age: the average age for the men was thirty-two; for the women it was thirty-five. The men were newer immigrants and tended to switch jobs more readily than the women. The men were also less experienced and tended to look for tasks that they could learn easily and quickly so that they could gain skills and make more money. The women tended to stay at their jobs for a longer period of time because they were more experienced, adapted quickly to their task, and took fewer risks when they had a relatively good job. The women averaged 6.4 years of work in the garment industry while working in five different factories. The men had an average of only 2.8 years in the industry and had worked in 4.1 places. Moreover, the men's average take-home wages were higher than the women's. Men and women coexisted in the garment industry at a time when Latinas were emigrating at higher rates. Young Latinas increasingly enter the United States for work, just as men had in the past. Changing cultural circumstances around the gendered expectations of women and work have given Latinas more freedom to pursue work (Salzinger 2003).

Changing expectations also allowed Latinos to enter an industry dominated by women. Men could negotiate their wages better because of their willingness to move from job to job for better wages and to ask for appropriate wages when they acquired new skills and experience. Young women were less willing to change jobs and ask for higher wages because their ability to be assertive had not caught up to the changing gender expectations of immigration and work.

YOUNG WOMEN

Like the Chinese women, Latinas enter the garment industry because it hires women. Moreover, interviewees told me that friends and relatives specifically advised them to try to find work in the garment industry. The undocumented Latinas have few work choices in New York City. Male-dominated work, like that in the delis and restaurants, dominates the wanted ads.[15]

Babysitting was the only other possibility that the women mentioned. However, the group that I interviewed was inclined to dismiss babysitting for middle-class urban families as an inadequate option. Babysitters quickly switched to the garment factory when they got the chance. The women came to New York for the same reasons as the men, that is, to find jobs that pay well, and the jobs that pay well are in the garment industry. Thus the majority of these women gravitated to sewing instead of babysitting. One Mexican woman who did try babysitting found that garment work had more advantages: "I went to work for them as a babysitter for one year. I was only supposed to do it for a month, but they didn't want me to go. The children cried for me and really wanted me to be there. I was paid three hundred dollars a week. I left on Saturday to go to my home and came back on Sunday night. I lived there with them. I make much more in the factory, and I can go and come as I please." (She was making $6.75 an hour in a garment factory.)

Moreover, these women would not choose to work in businesses where men predominate. First, they said that they were not physically capable of handling these jobs and, second, state that they would not be comfortable working in businesses dominated by men. An Ecuadorian woman in her thirties told me, "My brother told me that the restaurants were not for women. Only men work there—you have to move boxes of food, help cut food, and clean. I don't think I can do that, and I really don't want to be the only woman." Similarly, a Mexican woman in her twenties reported, "It's not safe to work with mostly men. They can tease you and make you very uncomfortable."

As it is, emigrating, working, and standing on the "for hire" corner looking for a job are enough of a challenge to traditional gender roles for these Latinas.[16] The same Latinas who discussed harassment in restaurant work also discussed the possibility of harassment in a garment industry job. A young Mexican woman noted, "When you don't speak English, sewing is the best. I tried, and others told me that you can be a waitress in a Mexican restaurant. But when the men drink too much, I don't like it. They tease you and try to play with you, and if you don't play back, you don't get a tip. Sometimes they just get crazy. In the factory, you have a foreman—sometimes, they can be terrible too, but most of the time they just want you to work, and they want everyone to concentrate on working. They don't care if you are a woman."

Others, like this Ecuadorian woman in her twenties, described the gender rules established on the street corner: "I don't like standing on the corner. It's embarrassing. In my country only the bad women stand on the corner. There are too many men there. Sometimes the strange men would bother me. And you never know. Right now I go there to meet with another woman—a Singer operator, so we can go look for jobs together. It is a different woman each time. I don't like going into the buildings myself anymore. Going by myself is dangerous. Have you heard the rumor that a woman got beaten up and raped in one of the stairwells? I don't go [by] myself anymore."

A young Mexican woman, who was standing on the northwest side of 37th Street, in front of a taco cart on Eighth Avenue, described the hiring corner: "The women always stand on this side of the street to wait for jobs. The men stand over there. We each have our sides. It's better this way. They won't bother us. We come early in the morning sometimes as early as seven A.M. Before, we used to go look and knock on doors, but now the owners come here to find us."

The Latinas who have been in the United States for some years told me that men working in the garment shops is a relatively new phenomenon, although the men discount that notion. Many Hispanics note that Latinos have been working in the *maquilas* back home since the early 1990s.

YOUNG MEN

> There are many Ecuadorians in the jewelry and garment industries, but I went to garment because even though I had friends in jewelry, I found out that it was easier to get a job in the garment industry. I don't know how to sew, but I can cut tags, threads, and bag the clothing. That is how I got started.   —*Ecuadorian man in his twenties*

In contrast to Latinas, young Latinos did not mention gender roles in the garment industry. While the women explained their presence in the garment industry as a result of a gendered division of labor in New York City immigrant communities—women did not work in the restaurants or groceries—men avoided or did not use any gendered interpretation. Men just assumed that they have always been in the garment industry and have a right to be there, with or without women. To the men the garment industry was just another place where jobs were available. The majority of the men whom I interviewed said it was easier to get a job in the garment industry than any other industry. Men, however, turned to the garment industry after they had been turned down by the small delicatessens and grocery stores that often hire Latinos.[17] The men did not acknowledge that they had entered an industry that was dominated by women. Instead, they stressed that working with machinery in a sewing factory was a way to earn higher wages. Latinos also stressed that the industry has room for fast promotions.

An Ecuadorian man told me how he came to work in the garment industry: "I got my first job in the Dominican factory through my father's friend. She helped me find the job in the garment factory. I sewed in that factory. I had experience at home. My father is a tailor; my mother and I help out [in] his business. Then in my second job, a friend told me about the factory. They hire men Latino workers too. We work hard. It doesn't matter that we are men as long as we know how to sew. They like men doing the heavier sewing—we are faster than women when we work with the thick cloths. We are stronger."

Garment shops offer more opportunity than the delicatessens, groceries, and restaurants by allowing advancement and higher wages if one learns more skills or sews faster. According to these men, small stores or restaurants offer few chances for advancement, noting that once "hired as a worker/sorter/washer in a deli, grocery or restaurant—always that." As one interviewee explained: "It's not that hard to find work—you can find work anywhere if you're undocumented. People work in restaurants, delis, grocery stores. And you can always find a job. So we are not afraid of leaving our jobs. But the garment factory gives you more of an opportunity to do better. In a deli, there may only be two levels. But in a garment shop you can always improve yourself and learn to make more kinds of clothing faster."

Moreover, the young men who had most recently arrived in the United States expressed a less rigid perception of male or female gender roles at work. They were more willing to try different kinds of jobs, even jobs that were once known as women's work. Lack of English and status as an undocumented immigrant relegated men to jobs that may be women's work back home. At the same time, while Latinas were pushing the boundaries by working and emigrating, they were still not willing to work in any occupation that had a majority of men. Latinas believe that this is an unsafe situation. One Mexican man in his thirties put it this way: "I'm not macho because I was raised very differently and even if you are when you come here, you can't remain that way. Because you learn fast that you have to help with different things around the home and accept whatever job they give you" (outside the home).

There is nothing in particular that makes garment work more suitable for men or women. Men and women enter the industry because of economic necessity, and the gendered image changes accordingly, as I noted in chapter 1.

Chinese women dominated the industry because so many women needed work. So long as the Chinese men have their jobs and are not being pushed out of the restaurant industry, and so long as there are jobs for the Chinese women in the garment industry, the Chinese sector will be defined as women's work.

However, because of economic necessity, Hispanic men and women are working together in the shops owned by Koreans. Women insisted that the garment industry was where they should work, but Latinos, who believed that the jobs were better than the other work available to them, were adapting and entering the industry without any stereotypical hesitation. Slowly, the sector was being redefined as being open to both men and women. Thus for Hispanics in Korean-owned garment shops, garment work is not particularly gendered; it is gendered only by those who enter the industry and define it as such.

In summary, all the individuals whom I interviewed—both workers and owners—entered the garment industry because they were told about it by others or knew of others who were successful in it. Throughout immigrant communities, information about where they can find work spreads quickly because it is of utmost importance. For the majority, working and earning higher wages are the reasons that they emigrated to the United States.

No one interviewed complained that too few jobs were available during the mid- to late 1990s, although many said that they were earning too little for the work they did. In the next chapter, I look at the two separate sectors, Korean and Chinese, and why the owners choose to have coethnic and noncoethnic workers.

CHAPTER 5

What Employers Want

We are more open than the Chinese. They [undocumented Mexicans and Ecuadorians] should be given a chance. They are excellent workers. Maybe we have learned to communicate with them and the Chinese haven't. It would be much better if the government, the workers, and us can come to an agreement. They should be able to give them some kind of paper so they can work, so I don't have to pay fines, and so the government can collect taxes. There has to be some in-between to accommodate them. It's not fair to them, me, or the U.S.

—*Korean owner in his forties*

We hire only Chinese. Some of the women have been here since the beginning. They watched my daughter grow up. And when their new relatives come over, we usually give them a job. They are good, they all teach them how to sew and everything. But some of these new ones from China are getting bad. They are very lazy, and think that everything is provided for them. It must be that communist society. The last few years has not been good.

—*Chinese owner in his thirties*

The Korean shop owners prefer to hire Mexican and Ecuadorian laborers, whereas the Chinese owners prefer to hire the Chinese. Why don't the Koreans hire the Chinese, who are immigrants as well as fellow Asians? And why don't the Chinese hire undocumented Mexicans and Ecuadorians, who actually have more experience sewing?

In this chapter I answer these questions by untangling some of the differ- ences between the coethnic and noncoethnic, racially mixed sectors. I focus on the hiring of workers and discuss how and why these groups separate them- selves to the point that there is little intermingling. This chapter draws on and extends the theories of immigrant incorporation (Portes and Bach 1985; Bonacich and Modell 1980), hiring preferences (Neckerman and Kirschenman 1991; Holzer 1996; Lee 1998), ethnic closure (Waldinger 1995), and opportunity hoarding (Tilly 1997). The literature on immigrant incorporation emphasizes the employment opportunities conferred on coethnics by both the ethnic en- clave and middleman minority economies (Portes and Bach 1985; Bonacich and Modell 1980).[1] According to both the middleman minority and ethnic en- clave theories, ethnic employers benefit from a large pool of inexpensive work- ers who are linguistically and culturally similar. The workers receive low wages but are compensated in other ways by coethnic business firms, including job training, prospects for managerial and supervisory positions, and eventual self- employment in the same industry.

However, the work by Waldinger (1995) and Waldinger and Lichter (2003) on ethnic closure and the work by Tilly (1997) on opportunity hoarding stress how one ethnic group's gain can be another group's disadvantage. Ethnic groups with access to an economic niche may in fact be hoarding opportunities for themselves. And, in effect, they may close off opportunities for other ethnic groups.

These scenarios can take a different turn when an ethnic group does not have enough members willing to work in certain industries. Korean Ameri- cans who want to be entrepreneurs need to turn to another group to find workers. Smith (1994, 1996) and Dae Young Kim (1999) stress how necessity brings together dissimilar ethnic groups, and the managerial group eventually accords its employees the status of "fictive coethnics." However, Smith (1997) found that positive benefits from "fictive coethnicity" were not always con- ferred by the Greeks and Koreans who hired Mexicans. He found differences between the Greek and Korean employers and between the grocery and restaurant businesses.

Practices used among the Korean and Chinese employers in this study can be linked to differences in the labor market and the type of work organization, employers, and industries. Garment shop owners need employees with more skills than the people that grocers and restaurateurs hire, so the garment indus- try hiring process is more selective. The organization of work is different in the Chinese garment sector (whole-garment piecework), where the owners hire coethnics; workers in the Korean shops are organized to do section work, are paid by the hour, and come from a different ethnic group than the owners do.

Furthermore, employers in both sectors have distinct preferences for whom they hire, and the garment industry, with its machinery and shop floor, is far different from the restaurant and grocery sectors. Many factors can inhibit garment industry employers from adopting the informal hiring practices used among coethnics that are cited in much of the literature on ethnic enclaves and middlemen minorities.

Employers have their own perspectives and tastes, both of which affect the kinds of workers they will consider and eventually hire. Because hiring practices are affected by bias, how employers perceive various ethnic groups is especially influential (Neckerman and Kirschenman 1991). This is especially true for the groups that the employers avoid. According to Holzer (1996) and Waters (1999), the general perception by employers, including the Chinese and Koreans, is that African Americans and Puerto Ricans do not work as hard and are more troublesome than immigrant ethnic groups. As a result, employers try to avoid hiring from those two groups (Holzer 1996; Waters 1999). In addition, the Chinese and Koreans share a preference for hiring immigrants over nonimmigrants, although they prefer to hire members of different immigrant groups (Cheng and Espiritu 1989).

EMPLOYERS' HIRING QUEUE

The hiring preferences of both Korean and Chinese employers are economically and racially motivated. Typically, the owners prefer immigrants to Americans and skilled workers who do not speak English, mostly because Americans and immigrants who know English are more capable of standing up for their rights. Owners know that Chinese immigrants and undocumented Mexicans and Ecuadorians have limited options and limited ability to complain to authorities. Employers can take advantage of these workers. In general, the employers offer the minimum or just above the minimum wage and only the benefits that the state and federal law require. Immigrant workers accept this compensation with little protest. Race also influences whom the owners or employers hire. Their preference for non-English-speaking immigrants is related to their encounters with English-speaking African Americans and Puerto Ricans, whom the owners and employers perceive to be lazy and demanding.

The Top of the Queue
Korean employers say they would in fact prefer to hire coethnics, but Koreans are too expensive and too few are willing to work on the garment shop floor.

The majority of Korean women who could have sewed have turned to the manicure business, which gives them an opportunity to become entrepreneurs or at least work in an industry that has higher status (Kang 1997). The few Korean seamstresses who remain in the garment industry are specialists who sew extremely detailed parts of clothing and are very highly paid. These women tend to be older and have worked in the industry since the Korean sector's inception, in the mid-1980s and early 1990s. The Korean seamstress is rare today, as a Korean owner in his forties attested: "Not enough Korean workers. Young Korean girls when they come here, they work in the nail salons or beauty shops. They make $600 a week easy, so why work in the factory? Nail salons are so much nicer, so we have to look for other workers. The older women who came over to start may still be in the factory but are not looking for jobs anymore. They are very good." Added another Korean owner, a man in his thirties:

> There were many of them [Korean sewers] ten years ago, but very few left. They are too expensive. Many came over as experienced operators. They worked in garment shops in Korea already. They get paid $10 an hour. My work can't have them. They are too expensive.
>
> For example, I make budget dresses— $75 to $100 dresses—wholesale is one-third to half of that. That means I can't afford to pay that much. But I know some Korean women who work at a Korean shop who only make [more expensive] garments. Those dresses retail for $100 to $200 They can afford to hire them.
>
> I have a few Korean women. They do specialized work that may have to be quick, like zippers and fancy collars. You won't see too many of them.

Usually, the only coethnics on the Korean shop floor are the husband-wife owners, their children, and close relatives who help to manage the shop. Korean employers, on the whole, have turned to another labor force, Mexicans and Ecuadorians. Korean employers believe that Hispanic workers have helped to make their sector competitive with the Chinese.[2] As one owner said:

> The other reason why we can have our business is the workers [Mexicans and Ecuadorians]. They are the hardest-working people; they just want to work. They make so little as is, that they want to keep all their wages. So I pay everybody at least minimum wage, I pay most above minimum per hour. I pay by the hour here. So long as they get paid, and they can make their income, my workers stay.

These workers make this garment district run. In my shop 80 percent of them don't have papers. Most shops are like mine. Can you imagine, let's say 70 percent of the garments in this garment district are made by people who have no papers. They deserve more than just getting a bad name. They put in so much hard work.

I have three problems here: the INS [Immigration and Naturalization Service], the taxes, and the [state] labor department. I am always having problems with them. They never give us a break, but what are we supposed to do? If the manufacturers paid more, then we can pay more to our people, and they would be willing to have taxes withheld from their checks. As it is, we just can't. We have to give them cash to make sure they get paid enough.

On the other hand, the Chinese factory owners have an abundant coethnic labor force. Immigration from China continues to grow. The garment sector still attracts thousands of Chinese immigrant women and supports ethnic immigrant enclaves (Zhou 1992) and informal training systems (Bailey and Waldinger 1991), where coethnic workers learn skills from each other. So many people want jobs that Chinese employers insist that all applicants be recommended by current employees.

The Bottom of the Queue

Studies of employer preferences have shown that they have a specific hiring hierarchy in mind when they select workers.[3] I found that garment shop owners rank prospective employees based on (1) the employer's personal attitudes toward race and ethnicity; (2) what they hear from other Chinese or Korean owners about workers from various ethnic groups; (3) their own experiences with African Americans and Puerto Ricans outside the garment shops; and (4) their experiences with their current workforce.

Korean and Chinese owners and employers in the garment industry will hire Chinese, Mexicans, and Ecuadorians before they will hire African Americans, Caribbean blacks, Puerto Ricans, and Dominicans. Although Dominicans are immigrants like the Chinese and Koreans, they seem to have a reputation among owners that is similar to that of blacks and Puerto Ricans. Chinese and Korean owners tend to associate Dominicans with blacks and Puerto Ricans because they often live in the same neighborhoods and want to be paid more than the minimum wage. Dominicans who are not legal residents are exceptions to this rule.

The Chinese and the Korean owners lack extensive work experience in the garment shops with people in these groups but still hold extremely strong opinions about them and why they will not hire them. Only one (a Chinese owner) of the thirty owners I interviewed ever hired someone who was black or Puerto Rican.

Both the Chinese and Korean owners believe that African Americans and Puerto Ricans will not take these jobs even if they are offered to them. The owners say that sewing jobs that pay barely more than the minimum wage in a crowded factory are below the standards of these potential workers. Furthermore, both Chinese and Korean owners say that blacks and Puerto Ricans will not work as hard as the Chinese and Hispanics because they are not immigrants. In any case, the owners admit that it is highly unlikely that they will offer a job to the African Americans or Puerto Ricans who come to call.

The Korean Employers

None of the fifteen Korean owners has ever hired African American or Puerto Rican workers. Three worked with Dominicans. According to these three owners, the individual Dominicans they hired were far more like their Ecuadorian and Mexican employees than like blacks and Puerto Ricans. The Dominicans accepted cash for their work, and some were undocumented, like the Ecuadorians and Mexicans. One Korean owner told me: "The workers I have are very similar. They all want their wages in cash, and they all speak Spanish. I want things to go smoothly and I like to pay like that as well. I don't really see that much of a difference between the workers I have. I have more Ecuadorian men than women. The Mexican girls are younger, and the Dominican women I have are mixed [various ages]. The Dominicans all have children."

The Dominicans were treated just like Mexicans and Ecuadorians, who seemed to be flexible and really wanted the garment jobs. All the Dominicans but one were undocumented and accepted cash payment like the Mexicans and Ecuadorians. The one Dominican worker who was a U.S. citizen wanted cash payments because she was working to supplement her Supplemental Security Income payments and the Medicaid benefits for her children. In these particular cases, the Dominicans' legal status and connections to the U.S. public assistance system made them as vulnerable as the undocumented Mexicans and Ecuadorians.

The bias held by many Korean factory owners against African Americans and Puerto Ricans is reinforced by stories that the owners hear from relatives and friends about the work practices of members of these two groups. For example, many of the garment shop owners have Korean friends who own grocery stores or delis in predominantly black neighborhoods and have hired black employees. One Korean owner in his forties told me, "I have friends that own stores who hire blacks, and they are just too lazy. They come to work in the beginning and work hard and then a couple of weeks later, they start coming in late, and [then they start] taking days off. I can't have that kind of person working here. We have deadlines to make. I'm not just selling things." Another Korean reported, "They [blacks] never stole anything from the clothing store, but they are not dependable. My friend had to hire someone every few months. They can't keep a job. You waste much time working with them." It should also be noted that none of the employers I interviewed had ever hired native-born blacks.

The Korean owners in fact make a clear distinction between black citizens and Korean, Mexican, and Ecuadorian immigrants.[4] Said one Korean in his forties: "Do you know what the main problem in the U.S. is? It is the Americans who are unwilling to do work like they [Mexicans and Ecuadorians] do at minimum wage. I don't know many Americans who will work like that. They never come here looking for jobs, and they just complain that they have no jobs. Give some more respect to people like [Mexicans and Ecuadorians]. Americans like black people, they don't want to do that kind of work. That's the last thing they want to do." In fact, the owners told me that they hire Mexicans and Ecuadorians, and sometimes Dominicans, precisely because they are undocumented, which means that they will work hard and are unlikely to complain.

Korean garment shop owners have even less experience working with Puerto Ricans than they do with African Americans, but the Korean owners lump these groups together because they often share the poorer neighborhoods of New York City. As one Korean owner commented: "I have never worked with African Americans and Puerto Ricans, but I know Puerto Ricans are like African Americans. They live in the same neighborhoods. They don't want to work in these immigrant jobs. They say it is not worth their time. They don't want to work."

Skin color is just one characteristic that the Korean owners I interviewed use to sort out workers they do not want. A black Ecuadorian woman recounted how she had tried to answer advertisements posted in Spanish in the midtown garment district where Korean garment shops are located. Although she applied immediately for advertised jobs, she was never hired. She never blamed her skin color for her difficulties:

I worked in the [garment] factory in Queens for only three days and never worked for any Koreans anymore. Yes, I tried to work for them, but I was never hired.

I went to the factory and said I saw a posting for a job on the street. The signs were usually in Spanish. And sometimes they said they already hired someone for it. Very few times was I allowed to come in to try for the jobs. And when I try, they tell me I'm too slow. Yes, I spoke in English and sometimes Spanish to try to get the jobs. Sometimes, I went by myself. Other times, I went with a friend.

A comment by one Korean owner, however, indicates that color was, in all likelihood, the source of this woman's trouble: "If a black person asked me for a job, I would not give it to them. I don't need the trouble they bring. I don't want to do anything more than I have to—to make the place efficient."

Owners consider skin color to be the best indicator in making hiring decisions because, they said, skin color is the only factor that signals African ancestry (Spence 1973). Korean owners did not make a distinction between black Americans and Caribbean blacks in answering my questions regarding black workers. They were unanimous in saying that no black worker, Caribbean or American, ever attempted to work as a seamstress. Thus they could describe their thoughts only in terms of the stereotypes they know. Black meant one thing, skin color, and owners lumped all blacks, including black Ecuadorians and black Caribbean immigrants, in this category. However, the owners are unable to use skin color to differentiate Puerto Ricans from Mexicans or other Latin Americans. Here, American citizenship and facility with English are the distinguishing features.

Puerto Rican workers rarely solicit jobs at the Korean shops, and they are rarely at the "for hire" corner. They are not hired if they try to get work—at least according to the experiences of the only Puerto Rican I was able to interview at the "for hire" corner. She had overheard parts of my interview with a Mexican and recounted how she had tried to get a job in one of these factories:

> I tell you the truth. Last October, I wanted a job. It was a couple of months before Christmas, and I thought I could make a little extra money. I saw this ad for piecework to trim threads. It's easy and I know I could do it. I did that in Brooklyn for a while and it is easy. So I went over there to ask for the job. I took the ad off of the wall. As soon as my mouth opened and I spoke English, I knew I didn't get the job. He asked me where my mother was from, and I said PR. And he said I got a girl already. I was there—there was no one there. I said where, he said, she's coming tomorrow. I knew he was lying.
>
> So I asked my sister-in-law to help me out. She looks Colombian. I told her about the situation and asked her to go try to get the job. I told her to speak with an accent. She used to sew so she knows everything about the factories. I knew she would not have a problem in terms of experience.

She went there and it almost worked. He was really nice to her. The accent worked. He showed her where she was supposed to work, and then as she started to work, he asked her where her mother came from. She said PR, and he said sorry I got a girl already. But he didn't have anybody. She was ready to start to work.

The Chinese Employers

The Chinese have a different constellation of attitudes toward and experience with blacks and Puerto Ricans. The Chinese owners did not mention any concerns about their work habits but did voice concern that blacks and Puerto Ricans might report violations in the shops and file complaints, which is the owners' major concern about hiring blacks and Puerto Ricans. Not one of the Chinese workers I interviewed ever reported a violation or complaint.[5] The Chinese owners are not worried about lateness because they already tolerate some unreliability from their Chinese workers. The Chinese workers are allowed to work flextime: they come in, take lunch, and leave according to their needs.

More than half the Chinese owners expressed a lack of confidence in their English proficiency and familiarity with U.S. laws. This makes them feel vulnerable in the presence of blacks and Puerto Ricans. To the Chinese, blacks and Puerto Ricans are Americans, capable of using legal and institutional means to get what they want when they need to (in other words, they refuse to be exploited). As one Chinese owner said: "They [blacks and Puerto Ricans] speak English. Why would they want to do a job like this? This is for people who can't speak English. I wouldn't hire any black or Puerto Rican. They would be watching everything that you do, making sure everything is fair."

What is considered fair in the Chinese shops may not be the same in other industries. For example, this owner also spoke of the special treatment that he may give to a worker who brings a new trainee into the shop. He may give her extra bundles of smaller-sized clothing to sew so that she can earn more money, allow her to recruit friends to the shop, and pay her in cash, off the books. The owners fear that these activities—which are the backbone of their training and hiring system—might be threatened if others perceive them as special favors for coethnics. Moreover, owners confessed that they would rather not deal with any person or organization that monitors their work. One told me, "I already have the union coming here all the time. I don't want to have workers that will cause more problems. . . . My friends who work with them in other places tell me [blacks and Puerto Ricans] are the first to complain." As this comment indicates, perceptions of blacks and Puerto Ricans are, in the main, based on hearsay, not from actual experience in the Chinese-owned garment shops.

Korean owners feel less nervous about having their informal practices observed. As I mentioned in an earlier chapter, Korean immigrants tend to be better educated, better versed in owners' and workers' rights, and more experienced in garment shop management than the Chinese. They have less fear that black and Puerto Rican workers will report their practices to authorities. One Korean owner said: "The [state] department of labor comes and visits. They just want to make sure everybody is being paid minimum wages. They look at the time cards and just check. I handle the department of labor all the time. They tell me what to do, and I follow what they say. If my workers complain, I try to fix it. I don't have problems dealing with them."

Moreover, Korean owners seem to be much more self-assured about their ability to succeed in business. This may be one reason that Chinese and Korean owners have different assessments of blacks and Puerto Ricans. Still, both the Chinese and Korean employers prefer to hire immigrants, who fit into their work scheme, over native-born members of minority groups.

The one Chinese owner who did hire a black American as a presser had only praise for him. But this one black worker was hired under unusual circumstances. The factory's Chinese forewoman had given the worker a personal reference; she had worked with him in a Jewish-owned factory in the midtown area, and her recommendation was the very mechanism that other Chinese workers used to get their jobs. It is unlikely that many more black Americans, Puerto Ricans, or Dominicans will be hired this way because little meaningful interaction occurs between Chinese immigrants and these other groups. The majority of garment workers live in the Chinese ethnic neighborhoods in lower Manhattan's Chinatown, Brooklyn's Sunset Park, or Flushing in Queens, and few non-Asians and nonwhites live in these areas. Moreover, there are very few older Chinese workers who might have worked with African Americans in an earlier period and who could recruit them to the Chinese-owned shops.

One would think that Chinese owners would hire Mexicans and Ecuadorians and that the Koreans would hire Chinese workers. However, it was clear from the interviews that ethnic employers have very strong preferences about whom they want to hire and they have no interest in changing.

Korean owners are just as vehement about not hiring Chinese workers as they are about not hiring blacks and Puerto Ricans. Two Korean owners had tried Chinese workers and both found them unsuitable in their factories:

> I don't discriminate, I hire everybody. . . . I tried the Chinese women a few times, but they are too slow for the work. They don't clock in the speed necessary. They are not as good as the Latino workers. Some operators are very good but they leave too. You know, believe it or not, they

come in as groups and all want to work together. If one leaves, they all leave. I can't do that. That's OK in a Chinese shop because they can just close down a section of machines. But here they mess up the system. I don't hire them anymore. Maybe they get bored with the section work; maybe they make more in the piecework; maybe they like the flexible time, I don't know. But they don't work out here.

The Korean shops are organized in a markedly different way from the Chinese shops. As I explained earlier, Hispanic workers work for a set amount of time on section work—that is, they sew just a seam of a garment and get paid hourly wages. Hispanic workers in Korean shops are seated, and the garments are passed from area to area until all the seams are sewn, like an assembly line. In the Chinese shops the workers sew practically a whole garment and get paid according to the number of garments they sew. Thus, if workers are missing from a shop, other workers compensate by sewing faster. If workers are missing from a Korean shop, the system has to be rearranged so that the seams can be sewn in an orderly, assembly-line fashion. Thus, if Chinese workers are trained in the Chinese shops, they need to be retrained for the Korean shops and vice versa.

The Chinese employers I interviewed did not have any experience with Mexicans and Ecuadorians, although twelve of the fifteen owners told me that members of these groups had come to solicit jobs. The Chinese owners had little to say about Mexican and Ecuadorian workers, apart from telling me that they are undocumented. The Chinese owners have never hired them because they generally do not hire workers without personal references. Moreover, Mexicans and Ecuadorians do not fit into the elaborate training system, which requires a knowledge of Chinese and a referral from someone who is also willing to be a sponsor and trainer. Finally, the owners do not believe that they would save money by hiring Hispanic workers. Newly hired, untrained Chinese workers earn very low wages at piecework scales—sometimes as little as $10 per day—in their first few days at work.

The Chinese have no need to turn to an outside group so long as Chinese immigration continues and there is an abundance of Chinese women who need work.

WORKERS' REFERRAL PROCESS

People who are interested in working in the industry, but who are not Mexican, Ecuadorian, or Chinese, have a hard time finding information about jobs because of the closed nature of the work culture. While the process of getting jobs in the Chinese and Korean shops differs, information about jobs is nevertheless shared among the coethnic Chinese, Mexicans, and Ecuadorians. Other groups, such as blacks and Puerto Ricans, are isolated from these informal networks. Any non-Chinese or nonimmigrant Hispanic who makes it to the factory door but is not hired fuels the negative image about the garment industry among his or her coethnics.

As Greico (1987), Waldinger and Lichter (2003), and Tilly (1997) found before me, coethnics both protect their own access to jobs and work to prevent blacks and Puerto Ricans from gaining information about jobs in the industry. While the Chinese and Korean owners' prejudices against blacks and Puerto Ricans are real, actual instances of rejecting individuals from these groups are almost nonexistent because they so seldom apply.

In any case, the information necessary to get a job in the industry is not shared with other ethnic groups. This is reinforced by strong coethnic communication through social networks that help create a labor supply by continuously channeling new immigrants into the garment industry labor pool. Very few noncoethnics (that is, among the workers—non-Chinese in the Chinese shops and non-Hispanics in the Korean shops) learn about job possibilities in these two sectors.

Most employees in each sector know too little about each other to be able to cross over—or to even change conditions in their own sector that would permit the incorporation of the other group. The few Chinese who have attempted to work for Koreans have not been able to persuade the Korean owners that they would be desirable hires; the Korean employers believe that the Chinese sewers are too slow and do not like the long hours. Likewise, Mexicans and Ecuadorians have not been able to convince Chinese employers to give them a chance to work in their shops. Unless Mexicans and Ecuadorians have a chance to succeed in the Chinese shops, and barring a labor shortage in the Chinese shops, it will be difficult to convince Chinese owners to hire people from these other groups. Nor will Mexican and Ecuadorian workers encourage coethnics to seek jobs at the Chinese factories. Similarly, in the absence of successful Chinese in Korean shops, it is unlikely that Chinese workers will go out of their way to figure out how to find work in them.

Chinese Workers

It is very hard for any group other than Chinese immigrant women to get jobs in the Chinese garment factories. The majority of the Chinese workers I interviewed had no idea that a Korean sector of the industry even exists. The few that did either tried working there themselves or knew friends who had tried working there. As one Chinese woman who attempted to work there told me:

> When business was getting bad, I thought I would try a Korean shop up-town. I heard about them from a Korean neighbor of mine. I went by my-self. I basically was fooling around in the elevator and joking when I said I was looking for a job. The elevator person told me to go over to this other building because there was a nice factory over there. And I went over there and tried out working for a Korean owner. I did not like it. There was no holiday pay, seven days a week work, no benefits, no over-time, and they would pay cash. You only get paid once every three or four weeks, but you get paid much more, about $10 an hour instead of the $5 to $6 I get now.
>
> When I got there, they gave me something to do to test my work. They saw that I knew how to sew and they offered me $10 an hour. They were watching me the whole day. If I got up to change the thread color, a person would come over to tell me to sit down, and they would change the thread for me. I couldn't take a rest and I didn't like that.
>
> I would discourage anyone from going there. It's much harder than I expected, and it's more stressful.

Another Chinese woman discussed her experience with me:

> A Chinese worker who worked there told me about it [the Korean shop]. She was also in the English class and worked there for a while. I was al-ready on unemployment and needed more money. She thought I could work there for a short while. I could work there to make a little more money. She told me the factory name and the address. The factory was cleaner than the ones I worked in Chinatown, and the work was easier [sewing just a seam, rather than putting together a whole garment], but I didn't like the hours. They are too strict there. And I couldn't understand anybody. After a month, I went to look for another union job in China-town.

None of these women had anything positive to say about the Korean garment shops, and none would suggest that a friend work there perma-nently. Another Chinese woman said she never discussed her difficult experi-ence in a Korean factory with people outside her family because it was em-barrassing to let others know that she had had to resort to working there. She explained:

They really don't like the Chinese there—if you work fast, you get put on the harder jobs. And they pay you the same rate, so everybody makes no more than a certain amount. I'm only telling you this; nobody else knows I ever worked at a Korean factory. Only when you don't have any other place to go, then you try Korean shops. The Latino workers are respected there but not the Chinese. The foremen pay attention to what the Spanish workers ask. They don't try to understand me. They make the job harder for me. Only undocumented go there. Only when you think there are no other jobs. I tried because I heard that you can get paid more, and I don't need health insurance. I thought working uptown would be better.

Few Chinese women who had information about Korean shops intended to share it, thus creating an information vacuum about those shops among the Chinese. On the other hand, the Chinese in the coethnic shops were more than willing to discuss their Chinese factory jobs with coethnics. This happens at many public places, such as during lunch in restaurants, at checkout counters in grocery stores, and at home among friends, as this woman describes: "I've been working in the factories for twelve years, and if you want to find out where to work, you need to find your friends. I try to have dim sum every few weeks with a group, and we always talk about work. We're all garment workers, and we're good sewers too. Factories that need workers would want us. We tell each other where the good factories are, and almost always, we know someone who works in these good places." Another stated: "All the shops are located close to each other. In the mornings we come to work on the train together, and somebody always knows somebody else. People tell each other which shops have work, and we all know which shops don't have work and which ones are paying people late. Everyone is always looking for something better."

Most of the workers I interviewed compared their factory to others in the Chinatown area. They spoke about which factories would soon go out of business because workers were leaving in droves. Workers frequently tell others not to seek jobs in factories where the pay is late and where work is extremely hard, given the pay rate. Thus the Chinese referral network also monitors shops and their conditions. For example, one worker told me:

My sister worked for another shop that closed. It was the first shop she found a job. When she first started it was a good shop, but the owners changed, and the new owners did not know what they were doing. Within six months, this shop lost all of its work and workers. My sister said that at first, the shop started getting less work. The shop would close on Saturdays. Because of that, a lot of women started to look for work at other shops. When the garment workers left, no one was willing to bring in new workers. Who wanted to be blamed for bringing someone to a bad shop? Then we were paid late. After that, everyone knew this shop was going to close. She would ask all her friends about other jobs and tell them about her current job. I even heard about her factory from coworkers of mine.

Clearly, rumors spread by Chinese women workers can devastate a garment shop. By the same token, praise can also land a shop hundreds of eager job applicants.

One can see, then, why the Chinese stay within the Chinese sector. Coethnics frequently and liberally share information about their own coethnic shops. This reinforces the social norms within the community and serves to sanction shops that are treating workers poorly and reward those shops that are doing well by their employees. Moreover, the information is also used to retain workers or attract them to the sector. It is hard for Chinese workers to leave the coethnic sector because little positive is said about the Korean garment shops.

Mexican and Ecuadorian Workers

The Mexican and Ecuadorian workers dominate employment in the Korean-owned shops. They do not have a personal reference and training system like the Chinese, but news spreads across neighborhoods in New York City and Latin America to family and friends about jobs that can be had in the garment industry. As one Mexican woman told me: "Everyone in Mexico always tells you how much you can make in a week here in New York. Everyone tells me about the garment work. For me it was easier to get to Los Angeles, so I went there first, but there were no jobs. I should have listened to everyone. In Los Angeles, there is no work at all, not even for $1 an hour. Here at least you can get something. There are less people going there, especially if you have family here."

And here in New York City, these workers also tell each other about their workplaces: "I know friends who know about this shop. It was next door to where another friend was working. I didn't go by myself. I went with my friends. No one introduced me, but it didn't matter. I know my work and could show anyone."

Even though these workers did not personally refer or sponsor another worker, they encouraged coethnics to join the industry.[6] As a result there is no shortage of workers from Mexico or Ecuador. The Mexicans and Ecuadorians are less willing than the Chinese to personally help a coethnic find a particular job, but they are willing to discuss the industry as a whole as well as the job prospects in it for any new immigrant. Many of these immigrants said that the garment industry should be the first choice of work for many Hispanics, and therefore they encourage garment work by discussing its virtues. A young Mexican woman told me, "I knew exactly where I was supposed to work before I came here. My mother sent letters telling me where I could go to get jobs before I came. I told my friends too. If you are going to New York, then you will find a job sewing." An older Ecuadorian woman said, "I can stand on the corner to wait for jobs, or I talk to everyone to find out about certain factories, but by afternoon I go and find the shops that were mentioned to me. I find out everything, usually at this corner."

Mexicans and Ecuadorians share information at the "for hire" corner at 38th Street and Eighth Avenue. Many make friends on the corner but are afraid to recommend their new friends for work in their shops (see chapter 6). On the street corners Mexican and Ecuadorian garment workers learn about the going wage, to whom and where to turn if there are abuses, and what is expected of them in the garment shops. Moreover, they share information and send friends to garment shops that may have openings. This creates an available labor pool so that Korean owners need not look at other groups—like the Chinese or African Americans—for workers. A young Mexican man said:

Many of my friends I know through playing soccer. On weekends, I play uptown. Some work in the garment factory. If they don't, they work in restaurants. Many of the people who I think have come recently are looking for work in the garment factories. Even though I have only been here for two years, many are asking me about the garment shops. It's a good place to work. There are more jobs. But they are often late with the pay.

I live uptown off of the number one train. There are many Mexicans there, but there are others too. I live with two other Mexican men in an apartment we share. They both work in the garment industry as well.

A Mexican woman in her forties, who has been in this country for more than ten years, told me:

Most of my friends are my family and the people that live near me in the Bronx. I tell them about work. There are many in my family from Mexico that still come. I give them advice. I don't have any close friends or real friends from the factories. But all of the younger Latino women do come to me to ask for advice. They treat me like their mother. I don't mind doing that. Yes, most of the women are a lot younger. They are in their twenties. I don't really trust them. They are very different from me [young and optimistic]. Many don't know what to do. They are just new to New York, so they are not dependable.

It is difficult for other groups to enter the Korean sector of the garment industry. Although the Hispanics share information freely with each other, they rarely do so with people in other ethnic groups. One reason (as among the Chinese) is that they meet very few people who are unlike them. As undocumented immigrants, Mexicans and Ecuadorians tend to live with coethnics or at least affiliate with a community that is filled with others from their ethnic group. There are no large, distinguishable Mexican and Ecuadorian communities in New York City, but there are sections in upper Manhattan, the Bronx, and Queens where Mexicans and Ecuadorians want to live. Moreover, a few of the male Mexican and Ecuadorian workers (5 percent of the Mexican and Ecuadorian workers I interviewed were men) play in the Hispanic soccer leagues across New York City and frequently share work information.

While Mexicans and Ecuadorians seem to get along on the job floor, it is not so clear that non–Spanish-speaking groups would mix harmoniously with them. My interviews indicated that fluency in the Spanish language is essential for getting along. Owners agree and often speak Spanish themselves or hire managers who can speak Spanish. One Korean owner explained how he chose the foremen in his shops: "I have Koreans who work for me, they are usually the foremen. I like to only hire Koreans who can speak Spanish. The other foremen are usually Ecuadorian or Dominican. They can speak in Spanish to the workers. When I have to, I will speak Spanish as well, but I rely on them to do that kind of work."

Although there are class and educational differences between Mexicans and Ecuadorians, these do not seem to cause a conflict on the job because the Korean owners tend to control most of the workers' interactions during the workday. And at the end of the workday, the workers travel back home to be with coethnics. One Korean owner limited the amount of interaction between the workers:

I am very involved with everything that happens in my factory. I watch out for quality, I make sure everything is completed ahead of schedule. The workers have to be able to work together. And do what I need them to do. If a worker causes problems, I just replace them. I want everyone to always work. If a worker is finished, she should check her work. The foreman will be there soon to give her more work. I don't like it if she starts talking with everyone and bothering the other people working. I don't like it if she just sits there. She has to keep herself busy. You see these [video] monitors. They have really helped. I've had them for three months, and everyone is working much harder. The finishers will sweep or do some other tidying up when they are done. They don't stand around and talk anymore. I think this is better. Before, when there was more talking, my workers would sometimes argue or there would be other problems. Now that they can't do that as much, they have to mind their own business.

Of the twenty-four Ecuadorians whom I interviewed, sixteen had held jobs before coming to New York City, such as selling medical tools or clerking in a store, that indicated that they had a higher level of education or more experience in the job market than the Mexicans. Indeed, the class background of the Ecuadorians was higher than that of the Mexicans.[7] The thirteen Ecuadorian men I interviewed were more highly educated than the eleven women. Many Ecuadorian women had never worked before they came to the United States. In contrast, ten of the twenty-seven Mexicans I interviewed were men. The majority of the Mexican men had worked in manual labor, for example, as mechanics or in construction. Most of the women had experience in sewing. According to an Ecuadorian woman in her forties, "The owners really prefer to hire workers that are young and inexperienced. That way they can pay them only $3 an hour. The women from Mexico are young, and they look like they do not know what they are doing when they first come in. But as soon as they learn they can get paid more, because they see that they are much better and experienced, they leave or ask for more money. They get what they want. They are good workers. But they are very rough [unprofessional] in how they carry themselves." An Ecuadorian man commented, "The Koreans really like the Mexicans because they are very marginalized. They yell at them and they just take it. They always get paid very little and don't know what to do about it. I know to tell the Worker's Center,[8] but hardly any Mexicans come there."

Just about every Ecuadorian I interviewed mentioned that his or her wages were appropriate and that only Mexicans were willing to accept lower wages. This is the only issue on which Ecuadorians tried to indicate that they were wiser and more adept than the Mexicans. As one Ecuadorian man said: "Mexicans who come looking for a job, just come in and say, 'I want to work' or something like that. They don't ask for a job. They don't know how. The owner thinks all Latinos are uneducated from what the Mexicans do. He treats them very low. The Ecuadorians know how to ask for a job, but the Koreans treat everyone the same."

While Mexican women may earn low wages to start, those with the most experience eventually are paid more.[9] Ecuadorians feel superior to Mexicans because of class differences in their countries of origin, the manner in which they emigrated, and the process by which they negotiate a wage. However, within a few months Mexican women with greater experience eventually improve their wages. As a Mexican man told me, "In a garment shop you can always improve yourself and learn to make more. For example, N. started out at $3.50 an hour but now she make $6 an hour. A friend of ours, from Honduras, makes $8 an hour and decides sometimes that she doesn't need to go to work. We would like to do that, to be able to work less hours and make enough money."

Pressure from the Chinese Community and the Union

The Chinese-owned shops hire mostly Chinese because of social pressure from the Chinese community and from the workers to maintain an ethnic niche. As I discussed earlier, Chinese owners in Chinatown prefer coethnic workers. Moreover, Chinese workers prefer that these factories continue to hire only Chinese so that training, sponsorship, flexible hours, and union benefits remain the same. A worker told me: "If the factory wasn't all Chinese, we would not have flexible hours. Uptown, everyone works on a schedule. Here the owners let us leave to take care of our children. But if the owner needs us to finish work, we have to stay late and work on weekends until we finish. We all do that to help each other. He gives us a favor and we help him out too." And another Chinese owner said, "We hire only Chinese. It is better to work with people who understand what you are doing and why. We're only here for the community. What good is it if we have jobs but they can't do the work? I like it when the women bring in new people. It really helps me so that I don't have to look for new people. I give them favors. We help each other."

Many Chinese workers and owners alike believe that their system of flexibility, training, hiring, and union benefits can be maintained only if the factories remain coethnic and coethnic cooperation exists between workers and owners. They believe that coethnic cooperation is good for their community. As I mentioned in an earlier chapter, one of the main reasons why so many women turn to the garment shops for jobs is that they can get health insurance as part of their union benefits. Garment shops represent the largest sector of the Chinese community that is unionized. Women workers flock to it because Chinese men usually are not in occupations that provide health benefits. For their part, owners rely on Chinese workers and their intricate training system.

The White Employer

The Chinese have the notion that working for a white employer is highly desirable—if they were to change sectors, they would not work for Chinese or Koreans but for whites. They see working for whites as a move upward. These jobs require that employees speak English and have excellent sewing skills. Thus those who work outside their ethnic niche are not new immigrants and have acquired skills since coming to the United States. One woman explained her ambitions: "I want to work uptown for a white owner. I think I can learn English and get paid by the hour. I would have benefits and vacation. I think it's better than sewing in Chinatown. I know one person who is a sample maker, and she likes working uptown very much."

Some Chinese workers suggested that Chinese employers were ruthless in terms of scheduling and pay. Because they are coethnics, some Chinese workers felt that they were taken advantage of. Others, however, thought that it was a natural progression to work for whites when they had learned English and gained more sewing experience. It was rumored among the workers that work conditions in the white-owned factories were better than in the Chinese shops. A Chinese worker told me: "I could work for a white person. I can sew pretty well. When you work for them, you don't have to work on Saturdays, and you'll get paid by the hour. But I can't find a job with them. I can't speak English. No, I don't know anyone that works for them, but others who do told me."

Unfortunately, only two of the Chinese workers I interviewed knew of any Chinese who worked for white owners. I located a few through union sources. They were all elite sample sewers—they do not sew clothing that is to be sold but clothing that designers and manufacturers use as samples, to show others a particular design. The three whom I located were very well paid and also spoke fluent English. They were very different from the majority of the women I met in the Chinatown garment shops, and I did not include them in the worker sample.

A documented Dominican who once worked for Jewish owners in the midtown area said that conditions and pay are much better in the Korean shops. She said that she makes more now in a Korean shop, by accepting cash from the Koreans and accepting welfare checks. This, she claims, has been necessary to make ends meet since her son was born.

On the other hand, undocumented Mexicans, and Ecuadorians feel that whites are unfair. They discriminate because they always want documentation, which they use as an excuse to hire a white person instead. A Mexican man told me, "I don't want to work in a unionized shop. They are mostly owned by white people, and they discriminate more against Latinos. Here they don't care if we are documented or not. We can have an opportunity to work. At the other places, we will not get the job. They prefer to hire others like them."

What we have seen, then, is that there are two ethnically and racially segregated labor markets that employ Chinese immigrants and undocumented Hispanics. These labor markets reinforce the stereotypes of hardworking Mexicans, Ecuadorians, and Chinese who are willing to accept low wages. However, they are still exploited, either because they do not speak English well or because they do not have documents—or both.

CHAPTER 6

Landing Work

The first place I worked, my sister-in-law helped me find the job. She was already working there when I arrived [in this country], and within the week after I arrived I was off working in this shop. She brought me there and introduced me to the others. I never sewed before, so I learned to sew in this shop. I learned watching my sister-in-law sew. It took me a while, but the boss never cared, you can sew slow or fast, but you only get paid what you can make—so it doesn't matter [to the boss]. It took me a while to learn. It was no surprise.   —*Chinese woman in her thirties*

No, I have never brought a friend to the shops. Many people ask me to bring them to the shop, but I don't. I'm afraid I will lose my job. There was a woman who worked there [her shop] for seven years and was making $7 an hour. She brought a friend to the shop. The friend wasn't experienced, so the owner gave her a job paying $3 an hour. The next day the owner fired the experienced worker.   —*Ecuadorian woman in her thirties*

Embeddedness in coethnic relations has a significant influence on all aspects of the immigration process. Emigrants come to New York City by way of information from family and friends. Both the undocumented as well as the documented depend on this type of informal information about where to go, where to live, and what to do when they get to New York. By emphasizing family sponsorship, immigration laws reinforce the importance of such communication among the extended family.

The goal of all the people I interviewed was to come to New York to earn and save money to be able to provide a better life for themselves and future generations—whether this was for family in New York City or back in their home country. Finding a job is, of course, an important step in the immigration process.

Getting a job is affected by the very social contacts who helped the new arrivals to emigrate. Contrary to expectations, embeddedness in social networks sometimes inhibits coethnics' ability to assist each other. Moreover, other factors limit the effective use of social networks. Indeed, embeddedness in social networks is not the only crucial factor in an immigrant's economic adaptation.

EMBEDDEDNESS AND GETTING A JOB

Embeddedness refers to the diverse economic transactions that affect the form and outcome of social interactions (Polanyi 1944). Mark Granovetter (1985) and Alejandro Portes (1995) have shown that social expectations can modify and even subvert the original intent of the transactions. Granovetter (1985) also distinguished between "relational" embeddedness, referring to an economic actor's personal relations with others, and structural embeddedness, referring to the broader network of social relations to which these actors belong.

Social networks are among the most important types of structures in which economic transactions are embedded. They are sets of recurrent associations between groups of people linked by occupational, familial, cultural, or affective ties. People communicate and trade to acquire scarce means, such as capital and information. Social networks are also important in economic life because they impose constraints on the unrestricted pursuit of personal gain.

In relational embeddedness, expectations of reciprocity are based exclusively on past knowledge of other actors and the ability of each individual to withhold resources or apply sanctions if expectations are not satisfied. In a broader network of relationships, economic transfers can proceed on the assumption that others will fulfill their obligations lest they be subjected to collective sanctions. For example, in a Chinese-owned garment shop, if a worker is not rewarded for her efforts to recruit and train a new worker, other potential sponsors will be reluctant to offer their services. Garment shop owners who fail to fulfill the social contract in this regard will have to resort to other means if they need to hire additional workers. Moreover, the owners will be responsible for training the new employees themselves.

According to Alejandro Portes (1995), immigrants should be regarded as members of groups and as participants in broader social structures (including social networks) that affect their economic mobility in multiple ways, not simply as individuals who come clutching a bundle of personal skills. The limits and possibilities offered by the society at large can be interpreted as being embedded in the process of immigrant settlement. The assistance and constraints offered by the coethnic community are usually mediated through social networks. They can also be defined as relational embeddedness.

Studies illustrating these concepts have shown that the Chinese in New York City's Chinatown have been successful in the garment business and other industries because of their ability to exploit social networks based on ethnic and cultural resources (Waldinger 1986; Kwong 1987; Wong 1987; Bao 1991; Zhou 1992). For example, Min Zhou (1992) has shown that Chinese employers' use of family and ethnic resources is a function of the social embeddedness of places of work in ethnic neighborhoods.

Moreover, Waldinger and Lichter (2003) and Tilly (1997) have stressed how coethnic social networks can keep noncoethnics out of jobs. As Waldinger and Lichter noted, the other side of embeddedness is that noncoethnics are clearly barred from the same opportunities that are offered to coethnics. In effect, Waldinger and Lichter discuss how a group can collectively discriminate against another group in the job market. At the same time, they point to the positive effects for coethnics of embeddedness in social networks.

Embeddedness in coethnic social networks helps immigrants get jobs, when jobs are available and networks provide access to them. This works in much the same way when coethnics assist each other in entrepreneurship. Immigrants in enclaves, those working in ethnic occupational niches, and middleman minorities all use ethnic networks as key sources for startup capital and employment opportunities. Likewise, coethnics can use the same contacts to seek job information, thereby facilitating finding a job.

Research on different Hispanic groups in New York City (D. Kim 1999; Smith 1994, 1996) has revealed the role of recommendations and informal networks in the hiring of other Hispanics in the grocery and restaurant businesses. A friend or relative of a current worker can easily bring in someone who can be taught how to move deliveries, sort or cut fruits and vegetables, or how to wash and bus dishes. On the other hand, the requirements in the garment industry are very different. Only a few are hired to sweep, cut threads, and package sewn clothing. The majority of garment shop workers are there to sew and are far more skilled. A Hispanic friend or relative of a current garment worker may not have the skills that the Korean garment shop owners want from their employees. Moreover, the Korean and Hispanic garment shops have no training system to help new workers learn the trade if they don't have skills.

While embeddedness in coethnic networks does have positive consequences for immigrant adaptation, the findings of my study complicate our understanding of embeddedness and show some of its limitations or liabilities. My comparative analysis of Koreans who hire Hispanics and the Chinese who hire coethnics in the needle trades shows that mediating factors—such as immigration status, lack of coethnic obligation on the part of noncoethnic employers, and work organization requiring specialized skilled workers—hamper the use of coethnic employee-only social networks in the contemporary New York City garment industry.

Moreover, workers see that very strong ties to coworkers also mean that personal information can leak out to authorities or to other workers. The pay system, work organization, and training reinforce what the workers and employers do. Thus some workers devise ways to circumvent the disadvantages of being deeply embedded in social networks.

Chinese Workers

> We were the only family [her mother, and sister also worked in the same factory], but everybody knew someone else. Someone always brought someone there to work. It's too hard if they get a job without knowing anyone else, because the workers make fun of them or give them a hard time. If there is no one else in the factory to help you out, the workers would all scramble and take the best work. The new person just gets hassled all the time. I wouldn't want to join a factory without knowing others there.   —*Chinese woman in her twenties*

For the Chinese workers coethnic relations support the processes associated with getting a job, where relative old-timers help those who are just a little bit newer. This referral process works not only for brand-new immigrants looking for jobs but also for those who are seeking a new job. Coethnic workers share information on potential job openings so that current workers can transfer. Only a few people whom I interviewed got jobs by walking in off the street, by answering an ad in the newspaper, or by reading a sign posted on the street. For the majority of Chinese workers, someone always brings them in. That is how a potential worker knows when a shop has "open seats." Unless it is a brand-new shop where all seats are open, a worker needs relatives or friends to gain information about job availability.

In my sample, nearly one-third of the workers were first-time job seekers.[1] A first-time job seeker is typically a new female immigrant who has just arrived in New York. She needs a job and asks everyone she knows, both friends and family, about openings at garment factories. Rarely does she turn down the first person who offers to take her to a shop. This usually occurs within the first month of her arrival. Thus she is the instigator of a chain of events that will lead her to a job on a shop floor with training and social support. A Chinese woman in her twenties told me:

> When we first came, my mother and I were both looking for jobs in the garment factories. My aunt knew this and took us to work with her. In her factory there was only one seat available. My mother and I both wanted to learn how to sew. My mother and I shared the seat. If my mother practiced sewing and learning on the machine, I would try to piece together the garment for her to sew. My aunt taught us how to run the machine and showed us how to do pieces. I learned quicker than my mother, so I ended up working there on the machine. My mother didn't want to go to a strange place by herself, so my aunt asked if she could stay to "cut threads" [do finishing work].

A woman looking for her second or third job also relies on this method. But because these seekers already have a job, they are more selective and will wait for a good opportunity. If a shop seems appropriate and the work does not seem too difficult for the pay given, these workers will ask a friend to bring them to the shop. Although they will receive less training from the friend, they will receive similar social support in terms of becoming familiar with the shop practices. A Chinese woman in her forties related:

> I worked in over ten shops in the years that I've been here. I've been to so many that I forgot how many. I've worked in Manhattan and Brooklyn, all for Chinese. In Manhattan, I've worked for big shops, new ones and old ones. The one where I work now is a new shop, opened for only a year.
>
> If I look for a job, I always ask around to see what kind of job I can get. I know a lot about the different factories. Even in this building there is a factory above us and another below. I wouldn't work for the one below us because I know they always pay late. I hear the women talking about it. I know enough people to find out which factory is doing well. I'll ask them to keep an eye out for me and to let me know when there is a seat and to bring me in. I like to have a friend who can tell me what the boss likes or doesn't.

Occasionally, it is not the potential worker who inquires about jobs but employers who ask workers to act as brokers to bring in new workers. According to Grieco (1987), employee referral is the lowest-cost method of obtaining labor. Because someone usually has a friend or relative to bring in, the employer need not advertise. Moreover, employee referrals provide an efficient screening mechanism. The employer spends less time and money on the hiring process. Owners reward brokers who are able to bring in new workers by giving them easier or smaller-sized clothing to sew, enabling them to sew more pieces in a given day and earn more money. As a Chinese owner in his thirties told me, "The good fast workers, I pay them some money, even on days when I get a little work. I don't want them going to another factory. I really want them to know that they are important. I can always get them to bring in workers when we get a big job. It really works. I give them some easier work and, if I can, I give them a *hung bao*' [bonus money in a red envelope] at the New Year."

In these small ways, those who make an extra effort to recruit and to train other workers get recognition. Workers who bring in new recruits are recognized as "elders," "big sisters," or sponsors, people on the shop floor who are willing to help out both workers and owners. Furthermore, they are expected to assist in the training and acculturation of the newcomer. Workers are willing to be sponsors and brokers because garment work in a Chinese-owned factory is organized in such a way that new workers (even experienced new workers) are not regarded as competitors, lower-waged replacements for the current workers. Piecework sewing is individualistic, and workers are more likely to push themselves to make more money than to compete with the person next to them.

Expectations Within the Shop

The shop owners and the new worker both expect the experienced sponsoring worker to take responsibility for the new person by training and accompanying her and helping her adjust to the factory's rhythms and routines. This informal training is somewhat similar to the training system that Bailey and Waldinger (1991) describe. They argue that immigrant employers are willing to support this skill-transfer system because they can rely on the relationships between their workers to keep newly trained workers in their firm so the cost of training is negligible.

Inside recruitment is nothing new.[2] The most important benefit of inside recruitment for employers is that it reduces risk. Having a referenced employee is clearly significant, because it reduces worries that the new recruit will cause trouble (Neckerman and Kirschenman 1991; Holzer 1996; Waters 1999). Workers or sponsors have an interest in making sure the new recruit works out because it increases their own status in the shop and the employer recognizes the contribution to production that they have made. Indeed, potential troublemakers can be restrained by those who brought them to the job in the first place. As one owner explained:

> We really like workers' bringing friends to work here. We don't have to watch them as much. They don't ask us as many questions. Their friends help them and they learn faster. They understand if we have to pay them late because they are learning. I know that the worker will get better. Sometimes the ones that walk in are just looking for any job and have never been able to learn to sew. They just go from place to place. They are the one that friends and family are not willing to sponsor or teach. Workers like that waste time. They are just looking for a shop that is sewing something easy. We don't have easy work all the time. They leave when the work gets hard.

Thus owners and workers both benefit and in the long term the training and recruitment increase the skill base of the Chinese community.

HISPANIC WORKERS

The personal, informal hiring and training scenario that characterizes the Chinese sector of the garment industry does not exist in the Korean sector. Although some Mexicans and Ecuadorians whom I interviewed did bring friends and relatives to their garment shops, the majority did not. The few who did bring friends said that they did it out of personal preference. One Ecuadorian woman explained: "I have brought friends to work there. I was one of the first workers when the shop opened, and I like to help when I can. I know many women who need jobs. The owner knows me well and doesn't mind when I bring others in."

The workers who bring others in tend to be better skilled, more confident, and more secure in their jobs and their lives than those who do not engage in recruiting friends and family. Moreover, the recruiters admit that they want to be acknowledged as the people who are helping others. One Mexican woman told me that she likes being recognized for her efforts by the others on the shop floor. But more often than not, workers are afraid of what will happen to them if new workers do not work out or if new workers are selected to replace them. A Mexican woman in her thirties told me, "I only tell people the address. I never introduce them to the owners. I don't like it when they [the owner] start asking me about them. The owners just need to know if we can sew—nothing else." And a Mexican woman in her twenties said, "I don't feel comfortable introducing a worker to the owner. What happens if they get the job, and it doesn't work out? It would be a bad reflection on me. I help only by telling them where they could go to find a job."

The most typical scenario is for Mexicans and Ecuadorians to send workers to shops other than their own where there might be openings. In general, a number of difficulties hinder the workers' job search, such as undocumented status and lack of coethnic employers. They do not rely on informal employer and employee personal connections like the Chinese do. Because they are keenly aware of possible exploitation, both workers and prospective workers take measures to limit their use of personal ties to get jobs. Potential workers still inquire about job openings, but very few receive the personal treatment or advice that the Chinese workers get.

What happens is that newcomers may tell friends and kin that they are searching for a job and ask for help. In return, friends and kin may mention that they know of openings in certain factories. The addresses may be exchanged, and the prospective worker is sent, on her or his own, to make an inquiry about the opening. Very often, experienced workers send new workers to shops other than their own because, as undocumented immigrants, they fear being exposed. Other times, prospective workers may be told about the area in midtown where the shops are located, and they are left to investigate potential jobs on their own.

One worker told me, "At my first job, a friend of mine told me where to go. He didn't introduce me to the owner or anything. I just came in and asked to see if they had a job." Another accidentally came upon the hiring corner: "In the spring I went to look for a job and came down to this neighborhood because friends told me there were many factories here. I came looking for a job. I was standing in front of the building. Then I saw someone put up a sign across the street, and it was a job posting for this factory. I came up to the factory and asked the man if I could have a job. He told me to talk to M [the owner's wife]. M asked me what I could do and asked if I could use a merrow machine that had two bobbins. I said no, I never did that. I worked with better merrow machines that had five or six bobbins. I was overqualified."

Hispanic workers prefer to be anonymous, for fear of being turned in to immigration authorities. Having relatives and friends in the factory only adds to the possibility that someone may leak information about them. Rarely did any of the workers have close friends or kin in the same factory. The majority of the Hispanic workers had friends or kin in nearby factories. As one wary worker told me: "I am friendly with everyone. It doesn't matter where they come from, but I don't have too many friends from the factories. I don't trust them because when it comes time to fire people, I don't want to be the one fired. I don't have papers. Someone can find this out and use it against you. The owner can go fire someone, and then the worker can say to the owner why not fire her instead, she doesn't have any papers. I've seen this happen. People don't help each other as much as they should."

Thus the way Mexicans and Ecuadorians find work is impersonal. While they rely on social contacts for ideas about which factories may have openings or even where prospective factories are located, they do not go the extra step of asking friends and kin to give personal references for them. Workers worry that if other workers know too much about them, the information could be used against them. Furthermore, a personal reference may not help in getting the job.

Korean owners would rather hire workers with few ties and social contacts within the garment industry. This is a sign to the owner that the worker knows little of what the acceptable wage is, and the worker has less support and usually is a relatively new immigrant. These factors make the worker more vulnerable and therefore more attractive to the employer. The employer can offer this new worker low wages, which the new employee often is willing to accept for a first job to gain experience. However, the employee leaves as soon as a better opportunity comes along. Employers take advantage of this, just as they did early in the twentieth century. German Jewish manufacturers felt the same about the new Russian Jewish immigrants. The manufacturers did not want experienced sewers because they knew the correct pay, but the fresh immigrants could not speak English and did not know where else to go. The employers allowed these novices to work hard for lower wages (Seidman 1942). A Mexican woman in her twenties told me, "I just got here and was looking for a job. I went to the factory, and the Korean man just said to me in Spanish, I'll give you $3 an hour to help bag the clothing. I took the job. I worked there for three months. Later on, other workers started telling me that they pay me too little. I'm supposed to get $4. I left after that and found another job." Because Korean employers do not appreciate or feel any obligation toward workers who bring in new employees, there is little benefit in stressing interpersonal connections. Twenty-nine of the fifty-five Hispanics whom I interviewed had been fired or had seen others fired and replaced by the newly arrived, who were paid lower wages. Ten of the twenty-nine reported that the experienced worker was replaced by a friend or relative. Not surprisingly, many Hispanic workers are reluctant to help these newer immigrants. Here coethnic assets become liabilities.

One worker discussed how her mother lost her job: "I came to New York City because my mother was here. She helped me get my first job by taking me to her factory. I worked there for eleven months until the factory went bankrupt. At that first factory, they fired my mother two months after I started. I sewed better than she. My mother and I have different ways. I don't know what she is doing now. I don't keep in contact with her."

A combination of factors, then, has led Hispanic workers and Korean employers to choose a casual and informal system of looking for work and workers. When I started this project in 1994, owners would plaster posters with help-wanted notices on poles throughout the garment district, and workers would look for the posters. As the district became more upscale by attracting higher-quality designers, and better maintained as a result of becoming a New York City Business Improvement District, the garment industry organized a central posting site, and it later evolved into the "for hire" corner.[3] In the mid- to late 1990s workers gathered at the corner of 37th Street and Eighth Avenue, in the center of the garment industry, every morning, waiting for employers to recruit them. Men stood on the south side of the corner and women on the north. An Ecuadorian woman who frequented the "for hire" corner told me her story:

> I haven't worked for three weeks now. But I come everyday to try to look for a job. I found out about this corner by accident. I just asked the people there why they were there. They told me they were looking for jobs. So I started to come around as well. I've made some acquaintances with the people on the corner.
>
> At one time there were posters put up on the bulletin board—but the police took them all down. They were notices that advertised for jobs at this corner. Even after the posters were taken off, people still gathered here.
>
> People do find work from the corner. Usually, it is the younger women who know how to sew with the Singer machines that get jobs. Once I saw a man come and take people's home numbers of people with documents. He wanted to pay everyone by check. I can't do that, I have no papers.
>
> Right now, only five older women are looking for jobs. Most of those women with experience are younger and can work the Singer machines. Whenever I see a younger woman here, I tell them that they should learn the Singer machine. There is an academy right here on Eighth Avenue—on the third floor that you can go to learn. It costs $300 to learn the machine for three weeks.

Since 1998 Mexican coethnics and other groups targeting undocumented Hispanics have opened employment agencies in New York City. These organizations are formalizing a process that supports the workers' need for anonymity and the desire not to use personal favors from friends or kin. At the time the Immigration and Naturalization Service seemingly ignored the employment agencies.

SECTOR DIFFERENCES

The structures of the Chinese- and Korean-owned garment sectors contribute to the employers' choice of mechanisms to recruit employees. They are different in all significant areas: ethnic composition, pay system, work organization, and training process.

Pay System and Work Organization

The way these workers get paid depends largely on how work is allocated and organized in the factories. Although the garment workers' union protested against the use of piecework a century ago, garment workers are still being paid both for piecework and at hourly rates. When a factory uses the assembly-line model, it can pay hourly rates because this system makes it easy to measure an individual worker's performance. However, if a worker is responsible for sewing a whole garment, and the average work speed varies among the workers, paying by the piece is often easier.

In the Chinese shops workers earn money for each whole garment sewn. New workers learning the skill and experienced workers who are able to teach can all earn money in these Chinese shops. Each worker can work at her own speed, and her sewing usually is not dependent on someone else's work. Any one worker—whether fast or slow—does not interfere with any other worker. And any one worker will get paid according to the number of pieces sewn. Chinese workers just learning how to sew need to become skilled at operating a sewing machine—that is, to be able to run the sewing machine with a foot pedal while manipulating the cloth with their hands—and to be able to put the pieces of cloth together like a puzzle so that the pieces form an article of clothing. Experienced workers who can do this are often sewing as many pieces as they can. Factories have a cadre of experienced career workers who do the bulk of the sewing, which has to be done fast enough to meet the manufacturer's deadline and quality requirements. Few factories have all experienced workers. Seasonal fluctuations, leaves, and vacations all contribute to worker fluidity in the shops. As one Chinese worker described it, "You see, every factory at full capacity can have close to fifty people sewing in it. But most of the time, there are only thirty or so people. There's always room to try a new person. It's no loss to the owner when he already has the room to have a new person come in. In all the shops I've been, there are always people coming in to work all the time. There's no contract, so the women come and go all the time."

New, inexperienced workers can join the shop floor without affecting the profitability of the shop. Anything a new worker makes, even if it is two or three pieces of clothing, will earn profits for the garment factory, though the worker in training may earn only $10 in wages. If a new worker makes mistakes, she is expected to learn from them by going back and making corrections. Therefore, as long as the factory itself can complete its orders, it does not matter whether the seats are all filled with experienced workers. If the factory has to stay open all night to complete its orders, the Chinese will do that and insist that workers stay. This, however, rarely happens. It is more likely that the shop will be open seven days a week so that orders can be completed.

In the Korean shops, wages are paid at an hourly rate and work is organized in sections. This means that workers are assigned to sew portions of the garments, and bundles of the partially completed garments are passed along to each section until the whole garment is finished. If workers are brand new, inexperienced, or extremely slow, the whole production process slows down. Therefore any new inexperienced worker can greatly affect the yield. Not surprisingly, these shops prefer to hire experienced workers.

As the Korean owners and Hispanic workers told me, experience or skill is very important. All workers need to be able to operate the sewing machine and manipulate the cloth at the right rate with both their hands and feet. It is not a terribly difficult feat, but it does require coordination and some "on the machine" training. It is very easy to have the fabric eaten up by the machine or have stitches too tight, wrinkling and puckering the fabric, or stitches so loose that the thread unravels. Although the task before each person on an assembly line (usually sewing a straight seam in a matter of seconds) is not that difficult, a person coming in off the street without any training or skills may find it very difficult. Here is where the Korean owner will make his choice. Experience and skill do matter because they affect the speed of his line and the final production that leaves his factory. One Korean owner explained:

> I have only section work. My workers only do one part of a garment and they do it fast. For example, a group will only do collars or only sleeves. Most Koreans are set up to do section work. They don't do piece rate work like the Chinese. The Chinese do pieces like that. But many [workers] leave for long lunches, leave early. I can't have that—this is team work and if one operator is missing, the work gets messed up. If any of them have trouble for not coming in, I want them to tell me the day before or even two days before. That way I can move another worker to replace

them. I can rearrange it so that my output is still high. The Chinese don't do that. They just keep their shops open all the time [have long hours until the orders are completed].

Labor Supply

How did these different types of work organizations emerge in these two sectors? Ethnicity and the ease of obtaining resources from coethnics are factors, but they offer only a partial explanation. In addition, the worker's preimmigration education and work experiences, gender, and coethnics' family composition in the United States also play a role.

First, consider the role of the worker's educational and work experience back home. The Chinese immigrant population includes people who want to be employers and those who want to be employees in the garment industry. Because many women seem to want to work in the industry, sewing is a successful ethnic niche. This is not the case for the Koreans. Korean men and women, on average, are more highly educated than the Chinese. Moreover, Korean women who want to be entrepreneurs look elsewhere for jobs, especially to the manicure salon business, as both owners and workers. In the absence of an adequate supply of coethnic workers, Korean garment shop owners must turn to another low-wage population, Mexican and Ecuadorian immigrants. One Korean owner in his forties says, "So many of them know that we need workers that they just come and knock on our doors."

Given these differences in labor supply, the work organization on the shop floor in each sector has been arranged to accommodate the groups of available workers. In order to retain Chinese women as employees, the owners need a work organization that accommodates their employees' responsibilities and family needs. A Chinese woman in her forties, who is enrolled in English classes and is on unemployment, told me, "My husband works in the restaurants in Chinatown. He's been working in different restaurants for the past ten years. Right now he makes $1,300 a month, which is good. I'm not working now, but I still have Blue Cross [health insurance from the union]. He never had any union. I work enough to get Blue Cross. Next month I have to look for another [unionized] job." A Chinese woman in her fifties related,

My husband came first. He came as a specialty cook for a restaurant in the suburbs. He worked and ate there. When we came, he looked for work in Chinatown. In Chinatown he didn't make enough for all of us. We didn't have enough money to get a bigger apartment. The five of us lived in a one-bedroom apartment on Mott Street. When I started working, we started to save money for a house in Brooklyn. I could only work because back then my children could come to the factory after school. I would take them to school and get to work by 9:30, and I would pick them all up. I had them do their homework in the factory. Later, I sent them to Chinese school after school, and I would pick them up afterward to go home for dinner. After dinner my oldest daughter would watch if I had to go back to the factory. Now it is different. Many people have the grandparents to take care of their kids.

And a Chinese woman in her late twenties said, "I don't know how to sew too well. I don't make that much money, but I make enough to help out. I only make about $100 a week. That pays for the groceries. I qualify for Blue Cross. My husband doesn't make that much. He's just a busboy. He's waiting for an opening to be a waiter at the restaurant. I think he can make more, if he starts getting tips."

The whole-garment piecework system is the most flexible in the industry. This system allows the woman to determine how fast and at what time she can work. Although a woman is paid only for pieces that are completed, she can be flexible about her working hours on the job. One former forewoman explained:

I was a forelady for a while, but that's not the kind of job I like. There are too many headaches. I don't like having to open and close the shop. The owner and I are always trying to predict if an order can be finished by a certain time. We can't ever predict it unless we rush everyone. The workers are always going in and out, especially the ones with children.

Sometimes, I have to let them bring their children to the shop in the evening. The inspectors rarely come in the evenings to check. Other times, I have to give them a *hung bao* to get them to do extra work.

Although the worker may show up for work at 9 A.M., and not leave till 9 P.M., she may have put in only eight hours of work. It is important to stress that this particular system is flexible because the women are being paid for a whole garment and not by the hours they put in at the shop. If the owner needs to rush out goods, workers in the shop will be told to work faster, and owners can request that workers return quickly from errands. Twenty of the Chinese workers with whom I spoke to stressed that flexibility is one of the attractions of working in this industry. Even Chinese women who live in Brooklyn stress the convenience of flexible hours: "I live in Brooklyn, so I can't go pick up my children from school, but I take them to school before I come to work. I don't get here till 9:30 or 10. I work till 6 and then get home by 7. My mother picks up my children. I do the shopping here in Chinatown. Two or three times a week I buy cooked meat, like a chicken or roast pork, to bring home. Then I have less to cook. It's convenient to work in Chinatown, especially to buy groceries. My bank is here, and I pay my gas and electric here at the bank too."

Korean employers have found that the whole-garment piecework system is not suitable for a workforce made up of undocumented Mexican and Ecuadorian men and women. These men and women emigrate without children and are less likely than the Koreans or Chinese to be permanent residents.

Given their particular immigration trajectories and family needs, the flexibility afforded by the piecework system in the Chinese shops is not critical in attracting Ecuadorian and Mexican workers. If Korean owners adopted the piecework system, their workers would have to put in longer hours to make up for the flexibility. Moreover, the whole-garment piecework system would require highly trained workers or the implementation of a training system to teach workers how to put together and sew a whole garment. Again, this does not fit the characteristics of the low-wage labor supply available to the Korean owners. Their labor supply consists of both high- and low-skilled workers. A Korean owner in his forties said, "I pay them by the hour here, and I pay them well. Many of the workers don't want piecework. I wanted to give them piecework rates for each seam they sewed, but many workers wanted to leave. If I paid piecework, it wouldn't be like the Chinese piecework, where they get dollars for each whole dress, but I would pay a few cents or a dime for a seam. The workers didn't like that. Almost all the Korean factories pay by the hour. I can't be different—I would lose all the workers."

The Koreans needed a system that allowed them to control the workers and accomplish the work necessary in the requisite amount of time. A section work system with hourly wages, based on the assembly line, affords the employer the most control. The work can be broken into minute segments, so that less experienced workers can sew a single seam. Any worker who is familiar with the sewing machines can quickly replace another on the line, if necessary. Moreover, the wages are determined solely by the employer. A faster worker might be paid the same hourly wages as a slower worker, in contrast to piecework, whereby a person who sews more pieces automatically gets higher wages. Thus the assembly line gives the owners considerable control over the workers.

These two types of work organizations and pay systems have different implications in terms of hiring and training. In the Chinese whole-garment piecework system, speed is not crucial, so brand-new workers can be accommodated and trained as long as there is room and as long as there are enough trained people to complete the work. The owner counts on the more experienced employees to do the bulk of the work, while new workers learn and earn meager wages. Moreover, the coethnic personalized hiring system means that workers monitor each other. New workers rely on their sponsors for training, and in turn the owners reward the sponsors for doing the training. Sponsors also encourage new workers to learn quickly, to increase the overall proficiency in the factory.

For the Korean owners to maintain the section work–hourly rate system, it is crucial that they hire workers who are semitrained or at least able to manage a sewing machine. An absolutely untrained person is not productive, but a person with machine experience is. A new worker need not be a professional garment worker but does need to be able to work a machine. In this kind of system, the owner has a vested interest in personally deciding who can join the assembly line and in calculating that person's wages.

Training

Given the pay system and work organization in each sector, it is understandable why Korean shops would rather not provide on-the-job training for novices. If there is an easy job—such as sewing a straight seam—then relatively new sewers are hired for that job. But otherwise, a Korean-owned factory is not organized to accommodate absolute beginners. Very little training takes place in Korean factories. If young women want to learn, they can go to the schools that have been organized to provide basic garment industry training. Absolute newcomers are not often given a chance to sew; they are instead given floor work, which consists of hanging clothes, cutting threads, and packaging the sewn items.

The Korean shop does not have extra machines for the training of new workers. All the machines are usually in use, to manage the minute sections of work that have to be completed. Moreover, no one is available to train new people. Owners, foremen, and forewomen are busy managing the workers and seeing that production is proceeding according to schedule. As a Korean owner told me, everything has to be organized: "I think my shop is very organized. I give the workers lots of room to do their work. I try not to have too many things around them. It makes them work faster. I don't like empty machines. They learn as they sew. I can't teach them. They have to be smart to learn when I show them what they are sewing. I try to have someone who has some experience at all of my machines. Someone who is very good has to be at every section."

As a result the owner arranges his shop so that the machines are in a particular order to maximize efficiency. Workers are required to work at a certain speed. Faster and slower workers are assigned to make different pieces of clothing, according to the requirements of the assembly line. Thus it is difficult for experienced workers to stop their work to assist a newer worker. In fact, stopping would mean slowing down the whole line or the whole production process.

Consequently, if a Korean owner hires an employee's friend or relative who cannot sew, the entire production process may be slowed down. A friend's recommendation does not guarantee a sufficiently experienced sewer for the Korean employer. Thus the Korean owners are more wary and more selective in hiring than are their Chinese counterparts. The Korean owners want to be able to test and see the worker in action for themselves before they offer a position. And they do not want to feel obliged to offer a job to this new person simply because he or she comes recommended by a worker in a shop. In fact, the Koreans do not want to feel *any* obligations to their workers. Workers get paid only for the hours they sew. If workers come in and there is little sewing to do, or if there is no work for the day, they receive no pay or are given only part of their daily wages. When there are many of these days in a row, workers frequently go off to find another job. One Mexican told me that new workers are given a short period of time, perhaps one day or one week, to show their skills: "I've gone knocking on doors, and I've stood here waiting for people to come hire me. It's the same either way. The owner asks what you can do, and you tell them. I can sew fast. They have never asked me for papers, just what I can do. They take you over to your job. At the end of the day, or week, they tell you how much you'll be making. If you can't do the job, then you're fired."

Moreover, Korean owners know that the majority of the Mexican and Ecuadorian workers are undocumented and believe that they do not want to stay in New York City for an extended period (see chapter 3). The Korean garment shop employers do not see the benefit of doing favors for their employees, because they may go back to their homeland. By not offering their workers any kind of incentive for finding new workers, however, the Korean owners end up discouraging coethnic support among the workers.

The Chinese shops, as I have explained, depend on experienced workers to train new inexperienced workers. This is especially true of those who bring in kin and friends to the shop. The Chinese owners expect the workers to do the training because they see it as a favor in return for hiring kin or friends. So long as a seat is open, the Chinese owners allow this kind of referral and training. The result is that new Chinese workers are always being trained to be garment workers.

In this way the structural dynamics of work organization reinforce the ability of the Chinese to use coethnic resources to help each other get jobs, and they explain why the Mexicans and Ecuadorians do not have this option. Mexican and Ecuadorian coethnic resources are circumscribed by conditions that can turn coethnic assets into liabilities.

Thus embeddedness in social structures and networks per se may not be helpful and in fact can be a hindrance. Embeddedness in social structures is just one factor that helps immigrants to adapt. Indeed, these networks have to be placed in a larger context, and seen in relationship to outside conditions that affect social connections.

CHAPTER 7

The Bottom Line

In a garment shop you can always improve yourself and learn to make more. . . . You learn more at each shop, and when you change, you can show them how much you know, to make more.

—Mexican man in his thirties

Here I put in nine or ten hours a day and I don't make so much. I get paid piece rate and if the item is hard, I can spend all Saturday here and not make many pieces. This past Saturday, I didn't go in because I have too much to do at home. I didn't make enough money last week.

You've seen the dresses I make, they are difficult with fabric that is hard to handle. They sell these dresses from $100 apiece, while I only get between 90 cents to $1.30 per dress. On average I can only make thirty or so dresses a day. That's only about thirty-something a day. On average I make about $170 a week. Rarely do I make more than that.

—Chinese woman in her thirties

Both the Ecuadorian/Mexican and Chinese garment workers earn low wages, yet this characterization is too simple and obscures important differences in what they earn—differences that, once again, are related to the structure of work organization in different shops. In this chapter I compare the pay that workers in the two sectors receive. On the one hand, as I discussed, the Chinese referral system is an effective source of labor for employers. However, recruitment through employees or sponsors acts as a form of control (Grieco 1987:37). On the other hand, the lack of this kind of system in Korean shops gives Hispanic workers more freedom in choosing employers and in rejecting low wages.

While coethnicity greatly enhances the ease with which a Chinese worker can get hired and trained, it does nothing to get her better pay than an undocumented Hispanic. Coethnic relations, as described in chapter 6, create boundaries that limit the kinds of behavior possible, and one such boundary is created by the sponsoring worker. She can exercise control over the new worker's behavior because of the obligation that the new worker owes her. This informal referral system has many positive aspects: workers support each other on the job and use flexible hours specifically designed for Chinese women workers. On the other side, the worker-sponsor relationships lead to constraints that inhibit the Chinese from demanding higher wages.[1]

In Korean shops the Mexicans' and Ecuadorians' very lack of loyalty to their Korean employers means that they often leave shops to look for higher wages elsewhere. This movement has created a median wage that is higher than that of the Chinese workers. Hispanic workers' ability to earn higher wages owes to the sewing skills of the workers, who are able to negotiate a higher pay. Indeed, Hispanic workers who feel entitled to better pay tend to change shops as a way to gain both better skills and greater pay at each successive workplace.

The coethnic advantages that accrue to Chinese in the hiring process do not translate into higher pay. The Chinese were paid for piecework, often resulting in a take-home pay of $200 a week, or about $4 an hour.[2] On the other hand, the Hispanic sewers received hourly pay of about $5.30 an hour, or $265 a week, which was 33 percent higher than the Chinese wage. Both Chinese and Hispanic workers average forty-five hours a week, from Monday to Friday, and five additional hours on Saturday. These hours do not include lunch breaks.

On the face of it, a purely economic, rational explanation that emphasizes market forces seems to account for the wage disparities. The supply of Chinese workers is greater than the demand, so wages in this sector are lower. The demand for skilled workers is greater than the supply in the Korean sector, so wages are higher. However, social factors are also involved in the different wage rates.

Because a new worker in a Chinese shop is obligated to the person who brought her in, she will not want to embarrass her sponsor by being "greedy" in asking for higher wages or causing a problem that would embarrass the long-term worker. The new worker keeps complaints to herself. Other new workers do not demand higher wages because they too are in similar layered sets of obligations. A Chinese woman in her fifties told me, "My sister-in-law helped me find this job. There is nothing wrong here. If I want to make more, I have to try harder. She has worked here for a long time, and the owner has always kept a job for her, even in slow times. If I don't like something, I would rather not complain. I don't want to complain to my sister-in-law. She got this job for me. Good or not so good, I have to take it. She thinks that this is a very good job. I would rather leave and have someone else help me find another job. She can tell the boss that I had to take care of my children."

For their part, the Chinese owners depend on coethnic sponsors to solve problems involving the new workers and any demands they might make. The Chinese employer expects the long-term employee to deal with anything that would disrupt the training and piecework systems in the shop. Moreover, sponsoring employees find themselves orienting new workers to the shop.

In the end, Chinese workers are resigned to their low wages because of the relationships that they developed during the informal hiring and training process and the resultant web of obligations in which they are entangled.[3] While the sponsor is really a worker, her interests lie with the employer. The close ties between the sponsors and new workers actually limit what all the workers can do to improve wages. While the social connections are strong, the shared information does not help to increase the pay of the Chinese workers. Moreover, aspects of the work, such as whole-garment piecework, the belief that the union is nothing more than a health insurance provider, and the continual changes in clothing styles (and therefore sewing patterns) reinforce the coethnic relationships of the Chinese that keep pay low.

Mexicans and Ecuadorians have never really had very close ties to each other or to coethnics in the shops where they work. They also do not have any particular obligation or ties to their Korean employer. Workers, however, are close to coethnics who work in other shops, and they are able to gather information about pay in this way (see chapter 6). Because they are not obligated to stay in any one shop, they apply for work at places where they can obtain better pay. Because the social connections are weak, they have no social obligations to remain in a particular shop. On the other hand, the information that is conveyed through their social network allows these workers to move to other shops to get higher pay. A twenty-four-year-old Mexican woman, who had been in New York for three years, told me,

At my first job, they treated me very well. I was paid $4.75 an hour. The owners were Koreans. They were two couples related by marriage. They spoke Spanish and everyone was treated well. I left because I heard that I could make more.

The ones who were there the longest were treated better. The newer people were treated worst. They didn't yell at people. The new people were only paid less, like $4.25 an hour.

I've only worked at five or six other jobs for Korean owners since then. They all pay me too little. I've been paid cash most of the time. I only work for a short while if I'm paid too little. I worked the longest at my last job—for eight months.

At my last job, I was paid $5.50 an hour and then given $7 an hour for overtime. I left because it was too little money. I think I deserve more. I think I can be paid more now—I have much more experience and can work in many more sections [of the garment shop].

Hispanic workers are free from most of the coethnic obligations in which the Chinese workers are entangled. Mexican and Ecuadorian workers are not in coethnic relationships with the Korean owners, nor do the workers rely solely on coethnic Mexican and Ecuadorian resources in finding a job. Both aspects free them from obligations to coworkers and employers. So how do the Korean owners determine their pay scale?

MEXICAN AND ECUADORIAN WORKERS

For Mexican and Ecuadorian workers pay depends on their immigration status, length of time in the United States, sewing experience, and ability to navigate the job market. Work experience is especially important in the hiring process because skilled Hispanics who are able to ask for higher wages are scarce. Hispanic workers in a Korean shop are not paid identical wages for identical work. Workers who can present themselves as skilled and knowledgeable, and who request higher wages, often get better pay. Korean employers take all these criteria into account when calculating the rate of hourly wages that they offer to their workers. For example, brand-new immigrants rarely receive the legal minimum wage unless they are experienced or know about the labor market for the New York City garment industry. Employers use the ability to speak English as a proxy for gauging an applicant's length of time in the United States and experience in the U.S. garment industry. Thus the better the worker's English, the greater the worker's wages will be. Moreover, having a reasonably good command of English makes Mexican and Ecuadorian workers more confident and therefore more willing to switch jobs, and they are likely to land a job with higher wages because of the confidence they exhibit at the next job search.

Legal Status and Length of Time in the United States

Legal status and length of time in the United States together greatly influence the wages of Mexican and Ecuadorian workers. In my study all but four of the

Hispanic workers were undocumented. Without legal status, it is difficult to get a Social Security number and therefore employers cannot pay wages by check—which would also require them to deduct federal, state, and city taxes, as well as Social Security taxes. Without check stubs, workers cannot join the union, which requires proof of wages from employment in a garment shop.

Korean employers generally prefer to pay cash wages to the undocumented. One Korean owner frankly stated that employers usually want to avoid paying Social Security taxes and dealing with the tax-related paperwork associated with paychecks. They would rather pay slightly higher wages in cash and depend on employees to pay taxes on their own. More often than not, Korean employers confess that they know that the majority of workers will not, in fact, pay taxes because they are undocumented.

Korean owners typically manage two sets of books: one recording actual amounts spent on wages and the other recording the wages of those who received checks with deductions. These workers are usually those with Social Security numbers, although they may be undocumented workers with fictitious identification. A seventeen-year-old Mexican woman told me, "One employer insisted that I get a check. I didn't want one. I was using somebody else's Social Security card. I did not want the check because I didn't know how to cash it, and it wasn't even in my name."

The cash system works because the workers want cash. They may not have a bank account or do not know where to cash checks, and many simply do not want to deal with identification cards and signatures. The majority of the Mexican and Ecuadorian workers believe that paying taxes to the United States is unreasonable because they are here only temporarily.[4]

Length of time in the United States is a factor as well. Employers prefer experienced workers, who command higher wages than those new to New York. The Mexican and Ecuadorian workers who were brand new to New York City told me that they often get paid only $3 an hour for their first job, no matter what kind of work they do or how well they sew. Their mannerisms and their lack of English signal to the Korean owners that they are newcomers and will accept any pay that is offered.[5] For example, Korean owners believe that they can tell whether workers are newcomers by how they carry themselves and how they ask for a job. As one owner told me, "New immigrants can knock on the door and say, 'I want work.' Sometimes, they are not sure what they can do. I can offer them very little money and they will take it. Others who have worked in the [New York City] factories will ask for certain machines or certain kinds of work. They can understand some English and understand what I ask them to do. If they are good, I know not to give them too little, or they will leave."

Workers said that only the newest immigrants will accept less than the minimum wage. This is supported by my discussions with brand-new workers. But within months these new workers have learned that the going wage is more than what they are being paid, and they willingly leave their first job in the hope of finding a better-paying position. Relatives and friends may be unable to help them get jobs, but they are very proficient at wage counseling. Moreover, contacts that the new workers make in the factory, at the "for hire" corners, and in eateries around the garment district counsel them about the going wages and about how to learn the skills that the Korean owners want:

> I got paid $3.50 an hour on my first job. I was really scared and took whatever she said. I sat down and didn't recognize the machine. It wasn't the same kind I learned on in Mexico. I thought she was going to fire me. I worked there for two months. I would always buy lunch at the same place, and one day someone asked me if they paid well at my shop. I told them I was only making $3.50 an hour. They told me I could make much more, especially since I was working a machine. I didn't know that and neither did my husband. I didn't want to ask for more money. They were not too friendly. After they paid me for that week, I never went back.

Occasionally, workers earn raises in their own shop. This has happened to four of the Hispanic workers I interviewed, all of whom had extensive sewing experience in Mexico and Ecuador. An Ecuadorian woman in her forties said,

> I work from 7:30 to 5 every night, for six days a week. I used to get $5 an hour, now I get $5.25. They just gave me a raise [to $330 a week]. I get paid cash every week and they are very good about paying on time.
>
> I was sick for a couple of days and didn't come to work. They gave me a raise when I came back because they were afraid that I was going to leave. That's what happens. Sometimes, workers come to work in the afternoon, for a few days. I know they were looking for another job. If they are not good, they will fire you. But if you are good, and they want you to stay, they may give you a little raise.

Sewing Skills and Experience

Having sewing experience, in fact, any skill in running the sewing machine, has a profound effect on wages. Anyone walking in off the street cannot sit on an assembly line and expect to operate a sewing machine to sew even the smallest seam. There are many gradations of skill that a sewing machine operator can have. And those variations can make a huge difference in terms of production for a garment shop.[6]

Any new worker without sewing machine experience is relegated to floor work, earning at most $4 an hour. Floor work is considered a beginner's job, and anyone with the least bit of ambition will try to move up to sewing work. Sewing machine operator is usually regarded as the entry-level position in the garment industry, whereas floor work is considered a dead-end job.

As I have emphasized, a training system is nonexistent at the Korean-owned factories. Korean employers do not spend the time and money to train new workers, and therefore employers look for experienced sewing machine operators. As I discussed in chapter 6, Korean employers are much more selective than the Chinese in their hiring. Almost all the workers I interviewed aspired to work at a sewing machine. This worker was offered a wage of $5.50 an hour in her third job in New York: "They sat me down with some work and [I] did it; they looked at it and said to keep working. I asked the man how much I would make and he said to ask M. She told me that I would find out at the end of the week. When my pay came, I found that I made $5.50 an hour. When other people come there, they do the same, they give them some work to do. They never test them, just work. If they don't do it well, they are asked to leave."

The workers coming into the garment industry with little experience as a sewing machine operator learn to sew in one of two ways. They either train at a friend's or relative's home where there is a sewing machine, or they take lessons at one of the many sewing instruction facilities in the garment industry. A seventeen-year-old Mexican woman told me that she taught herself to sew in a Mexican friend's house while she babysat for the children of other Mexican garment workers. Other aspiring sewers might borrow a machine and solicit help from friends and relatives. When Hispanics received assistance in learning how to run a machine, it was from a coethnic Mexican, Ecuadorian, or Dominican. In these respects, coethnic Hispanics do assist each other: "I'm from Mexico, and when I first came I was a student. I worked in restaurants, washing dishes and then helping the cook. I overstayed my visa. My wife then came over. She knew how to sew and she taught me how. She works in a factory on 38th Street."

Recently, a smaller cottage industry has developed in New York City's Hispanic neighborhoods and in the midtown garment district. Storefronts and lofts have become schools for sewing machine operation. Workers pay $200 to $300 for a series of hands-on classes in how to operate the sewing machines. Four workers confessed that after months of not being able to get jobs as sewing machine operators, they turned to these instruction centers. All stated that the training was well worth it. They all moved up from floor work to machine work. And once in machine work, they received higher pay.

The Job Market

The ease with which new undocumented immigrants leave their first jobs indicates that plenty of jobs are available, especially for those with sewing machine skills. Korean employers are looking for workers who have some skills and understand some English. These are the workers who are scarce. In this sense, Mexicans and Ecuadorians have a relatively good job market. Workers know that the pay that they receive in New York City is better than what they can make in their home country; they also know that the pay is better than what they can earn in other U.S. cities, like Los Angeles. Korean owners, for their part, know that it is imperative to keep the best workers. They pay better wages to workers who can sew well, in an effort to keep them in the shop. But, as the work slows, or if there are any personal disagreements, workers simply leave one shop to join another.

Korean employers put much effort into trying to maintain a steady work flow for their sewers. Once this cycle is interrupted and work slows down, workers are off looking for their next job. This seems to be the norm rather than the exception. To the Mexican and Ecuadorian workers, a good wage is just a promise; the garment shop needs to provide the hours and the work to keep the income stream steady. According to many workers, they choose not to be too loyal to the owner because their goal is a steady income—they would rather have a decent income than remain at a particular shop or with a particular owner when there is not enough work to keep them busy for forty-five hours a week. A Korean owner explained his problems:

> I pay by the hour and they get at least the minimum, [and their hours are] usually 8 to 4:30. I pay overtime and when very busy, I ask them to stay, sometimes till 8:30. And of course, they work on Saturdays. I have very reliable workers. Most have been with me for at least four or five years. They are very good operators. . . . I've increased their pay over the years. . . . But I find that it's hard to find good workers. If I look for one week, I will be lucky to hire two good operators. It's hard to find good workers. I keep the good ones.
>
> I pay them good wages. No one else around will give them what I give them. Some person may be willing to pay them more, but I have steady work. That means a lot. Even if it's slow season, I can give them work. This business is the worker—if you don't treat them well, then you

can't make your deliveries, [and] if you can't do that, then you will lose out on getting sewing jobs.

Although this employer tries to keep his good workers by giving them steady work, good wages, and occasional raises, the majority of the owners do not. Only four of the Hispanic workers I interviewed were offered raises to stay. The rest went off looking for another job to improve their pay.

For the most part, workers do not seem to have trouble finding better-paying jobs. Employers comply with workers' requests for higher salaries because workers will turn down jobs that do not pay within a reasonable range of their expectations. From the employers' viewpoint, when they have a job that has a deadline, they would rather pay more to experienced workers to meet that deadline. If the shop meets that deadline, the manufacturer probably will give the factory another production job—thus keeping work steady for the garment workers and profits steady for the owner.

Experienced workers understand these job cycles and willingly look for the factories with the busy production lines. They claim that demand for experienced workers is great and that job hunting is much easier for the experienced worker. On the average workers were able to gain 50 cents to 75 cents more per hour with each job move. These workers all claimed that a weekly increase of $25 to $37.50 for every job change is very respectable.

Although employers say they want experienced workers, they still look for workers they can pay $3 an hour. As a short-term bargain, these newcomers are very profitable for the owners. Many new immigrants want low-paying sewing machine jobs because these jobs get them in the door and offer the opportunity to gain sewing experience. However, these workers learn and leave quickly for better-paying positions. One would think that it would be better for the owners just to pay higher wages and give raises to the skilled and more seasoned workers. However, owners can find skilled workers among the new immigrants. And it is these workers that Korean owners want as replacements for higher-waged workers. Thus Korean owners often let experienced, highly paid workers go when a respectable, lower-priced replacement turns up.

THE CHINESE WORKERS

The situation of Chinese workers leads to a different set of questions: given that they are documented and work for unionized garment shops, why is their pay less generous than what the nonunionized Hispanics command? And shouldn't the close relationships that Chinese coethnics have with each other and the owner lead to higher wages? In fact, close relationships create obligations and benefits that actually reinforce the status quo wages.

In brief, a worker bringing in a new recruit creates obligations. As I described in chapter 6, to thank the sponsoring worker the owner usually provides easier work. This usually means sewing the same style of clothing as everyone else in the factory but in a smaller size, which means that the worker can sew more pieces faster and therefore make more money, a sort of in-kind bonus. Moreover, other workers on the shop floor give recognition to those workers who introduce a new worker to the shop floor.

In return, sponsors feel that they have to live up to their new reputation as elders, as people who can solve other workers' problems. Because they are compensated by the owner, they also feel obligated to shield the owner from any problems created by the new worker. Thus the senior workers exert control and intervene in the affairs of the new workers to ensure a smooth transition and adjustment period in the garment shop.

The new worker now has an obligation to the sponsor. For example, if disagreements occur between the sponsor and employer, the new worker may align herself with the sponsor because of the sponsor's past assistance.

As these layers and layers of obligations are created, they serve to reinforce limits on the already meager pay scale. In their quest to protect the owners from workers' concerns, workers who become sponsors respond to any questions that workers have about the pay. Their acquiescence to the owner's needs shows their tenuous position.

New Worker Orientation and Sponsor-Worker Obligation

> When I went to my first shop, my cousin showed me how to work the machine. I first sewed straight seams on cloth. Later I got braver and sewed some clothing from my cousin's bundle. She would explain how to do things if I didn't know how. After doing this for a long time, I started to get my own bundle of clothes to sew. —*Chinese woman in her forties*

Coming into a shop via coethnic relations provides many benefits to new workers. They automatically get a guide to the new workplace, someone who informs them of the rules and regulations and provides them with a social circle. In my interviews with both workers and owners, all agreed that the "sponsor worker" should act as the intermediary between new worker and owner.

Owners, for the most part, trust these sponsor workers and their methods for both training new workers and answering their questions. Owners say that seasoned workers understand the new workers better than the owners do, partly because sponsor-workers were once themselves new workers. One worker told me, "I only brought one person here to work with me. They stopped working here when their father got sick. I try to help when I can. It is hard when you first come to New York. Everything is so new. I remember when I first started, I had so many questions, and you didn't want to ask the forelady everything. I asked my cousin everything. Even before she got me this job, she told me about what it was like to work in a factory."

Any question that a new worker has regarding pay, vacation, and the appropriateness of bringing children to the shop can be answered by the senior worker without the involvement of the owner. The sponsors give basic orientation to the shop rules and the system of work. Most workers said that the person who brought them in was the one who gave them the most information and hints about life in the shop. The sponsors help answer a variety of questions: when and how to get some of the work that is distributed, where to put a finished bundle, how to get paid, where and when workers are allowed to eat in the factory, how to heat up their food, and how and when people can go out to lunch.

Sponsors feel obligated to train the workers they bring in, and owners want the sponsors to maintain the training system within the shop. Sponsors teach the newer workers about the sewing process, such as how to thread the machines and put together each of the many styles that arrive at the factory. Learning to put new styles together is a time-consuming task but is essential in learning the clothing-making process. Once a worker can piece together a whole garment, the next step is to sew the pieces together in a timely manner. This requires learning how all the parts of a sewing machine operate, as well as the art of clothing construction. A Chinese woman in her forties said, "I could piece together the dresses. That was easy. After a few times, I knew what all the pieces look like when they are flat and how the pieces can fit together to make a dress. That part is like playing. But the machine, it took me three weeks to work it properly, and I still sew it very slow. There are too many [mechanical] parts. And you have to learn to touch it right to get it to sew slow or fast or tight."

In treating these new workers so considerately, sponsors believe that they are shielding the owner from new workers' criticisms and questions. As for the newcomers to the factories, many told me that they appreciated the attention that they received from their sponsors. Said one, "We were the only ones that were family there, but everybody else knew at least one other person. It's hard when you don't know anyone, because people make fun of them or give them a hard time if there was no one else in the factory to help you out." Another newcomer mentioned learning the unwritten rules in the sponsorship game:

"My cousin answered everything for me. She also introduced me to everyone in the shop. I wasn't sure if I was supposed to go get my own bundle. I got up to do that once, and my cousin stopped me. She told me that the forelady parcels out all the bundles so that everyone gets a chance to sew the smaller sizes. I'm glad I didn't pick up my bundle, I learned later that they were giving my cousin more smaller bundles because she brought me in and I was a good sewer."

All the new workers I interviewed appreciated having someone to whom they could turn with their questions. Frequently, new workers find it easier to express concerns to a coworker before going to the owner. New workers also do not want to embarrass themselves in front of the owner; they would rather ask questions and make comments to other workers.

Moreover, new workers feel a certain loyalty to the sponsor who has brought them into the shop. If their sponsor leaves the shop, the new worker she trained often will follow along. The new workers realize the tenuous position that the sponsors occupy and do not want to do anything that will interfere with the sponsor's relationship with the owners. New workers do not want to cause trouble on the shop floor and bring attention to themselves or the people who brought them into the shop. As one worker told me:

> My husband's cousins who just came from China asked me to help them find a job. His cousin and her daughter wanted to find sewing work almost as soon as they landed. My boss let me bring the daughter to work. He wasn't that interested in having a fifty-year-old woman learn how to sew. I brought her daughter in to fill a seat. She was about thirty and really learned quickly. I told her that I would help her with everything, and if she had any questions to ask me. I told her that in this shop everyone tries to work things out for themselves. If there is anything bothering her, she should ask me. I've been here for five years and I know what the boss likes.

Because the shop floor is made up of women who know many others there, difficulties arise when a worker does not conform to the informal shop rules or shop etiquette. All the new workers have similar obligations to their sponsors, and likewise the sponsors have a certain obligation to the owner. Ultimately, the owner has the greatest influence in how his shop floor is run. Thus the obligations keep the new and more experienced workers from demanding a higher wage.

Owners are also unlikely to raise wages voluntarily and think that their workers will not seek raises; they believe, in fact, that their workers will have a difficult time asking for higher pay, given that the workers are paid by individual garments completed or by the piecework rate for a whole garment. Unlike hourly wages, the individual garment rate or piecework rate is not assigned by worker. Piecework rates are assigned to the tasks required in completing a garment. Every worker is paid the same rate for the same job. For example, all workers will be paid $2 to put together and sew all the seams of a certain dress. A new worker can work all day to sew five dresses and will earn $10. An experienced worker can make fifty dresses in a day and earn $100. To change the rate workers have to get together and agree that the rate is too low for the specific tasks or assignment in completing the whole garment.

To ask for higher wages each new worker first has to learn how to sew and understand that the wage structure, not her own sewing ability, is the basis of the low pay.[7] Workers often blame themselves for being slow, and not the wage structure, for their inability to make more money. Workers who want to change the rates will have to find others who agree that payments are too low. This is often difficult because the workforce includes both new and career workers. Moreover, even if the workers understand the underlying wage structure and no longer blame themselves for the low pay, they often do not want to cause trouble on the shop floor:

> I've worked here for five years now, and I think this is a good job. I make enough money. My friends are here with me. A friend of mine brought me here in the beginning. And, I later brought a couple of friends here when there were openings. And they have brought at least one other person here. If I ask for higher [per garment] piece rates, it'll make the person who brought me here look like they were irresponsible. You wouldn't recommend anyone who would cause trouble. Then, the people who I brought in will feel bad. I would be called a troublemaker, and the people who came with me will be the troublemaker's friends.

In Chinese shops, the training system and the recruitment and hiring process are based on relationships. Often an individual is obligated to too many others to feel comfortable asking the owner for higher wages. Because most other workers have similar sets of obligations, they will not support another worker's demands. Furthermore, many newer workers are unwilling to sacrifice their jobs, because they know that other new workers are waiting for an empty seat or opening.

Many workers who are sponsors and who receive favors from the owners aspire to become an owner someday or at least covet the owner's special treatment, for example, in getting smaller-sized clothes to sew to earn more money.

This special treatment is the only way that some workers distinguish themselves from the new, inexperienced recruits. As one newcomer told me: "I'm new, and I do whatever my cousin tells me. I listen to the workers who have been with the factory a long time. They know all about the owner, and many have worked in many garment jobs. I'm not the only one. We can all see that the owner likes them and treats them better. Some of them are like friends. My cousin still remembers what being a *then yee men* [new immigrant] is like, but many of them have forgotten. They remind us all the time that they are better off. Many look down on us so they will feel better."

On the other hand a sponsor-worker feels like she is receiving training in the business when she brings in others: "I have been working in this factory for six years and I know the boss well. I try to help out my friends and relatives when they need work. I like to bring in others to the job. My boss always asks me when he needs someone. He knows that I am reliable. I always do what he wants. I'm learning a lot from him, especially on how to manage other people. He teaches me and I watch him. I'm not like the new workers anymore. I'm trying to learn enough to open a factory in a few years."

On occasion, however, close relationships among shop floor workers provide the basis for solidarity in opposing the owner. If an owner tries to lower rates, and subsequently wages, too much, or if an owner cannot provide enough work or treats the workers badly, the Chinese workers will support each other and leave the shop. As one woman told me: "In the slow season, some owners will pay a minimum to the workers, but frequently after the slow season, if there is not enough work, the workers will still desert the owner to go off to another place. In Chinatown, the workers are relatively strong. They can determine if and when a garment contractor will survive."

Eventually, word will spread about an owner who goes too far, and sponsors will not want to bring workers to shops that do not have enough work or are not paying enough. The garment shop will have to close its doors because it cannot find employees. The workers are obligated to the owner only if he or she has work for them to earn money.

Employer-Employee Relations

Just as Chinese workers are unwilling to speak out against whole-garment piecework wages, they also do not complain much about their coethnic employers. When workers did complain in the interviews, they made clear that the job also had positive aspects. For example, when workers discussed their meager wages, they also mentioned the benefits of working in Chinatown, the flexible hours that piecework affords, and union health insurance coverage. When they mentioned the crowded and sometimes unsanitary conditions, they also mentioned that they received training in the shops. Moreover, they spoke of how they were allowed to bring their children to the shop when the children did not or could not go to school. All these aspects of work reflected the trade-offs and compromises that were necessary in their daily lives, given the circumstances they faced as immigrant women and mothers who did not speak English. One worker summed up her situation: "I have only been here for a year, and I already know the boss uses us to earn money. Everyone understands that. That's the way it is. It's much better here than at home [in China] [*Oh coy, ho ge oh kee*]. We don't make much money. At least we can work and work in a place where we can speak Chinese. Many of the younger women would not be able to work if they didn't have those hours."

Most Chinese workers mentioned how they, along with the owners, were complicit in a "check-splitting" scheme, whereby workers were assured some wages in cash along with their wages officially paid by check. Most Chinese employers brought in union work. However, when there was not enough work, the employers often bid on nonunion work for which they would pay workers in cash. Most often, this arrangement helped workers who did not qualify for health benefits on their own (Bao 2001). To be eligible for union health benefits, workers need to earn a certain minimum that is recorded by check. Some new workers cannot work fast enough to make the minimum of $3,500 during the first six months of work to qualify for union-sponsored health benefits. To help most workers qualify for health benefits, employers sometimes pay in cash those workers who make enough to easily qualify for benefits. Then they transfer the "check wages" to another worker who needs extra earnings reported in order to gain health benefits. Employees saw this arrangement as positive support for their work. However, in the long run this type of pay transaction did not improve the Chinese women's overall wages, which remained below that of the Hispanics. As one worker told me: "Many workers get cash for work that is for nonunion manufacturers. And many others also split checks. I sew a lot, and some of that gets credited to a friend's check so that she can qualify for union benefits. I get some money in a check, enough that says I qualify for health benefits, and the rest in cash. I don't mind doing this because when I get cash, there are no taxes taken out."

Hispanic workers, by contrast, were very straightforward in their complaints about Korean employers. They were not bound by any coethnic relationship. They did not have shared coethnicity to mask abuses or to smooth over rough relationships. Hispanic workers were more willing to go to the state labor department over back wages than were the legal Chinese immigrants. As one

Ecuadorian man told me, "A couple of the workers who worked here before were paid a month late and then were fired. They went to the department of labor to complain. Here at the Workers' Center [Garment Workers' Justice Center], someone knew of somebody they could talk to. There are people at the department of labor who speak Spanish. After they complained, the department of labor sent inspectors to the shop and gave the owners a fine. From then on, they [the owners] watched how much they were paying the workers."

Some Hispanics praised their Korean employers for lending workers money, promising to hold jobs for them until they returned from visits to their homeland, and even, in a few cases, helping them to obtain citizenship. One Ecuadorian woman said, "The owners are extremely nice. They have loaned me money when I needed it and tried to help me out when my family needed extra money. I had to send it home because my mother was sick in Ecuador. I slowly pay them back every week. I give them some money. I would gladly return the favors, but the chance has never arisen."

Yet the Hispanic workers also had many gripes and difficulties. They complained that Korean owners often yelled at them on the shop floor. Said one, "Today the owner was yelling at me to work faster and faster, but I couldn't because if you do, you can make mistakes. And they don't pay you when you make mistakes. I left early yesterday because I didn't like him pushing me around. I didn't go back to work today. I don't plan to go back. I'll look for another job."

Some Hispanic workers ignored this yelling and blamed it on language differences. Some said that owners yelled to try to communicate when they could not find the words to express their feelings in Spanish. Others complained that the yelling was the worst part of the job. Yelling is, in fact, the most common abuse faced by the Hispanic workers.

More serious is nonpayment or late payment of wages. Hispanic workers are not tolerant of this at all. If they suspect that wages will not be paid at all, they will just get up and leave the factory, leaving the employer unable to meet his production deadlines. Some workers who are owed back wages file complaints with the state department of labor. Others just move on to other jobs.

Nonpayment or late payment also occurs in the Chinese shops. Only if it is a persistent problem will they find another job rather than bring the situation up with the owners. According to union officials, 99 percent of the jobs in Chinatown are unionized so the women in delinquent shops just ask friends and family if there are openings elsewhere. The women do not claim their back wages, because they believe that they may be singled out for reprisal by Chinese owners and blacklisted from other jobs in the garment industry. None of my informants reported reprisals, but interviews by Xiaolan Bao (2001) and work by Peter Kwong (1987) indicate that this happens.

Both Hispanic and Chinese workers understand their situation as underpaid workers. However, their reactions and responses are different because of the relationships they have with the owners and other workers—relationships that, at base, are structured by the nature of the work organization.

Sector Differences: Cash Versus Check

There is yet another complication in comparing wages in the two sectors. If the Chinese were paid only off the books, in cash wages, they could in fact take home almost as much as the Mexicans and Ecuadorians by simply not paying taxes. But it is not so simple for documented Chinese workers to accept cash wages. Interviewees mentioned that they would accept a portion of their wages in cash but not their entire salary this way. There are many reasons why it is important to the Chinese to receive documentation of their pay. The union requires documentation for membership. Bank accounts and income tax returns are necessary to sponsor relatives who want to move to the United States. Moreover, financial documents are necessary to purchase a home.[8] The check stubs help legitimize them as members of U.S. society.

As I discussed earlier, the Chinese immigrants are permanent immigrants, and their outlook and orientation are toward building a life in New York City and the United States. Many are also trying to bring family here from China and are working to earn a stable income and learn enough English, American history, and civics to be able to gain U.S. citizenship. Some of these immigrants are their family's only connection to the United States. As one Chinese woman mentioned: "I'm taking this English class because I want to get my citizenship. I heard that sometimes they make you read during your test. At home, my daughter practices the questions with me. Who is the president of the United States? What are the colors on the flag? How many stars? How many stripes? What does each star represent? What does each stripe represent? Who are the senators from New York? My sister has been asking me to get her here since I first got here. She really wants to come, and I'm the only 'thread' that can connect and tow her to the U.S."

Working and paying taxes and Social Security are all part of showing that one has an interest in becoming a citizen of the United States. Moreover, immigration laws require documentation of assets as well as income to bring family members over. Check stubs, income tax returns, and bank accounts are all used to show net worth and the ability to support oneself and perhaps others. As another worker mentioned, she has been preparing for quite a while:

My brother and his family will be coming here in a couple of years. If I'm still here [in this garment shop], I will bring his wife here to get her a job.

I already told the boss that I wanted to do that. I want to make sure that they have a job and to be able to start earning money to support themselves.

I'm responsible for them. When you apply for immigration visas, you have to show that you have money to support them in case they can't find work. You need to show them your income tax statements, and if you have a house, it's easier. It means you were able to save money. It costs us a lot of money to bring them.

The Chinese workers want evidence to help establish their legality and capability to be naturalized citizens. The sooner these immigrants can show that they have earned income, the sooner they can buy a home or bring relatives from China. Thus the orientation of the Chinese workers is very different from that of the Mexican and Ecuadorians who work for the Koreans.

Only four of the Hispanics I interviewed were documented, and, as I mentioned earlier, the majority prefer cash wages. Because of their illegal status, it is easier to manage cash than to deal with check cashing, bank accounts, and other documentation. Their goal, unlike the Chinese, is to earn money to send home; although the Chinese send money home, their goal is to establish their life in the United States. Most Hispanic workers want to make enough to eventually open their own business or to buy their own homes in their home country.

Wage Minimums, and the Influence of the New York State Department of Labor and the Union

Wage minimums on the shop floor are also influenced by two outside forces. In the Chinese-owned shops the Union of Needletrades, Industrial and Textile Employees (UNITE) is influential in setting wages. In the Korean-owned shops the state labor department plays an important role in policing wage minimums. Both organizations have rules and contracts that the garment shops are supposed to follow. However, my interviews revealed that Chinese shop owners regarded union contracts and federal law as nothing more than guidelines that help create a wage ceiling.

THE UNION

The Chinese workers' permanent orientation to the United States serves to influence them to become members of the garment workers' union. As I explained earlier, the Chinese women provide the family with health insurance through the union. According to union representatives, any garment worker, documented or undocumented, is eligible to be a union member so long as the shop in which the worker is employed has a collective bargaining agreement. Any business agent can sign a worker into the union so long as she has worked for thirty days. A worker usually shows four check stubs as proof of her work history at the shop. She then pays dues of about $18 a month. Benefits include not only eligibility for health insurance but also paid vacation, and eligibility to meet with social workers and immigration counselors.

The union and its salary requirements for membership have unintentionally—and negatively—influenced the pay that Chinese workers receive. Union salary guidelines are extremely low, low enough so that even a low-skilled worker can qualify for membership. A new union member could qualify for health benefits—which in 1995 she could purchase for her family for $300 a month—if she made $3,500 in her first six months of work. To continue to qualify, a worker had to make $7,000 in any four of the previous six quarters of work. That meant that the worker had to average pay of $583 a month, or $146 per week, or $2.92 an hour for a fifty-hour week. The low salary guidelines were instituted to ensure that even the lowest-paid garment worker could receive health benefits, but they also have had the effect of depressing wages: owners calculate the minimum pay that workers will accept. Workers always strive to have the health insurance coverage, given how expensive medical costs can be:

> My sister-in-law would show me how to sew the pieces and how to turn on the machine. The machine was so loud it scared me. Now, I can sew but still very slow. I make a little money, enough to help buy food. I don't think I could have found another job.
>
> I'm trying to earn enough to have Lom Sup Kee [Blue Cross]. I went to see the doctor to get glasses and I had to pay over $100. What happens if I get sick? I went to the doctor because I get nose bleeds, they wanted to send me somewhere to see a doctor who would shine a light [laser] in my nose to stop it. I didn't do it—that was going to cost $750.

Chinese employers believe that most workers are satisfied with a salary that will qualify them for health insurance. The owners have no incentive to pay workers better because the owners understand that most are already resigned to the low levels. That is so because of the combination of ethnic relations (the conformity that is expected of all Chinese workers) and structural relationships (especially the training/sponsorship relationships) that exists in the garment shops. Moreover, the abundant supply of workers willing to take these wages has also kept garment wages low. A union alone cannot raise wages.

New York State Department of Labor

The New York State Department of Labor keeps tabs on wages in the Korean-owned factories. Korean owners might well want to pay below the minimum wage, but the state labor department has generally been able to prevent this.

According to labor department officials, they do not enforce immigration law, but they exist to ensure that the Korean factory owners abide by wage and safety standards. This agency fines the Korean owners if they pay workers less than the minimum wage. The labor department does not care that workers are undocumented. What the agency does care about is that undocumented workers who are paid less than the minimum wage undercut the wages of legal workers. And garment workers, UNITE officials, and union members have frequently complained to the Labor Department about that practice. Moreover, a few undocumented workers have also lodged complaints with the state labor department regarding nonpayment of back wages.[9] An Ecuadorian man in his thirties told me, "When we started, the owner used to pay people only $3 or $3.25 an hour, but he got scared from the [state] department of labor. This owner now pays everyone minimum wage at $4.25, but there are still many who only pay people $3 or so. These workers only make $180 per week for fifty to sixty hours of work. Where I work, many people have worked before, so many are experienced."

The state department of labor, however, has little influence on the Chinese-owned shops. Because Chinese workers make fewer complaints, labor officials rarely visit the Chinese shops.[10] Because they are unionized, the Chinese workers tend to complain to the union business agents before they resort to filing a complaint with the state agency (and the only complaints that workers told me about were for nonpayment of wages). Union business agents of the Chinese-owned shops are Chinese and speak Chinese, and most were once garment workers. They are at ease with the Chinese workers and will be approached by the workers.

Mobility Ladders

> I make about $20 a day. I have never made more than $200 week. I just make about $100 a week and that's not enough. They keep changing styles. So as soon as I pick up on one, they change it again. You get the same no matter which factory you go. Everyone says owners are getting the best rates for you, but don't you think they are doing better [than we are]?
>
> —Chinese woman in her forties

I've worked in seven jobs in the last fifteen days. I asked for work as a floor lady. I've gotten as little as $2.70 an hour and now I am up to $4.25 an hour. I left my first job after I found out how little I would be paid.

—*Mexican woman in her twenties who had been in New York for fifteen days.*

Mobility ladders within the Chinese and Korean sectors also greatly affect wages. Mobility ladders, which imply movement to a better job or higher wages, are almost nonexistent in the Chinese sector but exist in the Korean-Hispanic sector. The piecework per garment pay system that prevails in the Chinese sectors serves to depress wages: As the sewers learn the sewing movements for each style, they begin to sew each piece faster and make more money as they gain experience with it. But they face this learning curve with each change in style. The continual changes in style prevent workers from making substantially more. Unless piece rates are increased, these workers find it quite difficult to earn much more on average.

Moreover, the majority of the workers remain machine operators on the shop floor. It is difficult for them to move out of the Chinese-owned sector, even though they aspire to work for white owners (see chapter 5). Only two workers told me that they knew of others who moved out of the Chinese-owned sector, and they worked as sample makers for manufacturers. In a Chinese shop one can move up to become a sponsor-worker or eventually a forewoman, helping to coordinate the sewing. These are very limited choices. One does not make that much more as a sponsor, and very few become forewomen. In every garment shop of forty employees, there is usually only one forewoman.

On the other hand, the Mexicans and Ecuadorians have a strategy for gaining higher wages: they work for low wages in their first jobs and then leave to find another, higher-paying job. All the workers use this strategy, and the Korean owners know this strategy as well. Employers are willing to pay skillful and experienced Mexicans and Ecuadorians higher wages. Thus these workers are able to earn more if they work hard and learn the correct techniques. All the garment shops need skilled workers. Some workers shop around for the best wages, and others are willing to accept any rate because they do not know any better. When experienced workers find a job that offers fair pay for work done, they tend to stay put.

CHAPTER 8

Immigrants and the Economy

This book highlights how one industry can satisfy the employment needs of a number of immigrant groups in New York City. The interplay of immigration status, gender, and ethnicity is extremely important in organizing the work life of New York City garment workers and employers. From the garment industry's inception, researchers have discussed ethnicity and work. However, the questions they asked were different from those addressed here. Previous research focused more on how ethnic groups changed the garment industry and how they assimilated into American economic life. Other researchers were interested in immigration, how certain ethnic groups became entrepreneurs, how they came to occupy their niches, what their work conditions were, and the role of the union. They were, however, less concerned with ethnic relations and how immigrant status and gender may affect working conditions and the workplace. I have tried to determine how these characteristics affect the relationships between owners and workers, and the workplace structure.

My initial thought was that immigrant economies (no matter which ethnic group) would operate in similar fashion. For example, New York City garment workers make very little money no matter who they work for. Certain groups were always channeled into the garment industry. Certain groups, like women or the undocumented, seemed to be more vulnerable to exploitation. However, on closer inspection I found more negotiation and more movement within the Korean and Chinese sectors of the garment industry than I had imagined. Workers from all the different immigrant groups that were being hired tried their best to negotiate better terms for their jobs. Immigration status, gender, and ethnicity all had a role in determining their wages and work conditions.

IMMIGRATION STATUS

Researchers have not really examined immigration status, that is, documentation and length of time in the United States. While immigration status cannot be totally disaggregated from the gender and ethnicity of the workers and owners, immigration status is important in a few situations. It can shape the outlook and desires of both workers and owners in the garment industry. In a comparison of mostly documented Chinese and undocumented Hispanics, immigration status is a mediating factor in the kinds of work that immigrants are willing to do. Moreover, immigration status is a factor in the kind of work offered to the immigrants. I found that being undocumented puts one at risk of exploitation because the workers fear being identified by the legal authorities. Newcomers to the industry are easy targets for exploitation. However, being undocumented does not limit the chances of getting a better job in the garment industry. In turn, having legal status, even when working with coethnics, does not guarantee one a better job.

Legal immigrants, like the Chinese garment workers, were most likely to have family (spouse and children, in addition to extended kin) here in the United States, and the orientation is for the whole family to settle and sponsor others who want to emigrate. For the Chinese this creates many dilemmas in their quest for a job. Like native-born Americans, they find certain conditions unacceptable. These workers want their pay issued by check so that they have proof of their wages in order to sponsor a family member still in China or to establish credit for a home mortgage here in the United States. The workers want union membership so that they may obtain health insurance coverage for their families. The women want flexibility in their job hours so that they can manage work and household duties. While garment work in Chinatown has low status and low pay, the job has benefits. The women's immigration status and their desire for long-term settlement in the United States have pushed the employers in this sector to be more amenable to some of their workers' wishes. Also, the owners are coethnics who share many of the same needs.

On the other hand, most of the Hispanic garment workers were undocumented. Of those I interviewed, the majority did not say that they were planning to stay. Most of the workers I interviewed did not bring children with them. This was true even for married couples. The undocumented Hispanics think of themselves as workers who are providers for their families in their homeland. Their interests lie in earning high wages. Thus as undocumented immigrants they had no need to be paid by check; cash was just right. Surprisingly, undocumented immigrants are less likely to help each other get a job in the garment sector. Most did not want to work in a factory where others know them or their kin. Interviewees believe that it is safer for their kin and friends to be separated. If one person is arrested by immigration authorities, at least the others can still remain in the United States to work and send remittances home. Moreover, the Korean owners make it very difficult for a worker to bring other friends or kin to work in the same shop. The Korean owner is looking to hire someone who is new to the United States and who knows little of the pay scales. The Korean owner can then pay the new immigrant low wages. However, tension exists between Korean owners and their workforce, because Korean employers are always looking for the least expensive workers. Undocumented Hispanics who are experienced in sewing and no longer newcomers can move up to better-paying jobs on the factory floor. Korean employers often give Hispanics a chance to work and are willing to pay more to those who have more experience and are able to negotiate. At this level, immigration status is very complex and does influence work choices. As a result immigration status is just one factor that influences the role that immigrants play in the U.S. economy.

GENDER

Gender is another important variable in the garment industry. People tend to assume that women gravitate to this industry because they have sewing skills. However, I found that gender comes into play in relation to immigration status and ethnicity. Chinese women need to work in this industry because the men in their lives do not have access to jobs with health insurance. Their husbands are also immigrants and have limited access to job opportunities. The Chinese are interested in staying permanently in the United States with their children. When they have children, health insurance is especially important, as are flexible work hours. That is why Chinese women gravitate toward the Chinese sector of the garment industry. Some coethnic owners share similar needs, and the work organization reflects them.

In the Korean sector the workers work a very rigid schedule. Hours are not flexible, and the workers are paid only for the hours they are at the factory. Men find the hours and job amenable because they work in a "factoria." Working in a factory carries some status. Most of these men were farmers in their home country. Because Hispanic women do not have an edge in this industry, Hispanic men have recast sewing as an acceptable trade for either sex. Men are just as likely to work in this particular sector as women are. Gender, together with immigration status, puts men in the position where a low-status job in their homeland becomes a higher-status job in the United States.

ETHNICITY

Researchers of ethnicity in the workplace have studied how coethnic networks can limit other groups' access to jobs. Evidence here supports all that they have said—that lack of information from important networks, especially coethnic networks—can limit outside groups' access to jobs and job niches. If you know few people in a certain job sector, it is highly unlikely that you will gain information about job openings in that sector. In addition, if hiring within an ethnic group occurs as a result of personal recommendations, someone who is not of the same ethnicity will find it even more difficult to gain access to those jobs. This is the case for blacks and other minorities in the contemporary garment industry.

The Korean and Chinese owners in this study tend to lump African Americans and Puerto Ricans together. Even though the Korean and Chinese employers have had little work experience with these groups, their preconceived negative notions affect their relationship with them. Both Chinese and Koreans believe that blacks and Puerto Ricans would not take garment industry jobs if they were offered because sewing jobs pay too little, only a little more than minimum wage. The general perception is that blacks and Puerto Ricans are lazier and more troublesome than immigrant groups. Although few African Americans and Puerto Ricans apply for these jobs, they are already ruled out. Thus they are relegated to the bottom of the hiring queue. Because hiring practices are subjective, the employer's perception of blacks and Puerto Ricans is influential.

As I have shown, employers' opinions rule out hiring African Americans even when the owners tend not to rely on coethnic network assistance to find new employees. The Korean employers hire exactly who they want according to their own needs. These employers go to the street, to a hiring corner, to find their workers, and African Americans and Puerto Ricans could also visit these spots if they knew that hiring occurred there. In hiring workers, these employers avoid people with dark skin and those who speak English, because both qualities may mean that these individuals were born in the United States and likely to assert their rights. Korean employers also look for the least expensive person they can hire, usually a new immigrant with little knowledge of English and U.S. laws. They want complacent workers, and African Americans are unlikely to put up with an unstable employment situation—workers may be fired at any time—that demands that they keep up with the speed and tempo of the line. Although work may not be pleasant in these garment shops, workers receive more than the minimum wage, and these may be better jobs than other service-sector jobs that blacks hold.

The Chinese sector is dominated by Chinese workers. Rarely will the owners hire non-Chinese or even consider doing so. The elaborate training and work scenario leaves little room for anyone who does not speak Chinese or who is not related to another worker in the shop. The Korean sector tends to be similarly closed to outsiders. The Chinese rarely hear about job openings in the Korean sector because few Chinese work there.

Mexicans and Ecuadorians who work for the Koreans also tend to avoid using their personal social contacts to help coethnics get jobs. These workers do not bring new workers in, although they will at least mention that jobs are available in the garment industry. In turn, the knowledge that coethnics can find jobs motivates many Mexicans and Ecuadorians to seek out the garment district. Coethnicity or ethnicity and the use of social ties matter because they provide information about which factories are likely to hire Hispanics. However, the connections are not as personal as those used by the Chinese, who personally introduce the newcomer to the owner.

Thus closure exists on two levels, first on the hiring level, where coethnics induce employers to hire workers' kin and friends. Closure also exists because of sheer knowledge. It is easy to exclude a group from jobs when no one in the group knows anyone who could even provide ideas or suggestions about how to find a job in the garment sector. When such closure exists and ethnic groups have little contact, stereotypes and inaccurate images persist.

CONTROL AND WORKPLACE ORGANIZATION

The history of the garment industry shows that the structure and organization of the workplace changed as the shops changed hands, from coethnic to non-coethnic employees and employers. At the turn of the twentieth century, when garment shops were hiring coethnics through word of mouth, employees were highly skilled and worked in small family-like shops with their coethnics. Coethnicity and, as a by-product, shared language both facilitate training and certain forms of recruitment and work organizations because they aid communication between workers and those who can train or hire them. People without much skill rely on their coethnics to lend them a hand.

As immigration increased, unskilled coethnics and noncoethnic workers, two groups that were willing to accept low wages and nonunion jobs, entered the garment industry and looked for work along with the skilled. At the same time many coethnics turned to other, more profitable or upwardly mobile jobs. Employers had to reorganize and restructure the workplace to accommodate mixed ethnic groups (and therefore several languages) and those with fewer skills. Employers could no longer rely solely on workers to recruit coethnics for openings; instead, employers had to place newspaper ads and frequent employment halls to fill those openings.

Early in the twentieth century a form of assembly line became the work organization of choice. Anyone could work on an assembly line after learning some basic maneuvers with the sewing machine—what language you spoke, who you knew, and what skills you had did not matter. The assembly line was especially efficient for a group of workers of mixed skill and ethnicity. Communication was not crucial, work was simplified, and the speed and path of the line determined the number of orders completed on the shop floor.

Today, however, the assembly line is not the only work organization that employers use because the garment industry has once again attracted coethnic employers and workers. Coethnic social ties and reciprocity have once again gained importance in the workplace. Employers take advantage of workers' social ties to organize an entire production system using whole garment piecework. Although this system uses the same sewing machinery that is available to workers on an assembly line, the work organization depends on the obligations and favors that exist between workers on the job floor.

As I explained in earlier chapters, this system requires training and conformity, both of which are made stronger by long-term committed relationships. For example, Chinese employers hire coethnic workers' relatives and friends upon their workers' recommendation. Employers also encourage the long-time workers to train these new employees. Long-time workers are reluctant to refuse requests from the employers because they are obliged to the employer for hiring the newcomers. Thus whether the newcomers are skilled or not, they are under the wing of the long-time employees and dependent on their favors.

In this system, the bulk of the work is done by one person, even though it resembles an assembly line in some respects: finishers or buttonholers or trimmers are required to add the finishing touches after most of the garment is sewn. The sewing work itself is more skilled because it requires the worker to piece and sew together most of the pieces that make up a whole garment. Then it is passed on to the finishers. New employees usually learn this procedure from their sponsor. The elaborate training, hiring, and sewing process creates a context in which the worker is inherently controlled by the social relationships among other workers and the employer and not by the constant rhythm of the assembly line.

When workers are hired solely because of their skill or undocumented status, no one is beholden to anyone else, and the employer can simply assign these new workers to a place on the assembly line. The employer and other workers have few responsibilities for the new worker, and the new worker similarly has no or few obligations to the others in the shop. In other words, without coethnicity and coethnic hiring, no previous relationship exists that can induce obligations or favors between the employee and employer.

For example, Korean employers prefer not to hire Hispanics who are recommended by someone else in the shop. Instead, the owners would rather choose Hispanics who are the most skilled and/or compliant. Korean workplaces are organized so that workers have small tasks in a clear division of labor. Hispanics with no skills whatsoever will have difficulty obtaining a sewing machine job because no training is available in the shop, from coethnics or anyone else. However, because Korean owners are the only people involved in the hiring decision, their employees recognize that the owners hold all the power (to pay or withhold wages, to fire, and to hire). The workers do what the owner requires and do not help out their coworkers or even recommend others for jobs.

The coexistence of an assembly line in the Korean-owned shops and whole-garment piecework in the Chinese-owned shops is quite significant in that it reflects flexible use of organizations of production. Moreover, both systems are profitable and competitive with each other. The implications are that a production system based on coethnic ties and employer needs can be as competitive as those based on Fordist principles of manufacturing. Coethnicity and the resultant relationships in the workplace are as inherently important as the technological improvements that allowed the formation of the assembly line.

As I have shown, coethnicity, along with gender and immigration status, effectively limits and controls the production line. The Chinese will probably not move to an assembly line like the Korean owners so long as coethnics are willing to fit into the current scheme of social relations and production. Ethnicity, along with immigration status and gender, shapes the relationships associated with the process of getting a job. They have become so instrumental that few owners would consider any other way of organizing their shop. Ethnicity and the relationships shared by the Chinese workers and owners support not only job search, job location, and information gathering but the actual garment production process itself. The economic prosperity reaped from these relationships in the Chinese shops is quite likely to continue until the number of coethnic workers is insufficient to fill openings.

In conclusion, immigration status, gender, and ethnicity are extremely important in the immigrant economies. These features are connected in myriad ways. The New York City garment sector illustrates how important these features are to the economic well-being of this manufacturing sector and to the immigrant groups that are in it. Moreover, to extrapolate, certain sectors, like the garment industry, are comprised of a social arrangement of various groups that respond to New York City's economy. They use a social process to sort themselves out within the industry. Thus, in the greater picture, immigration status, gender, and ethnicity are crucial for understanding what kinds of job opportunities are available and, subsequently, what role each of these immigrant groups will play in the economy.

Industry Ups and Downs Since 1998

Chinatown and the midtown garment industry have changed enormously since 1998. As of this writing, in spring 2004, both Chinatown and midtown Manhattan have significantly fewer garment shops and fewer workers. In chapter 2, I mentioned that Chinatown had about 400 garment shops employing 20,000 workers and that midtown Manhattan had about 300 garment shops employing 12,000 workers. I estimated that there are about 150 shops left in Chinatown, still employing coethnic workers, and probably an equivalent number in midtown Manhattan (Chin, forthcoming). Most of the shops in midtown that closed were owned by Koreans. While the number of shops in Manhattan has decreased since 1998, the Chinese have been opening shops in Sunset Park, Brooklyn. Some of these shops moved from Manhattan's Chinatown, and others were brand new. These shops first appeared in the late 1990s, following the establishment of the Chinese community in Sunset Park (Hum 2003). Each shop is smaller and employs only half as many workers as those in Chinatown. Estimates of the number of shops in Sunset Park vary from one hundred to 250. The number fluctuates according to the health of the city's economy and the garment industry.

The Manhattan sector of the garment industry has always been known for quick turnaround times on relatively small orders of a few thousand pieces. With computerized inventory control most stores know exactly when to reorder. Within the confines of Manhattan orders can be completed quickly and easily because everything that the shops need to assemble the clothing—

textiles, buttons, and zippers as well as skilled workers—are readily available. Production managers easily commute to the midtown or Chinatown locations to monitor the quality of clothing construction without having to plan an expensive and extended trip to Asia. The proximity of all the players allows for a relationship that is difficult to duplicate overseas. But even with these strong associations, garment production has waned in Manhattan.

Three factors explain the decline of the sewing shops in Manhattan since 1998. Many New York City manufacturers and designers were quite satisfied with producing 100 percent of their clothing locally. However, as the cost of production increased and clothing prices remained the same, manufacturers and designers started sending some of their work overseas. Manufacturers and designers diversified their production arrangements to protect themselves. If there were large orders, overseas production was less expensive. Smaller orders that have to be assembled quickly were more economical to produce locally in New York City. Over time, as manufacturers developed better working relationships with overseas contractors, more production moved overseas.

The late 1990s also saw the rise of new media, especially the rise of the dot-comers. These new firms were eager to rent loft space and quickly helped drive up rental costs for Manhattan garment shops. New media firms were in fact attracted to the loft spaces that held the garment shops. They would rather locate their offices in trendy, edgy places over Chinese noodle shops or midtown button shops than in the office spaces that more traditional businesses occupied. Garment shop owners looked elsewhere to procure lower rents. Sunset Park, Brooklyn, was the answer. Not only were the rents cheaper but Chinese owners found that they could escape the union, UNITE. Some Chinatown owners opened a second branch in Sunset Park, whereas other shops just relocated. The union's presence in Brooklyn was not as strong as in Manhattan. Most garment shops in Brooklyn were not organized because the owners as a group were against unionization. Certain Chinese workers, on the other hand, were willing to work in the Sunset Park shops without union benefits. These two reasons alone accounted for the loss of twenty-five to fifty shops each year between 1998 and 2001. The most drastic losses came after September 11, 2001.

Although few people realize it, the terror attacks of September 11 had a devastating effect on the New York City garment industry and especially on the Chinatown sector of the industry. The consumer saw no shortage of merchandise and no real increase in prices of clothing. However, in the months following September 11, many in the garment industry lost their jobs because fewer garments were made in New York City.

CHINATOWN AFTER 9/11

The Chinese garment workers and Chinatown in particular faced challenging conditions in the aftermath of the September 11 attacks. The physical and economic conditions right after September 11 made it very difficult to conduct any business in Chinatown (Chin, forthcoming; AAFNY 2002a, 2002b). Chinatown is located just ten blocks from the World Trade Center site and less than five blocks from New York City's Civic Center, site of City Hall, the New York City Courthouse, and many other government buildings. Increased security and roadblocks hindered the movement of materials and clothing into and out of the Chinatown garment factories. Chinese workers who lived outside Manhattan and in other boroughs had a difficult time reaching their places of work. No one could place orders; orders that were in midproduction when the attacks occurred could not be completed; and no one could pick up completed orders. Many orders for "Holiday 2001" production were canceled, causing massive unemployment among garment workers. Six weeks after the attack every factory with a UNITE contract had laid off workers or reduced their working hours. Garment workers turned to the unemployment lines.

Chinatown was also plagued by a whole host of infrastructure disruptions, from phone service to subway service to parking restrictions. Full phone service in the Chinatown area was not restored until mid-December 2001. The N and R subway line did not service the main Chinatown stop—Canal Street—for six weeks. Sections of streets in Chinatown (Bowery, Henry, and Madison) were closed until January 2002. As of spring 2004, Park Row, a major thoroughfare that connects Chinatown to the Civic Center, remained closed. A four-hundred-car municipal parking garage on Police Plaza, on the edge of Chinatown, which had been used by both tourists and ethnic Chinese shoppers and visitors, remains closed to public use for fear of a terrorist attack. These changes turned away many tourists and restaurant diners, along with the ethnic Chinese who normally do their shopping in Chinatown. The economic effect of 9/11 on Chinatown was tremendous. Most retail shops reported a 20 percent decline in business in the one year after 2001 (AAFNY 2002b). Most garment workers' income declined by 50 percent from the previous year to $16,000 a year (Chin, forthcoming).

At the same time federal assistance was not forthcoming to Chinatown during the first six to nine months after the attacks (AAFNY 2002a). This was very different from the experience of the wealthier neighborhoods (Tribeca and Battery Park City) that bordered the World Trade Center (Kasinitz, Smithsimon, and Pok, forthcoming). In defining the "disaster zone," federal agencies used Canal Street, which runs right through the center of Chinatown, as the northern border. For at least six months those who owned businesses, worked, or lived north of Canal Street were ineligible for government aid (AAFNY 2002a). This alone had a tremendous effect on the garment industry. More than 80 percent of the factories were located just north of Canal Street. For the garment shop owners aid in the first few months would have spelled the difference between remaining opening and closing forever—most factories had a small profit margin, and each month of lost business pushed more and more shops out of business. For the workers, aid was also difficult to come by, even for those who were eligible, because there was no single source of information about the kinds of aid available. While there were plenty of translators—the procedures and the rules were extremely complicated—many owners and workers who became eligible after the zone expanded in April 2002 never reapplied for government aid because they were so frustrated by the process (Chin, forthcoming).

However, more funds were made available after the inequities were publicized. For example, the September 11 Fund was able to assist many Chinese workers after hearing about their plight. Many workers were able to find some retraining and take ESL classes, and they obtained information about health insurance from organizations funded by the September 11 Fund. Many other programs and organizations, like the Garment Industry Development Corporation (GIDC) received funding to assist the Chinese garment workers and others in the community after the Asian American Federation of New York published a study in April 2002 that detailed the economic devastation to the community.

Worse, the events of September 11 accelerated the trend toward overseas production that was already underway in the industry when the attacks occurred. For the industry overall, manufacturers who needed to supply clothing to stores sent their production work out of the country. Large orders were consolidated, so that orders of similar items, which were once distributed to both Chinatown and midtown factories, were shipped overseas for production.

In the four months after September 11 as many garment shops in Chinatown closed their doors and laid off as many workers as in the previous two years. By the one-year anniversary twice as many Chinatown garment shops had closed as in the previous two years. By the two-year anniversary Chinese garment workers were still not sure if they could return to the industry. The huge downturn in Chinatown sent ripples throughout the midtown industry.

TRYING TO RECOVER

The Chinatown and midtown garment sectors are still trying to recover from the traumatic effects of September 11, 2001. Almost three years later, as many as eight thousand garment workers, mostly immigrants, had left the industry. While the midtown sector of the garment industry was not as affected as the Chinatown sector—simply because midtown is farther from ground zero—the decreases in overall production, and the manufacturers' and designers' decisions to diversify production by sending work overseas, also hurt the midtown shops.

On the other hand, garment work increased in 2004 because the economy had recovered somewhat. Consumers, who were not buying because of the recession, were feeling more comfortable with their economic situation. They were once again willing to spend money on clothing. Clothing production orders placed in late 2003 at overseas factories, in anticipation of U.S. spring and summer retailing, were too small to meet demand and sold out quickly. Clothing production reorders were quickly sent to the Manhattan sewing shops to replenish the supply. All my sources have told me that the remaining Chinese and Hispanic garment workers were quite busy during the first half of 2004. In fact, garment factory owners complained about a shortage of workers. And the workers themselves said that they had more than enough work. However, they were fearful that the 2004 boom would not usher in a full recovery.

Meanwhile, industry experts were looking for ways to bring garment production back to Manhattan. It may be too late to lure those workers who retired or entered other industries. But there might be room for new workers from different ethnic groups—so long as industry experts can assuage their concern about an unstable work situation. The industry is remaking itself once again. New York City production, which formerly concentrated on women's outerwear, is diversifying. Uniforms, especially U.S. government–issued military uniforms, and city police, sanitation, and mass transportation uniforms, played an important role in the small revival of 2004. Garment industry experts were lobbying for these products, and there was support from other sectors of the city's economy, such as fashion and retail luxury goods, that want to see the garment trade survive. Experts hope to rebuild parts of the industry with these new products.

In another few years the industry will have changed again. With different kinds of clothing, with changes in the union, and with new immigrant groups, the garment industry will once again evolve into something very distinct from its past incarnations.

Research Design and Methodology

A Comparative Study

I chose to compare two sectors in the garment industry, the Chinese, who hire Chinese, and the Koreans, who hire mostly Mexicans and Ecuadorians,[1] because these are the major ethnic groups in the garment industry today, according to union sources. Moreover, a comparative study would allow me to investigate the similarities and differences of these two sectors. They are actually very similar in the role they play in the manufacturing hierarchy. The two sectors produce similar goods and respond similarly to changes in the industry (see tables 2.2 and 2.3).

Methodologically, I use these two cases to illuminate how different types of work organizations and strategies (including the hiring of undocumented workers) practiced by the shop owners may or may not have been influenced by the use of ethnic resources. Moreover, I try to understand how they run garment shops that survive in New York City.

These two sectors provide the bulk of garment industry employment in Manhattan and have been relatively stable. They compete with each other to attract manufacturers that are looking for shops that can produce short runs of fashionable items, that want a "Made in the USA" label, and that have enough experience to sew mostly moderate-priced clothing.[2] Manufacturers say these two sectors have helped keep garment manufacturing in New York City.

Yet these two sectors also are different. The Chinese coethnic sector is unionized, has an informal training program, hires mostly documented workers, and bases its pay system on piecework. The Korean shops, which hire Hispanics, are not unionized, do not have a training program, pay an hourly rate, and hire mostly undocumented workers (see table 2.3).

These two sectors are also located in two different areas. The Chinese-owned shops, which hire Chinese from Hong Kong or the Guangdong region of southern China almost exclusively, all are located within a few blocks of the heart of Chinatown in downtown Manhattan. On the other hand, the Korean-owned shops, where Hispanics work, are located about two miles north in the midtown garment district, which is an ethnically diverse area. No one ethnic group predominates in the midtown area. Although one street in midtown—32nd Street between Broadway and Fifth Avenue—is dominated by Korean-owned restaurants and retail stores, however, that is not where the Korean-owned garment shops are located. They are located primarily between Seventh and Ninth Avenues from 37th to 40th Streets (just south of the Port Authority Bus Terminal). Koreans initially opened import/export businesses on West 32nd Street (along with other wholesalers). Other Korean businesses, like banks and restaurants, started to congregate along 32nd Street to serve the Korean business owners (I. Kim 1981).

Both the Chinese and Koreans located their shops in buildings with loft space large enough to accommodate about forty workers, sewing machines, and space for pressing and finishing work—usually two thousand to eight thousand square feet in all. When other manufacturers left both the midtown and downtown areas, the loft space became available at reasonably low rents for both the Chinese and Korean entrepreneurs (Abeles et al. 1983).

The Process

I used the following multifaceted qualitative approach in collecting data: (1) informal observation at four garment shops, (2) informal, in-depth interviews with 57 Chinese workers and 55 Hispanic (Mexican, Ecuadorian, Dominican, and Central American) workers, 15 Chinese garment shop owners, and 15 Korean garment shop owners, and (3) interviews with union officials, New York State Department of Labor employees, and ethnic business association officers and support staff.

Because of the nature of the study population, mostly new immigrants, more than a third of whom were undocumented, and because all the owners participated in some off-the-books activity, I did not think it appropriate to tape-record the interviews. Although gaining entry and information was not difficult, I felt that the introduction of a recording device would have discouraged and frightened many of the informants, preventing them from discussing sensitive matters that were crucial to my study. Usually, I typed up the interviews and observations within a few hours of our meeting.

Even though garment factories were noisy, and owners and workers were too busy to take time away from their work for extensive formal interviews, I conducted informal observations in garment shops because I was interested in the interactions between workers and owners and wanted to be able to discuss on-the-job interactions readily. The workplace was the only setting where I could observe this.

Interviews with workers took place in various locations. I interviewed the majority of the Chinese workers during lunch hour in the various eateries in Chinatown. I interviewed some right before or after their English-as-a-Second-Language (ESL) classes. I would follow up on our conversations with a telephone interview.

I used the same procedures for finding and interviewing Hispanic workers. The major difference was that I did fewer telephone follow-up interviews. Only about a quarter of the interviewees (twelve of fifty-five) received a follow-up telephone interview. The majority of these telephone interviews were conducted by a translator who was given very specific questions. Telephone interviews proved difficult because these Hispanic workers were hard to keep track of by phone. Frequently, phones would be disconnected, or the individual would not be home. Until I ran into this problem, I had no idea that conducting follow-up interviews by telephone would be so difficult. After this happened a few times, I adjusted my protocol to conduct longer and more in-depth in-person interviews with Hispanic workers (I would spend nearly two hours with Hispanic workers, whereas my interviews with Chinese employees usually lasted only about an hour).

INFORMAL OBSERVATION

During my informal observations at the garment shops, I frequently asked questions to clarify what workers were doing. I tried to remain as much of an observer as I possibly could. For example, if I was following the owner for the day, I sometimes helped by answering the phone, moving clothing, or doing whatever else seemed necessary just to keep our conversation going. I tried to act natural. I joked and kidded with the workers and owners. I did not just sit there and watch them work. That would have made them uncomfortable. I stayed out of the way of most operations because I was not qualified to do them, and I did not want to get in someone's way. When it looked like I could help, I did. Meanwhile, I questioned the owners about their hiring process, how they distributed work, and how they figured out their payrolls. The purpose of my observations was to learn the day-to-day interactions and activities in a garment shop.

The advantage of nonparticipant observation was that it allowed me to get closer to the people in their everyday work setting. When workers are hired, fired, or reprimanded, or when work is distributed unfairly, the resultant interactions are all observable. These interchanges served as a basis for my interview questions. Workers in the shops also had a chance to learn about my background and my interests before I interviewed them. This helped to set them at ease, and thus they seemed open and volunteered information during the interview.

I visited four garment shops to observe and to learn the work processes. The two Chinese shops were like the shops that I had observed two years earlier in another field project in terms of size, daily routine, and jobs that were sent to them from the manufacturers. The Chinese shops had many similarities, especially in the hiring and training processes. The two Korean-owned shops had some differences. One clearly had much more space and was cleaner. Workers seemed more relaxed there. However, the two shops were similar in terms of size, daily routine, and the jobs they accepted from the manufacturers.

While I was in the shops, I spent most of my time talking informally with all the workers as well as with foremen, forewomen, and owners. I spent on average four hours every other day for six weeks in each of the four shops. I varied the days and hours I visited. During the first week I stayed close to my key informants, although I also began to converse with other workers, foremen/women, and owners. By the end of the first week everyone in the shop recognized me and knew exactly what I was doing. This laid the groundwork for some in-depth interviews that I conducted off-site, either at a restaurant or over the telephone. The most crucial part of being at the shops was observing daily interactions between workers, owners, foremen/women, and sometimes union officials. This proved to be significant because it ensured my exposure to day-to-day aspects of work that informants might not have considered important to report to me. This allowed me to ask about certain aspects that no one happened to mention in our interviews.

GATHERING INTERVIEWS

I gathered most of the data through interviews. The main criterion guiding my selection of informants was that they represent the widest range of garment shops as possible. The interviews with the workers and owners were unstructured and covered five broad areas: background before emigration, arrival and family circumstances in New York, hiring or finding a job, first and subsequent jobs, and relationships to workers and owners. I interviewed owners, union officials, state labor department officials, some garment workers, and others connected with the garment industry during the winters of 1994, 1995, and 1996 and again in 1999 and 2000. I interviewed the majority of the workers beginning in the summer/fall of 1994 and continued this process through 1996. I reinterviewed some workers and additional owner/employers during the second round in 1999–2000.

BUSINESS ASSOCIATIONS, UNION OFFICIALS, NEW YORK STATE DEPARTMENT OF LABOR

As part of my research on the background of the garment industry, I decided that I should also interview as many people connected to the industry as possible. This included individuals with the business associations who are in contact with the owners, union officials who deal with both workers and owners, and the New York State Department of Labor, which regulates the different shops.

I initially had difficulty gaining entry into the Korean Contractors' Association (KCA).[3] The secretary always told me that the officers were very busy. I even tried interviewing a former president, who refused to participate because he was no longer a "spokesperson." This was the answer he gave even after I asked if I could interview him as an individual garment shop owner. KCA representatives postponed many meetings, until I finally spoke with the president of the association on the telephone. He was impressed with my background, mostly my Ivy League credentials, and am a daughter of a former garment worker. After he learned of my background, he invited me to his office. He was also very helpful in lining up Korean owners for me to interview.[4]

I also interviewed members of the Greater Blouse and Sportswear Association. The Greater Blouse and Sportswear Association is the Chinese contractors' primary source of information about the garment worker's union—all the association's members are union-affiliated contractors—and it has a majority Chinese membership. Through these initial contacts, I found the eleven remaining Chinese contractors.

During the early part of my research, the International Ladies' Garment Workers' Union (ILGWU) had not yet merged with the Amalgamated Textile Worker's Union to become the Union of Needletrades, Industrial and Textile Employees (UNITE). Thus the majority of my interviews were conducted with ILGWU officials, and when I refer to the union, I usually mean the ILGWU. Its officials were very helpful in providing information and allowed me access to the ESL classes conducted by its Garment Workers' Justice Centers. The union was much more helpful in providing information about the Chinese workers than the Koreans and Hispanics. The union was able to provide background information on the Chinese owners, as well as data on the number of workers and what benefits they received. The organizing department of the union, especially the director, was the most informed about the Korean shops, although it did not have any statistics, only anecdotal information or information gleaned during its organizing campaigns.

I decided to interview officials at the state department of labor because KCA officials told me that labor officials had addressed the group about wage minimums and hiring issues. I wanted to find out what the state labor department knew about the Korean-owned shops.

WORKER SAMPLE

Forty-five percent of my interviewees came from the ESL classes sponsored by the ILGWU and by the Garment Industry Development Corporation (GIDC) (table A.1). I recruited almost equal percentages of Chinese (47 percent) and Hispanic (42 percent) workers from these ESL classes. This was one of the two places where garment workers gathered outside the factories (the other was the "for hire" corner). The factories were a difficult place to recruit. Unless an informant brought me into the shop and helped me recruit interviewees, workers were reluctant to interrupt their work to talk to me. Moreover, there is no period in the factory workday when I could have announced my intentions and mingled with the workers to explain the study. The ESL classes were ideal in that they were structured with a fifteen- to twenty-minute break in the middle of class. Right before the break, union or GIDC officials would allow me to make my announcement in either Chinese or Spanish. During the break workers asked questions, and those who were willing signed up for interview appointments.

The ESL students, both Chinese and Spanish speaking, are a self-selected group. These garment workers who want to learn English are bolder, more independent, and probably more upwardly mobile than the rest of the inter-

TABLE A.1   *Worker Informant Recruitment Locations (Percentages)*

	*ESL**	*Shops*	*For Hire Corner*	*Friends*
Chinese	47	29	0	24
Hispanic	42	11	40	7
Everyone	45	20	20	15

*English-as-a-Second-Language classes sponsored by Garment Industry Development Corporation, the garment workers' union and its Garment Workers' Justice Centers.

view group. These workers carved out a few hours from their busy work schedule to attend ESL classes. Their family, living, and child care situations were much more stable and predictable, which allowed them to arrange to be at twice-a-week ESL classes each semester. These workers also expected that being able to speak English would make a difference in their lives. My analysis relies heavily on what they told me and thus represents more of the ESL participants than any other group in the analysis.

Within the Chinese and Hispanic groups, there are differences between the ESL participants and the non-ESL participants. The Chinese ESL participants are interested in becoming U.S. citizens more quickly than their Hispanic counterparts. These Chinese workers had access to family members who lived nearby, usually grandparents who could look after children while the parents attended these classes. These ESL participants were also more interested in finding jobs outside the Chinese garment sector. The Chinese ESL group had more resources and was striving to gain U.S. citizenship to bring other family members to the United States. There were few other socioeconomic differences among those who took ESL classes and those who did not.

Among the Hispanic workers, those from ESL classes were overwhelmingly Ecuadorian, and the workers from the "for hire" corners were overwhelmingly Mexican. The Ecuadorians who were in the ESL classes had lived in the United States for about six months longer than the Mexicans and also had more education and came from a higher socioeconomic level back home.[5] As a result the average educational level of the Ecuadorians was higher than that of the Mexicans in my sample. The Ecuadorian workers who took the ESL classes also believed that they could become foremen or forewomen in the garment shops. They aspired to that position because the jobs are of higher status and pay much more. The Ecuadorians were more upwardly mobile than the Mexican workers.

Although the Ecuadorians in the ESL classes discussed their experiences at the "for hire" corners, I recruited very few from those sites. In retrospect, I may have missed some Ecuadorians at the "for hire" corners because they may have been hired very early in the morning.[6] Or perhaps fewer Ecuadorians were looking for jobs when I was doing my fieldwork. Or Ecuadorians may have avoided being interviewed or recruited from the street corners because they did not want to associate themselves with the Mexicans, who dominated the "for hire" corner. Because of their higher socioeconomic status back home, the Ecuadorians may have wanted more anonymity and may not have wanted to admit that in the United States, their status is very similar to that of the Mexicans and that, like the Mexicans, they have to resort to the "for hire" corner to find jobs.

From what they told me in the interviews, the Ecuadorians were no more likely to stay permanently in the United States than were other Hispanics who did not take ESL classes.[7] At least, they did not tell me that at the time of the interview.[8] Their experiences in the Korean shops are really no different than those of other Hispanics, except that the Ecuadorians seemingly had a more stable living situation here and thus an ability to navigate their way to these ESL classes. They may do better economically in the long run than the Mexicans. Much of the information that I gathered came from either the Ecuadorians I recruited from the ESL classes or the Mexicans I recruited from the "for hire" corners.

While all the Chinese workers I interviewed had working telephones, this was not the case for the Hispanic workers; many Hispanic workers periodically lost their phone service after they failed to pay their phone bills. Thus the data that I analyzed are skewed toward the information given by those with phones, people who therefore may have had a more stable income and home life than other informants.

Chinese Workers

I obtained the majority of the interviews with the Chinese workers through purposive sampling. I purposely chose different sites to recruit workers so that I could interview as wide a variety of workers as possible. I recruited workers who were willing to be interviewed at the ESL classes, at certain garment shops where I had personal contacts, and at the garment shops where I visited. I would recruit informants from the ESL classes by making announcements and asking for volunteers. At garment shops I would approach friends of my informants, as well as talk to individuals when they were on lunch breaks. My informants came from these three sources: twenty-six from ESL classes, sixteen from the garment shops, and fifteen from referrals by their friends, who I also interviewed.

Hispanic Workers

I obtained interviews with Hispanic informants much as I did the Chinese informants. Twenty-three interviewees came from the ESL classes, twenty-two from the "for hire" corners, and six from the shops I visited. The rest were friends of other interviewees. I will discuss differences among these groups of Latinos in the sections that follow.

GAINING TRUST: KEY CONTACTS AND TRANSLATORS

I was confident that I could easily gain the trust of the Chinese garment workers and the employers because I speak Chinese, am the daughter of a former garment worker, and my parents hailed from the same region as the majority of the garment workers. Moreover, I had a grant that allowed me to give $10 to every worker I interviewed. I felt that this was appropriate because I was using up their valuable time.

In an earlier study I encountered problems interviewing Chinese workers because I tried to interview them during their workday. They were reluctant to speak to me because they wanted to concentrate on sewing. And because they were being paid for piecework, interviewing them during work hours interfered with their earning capability. I changed my tactics this time, such that I did not interview workers on the job but only recruited them there. Workers were much more willing to talk outside work hours. I also recruited from ESL classes sponsored by the union at the Garment Workers' Justice Center on 40th Street. The program was discontinued shortly after the formation of UNITE.

I did not encounter many problems in recruiting Chinese workers. I did not expect that every worker would be willing to be interviewed, and I encountered few problems in gaining the trust of those who consented to be interviewed. I found that I needed to speak to each informant personally before she would agree to an interview. By being able to offer the interviewees $10, I was able to "buy" a few more minutes of their time to listen to my entry script.[9] I believe these extra minutes were crucial in gaining their agreement to be interviewed. The least guarded were the thirteen people who were friends of people I had already interviewed. More than half (thirty-two of fifty-seven) of the Chinese truly felt that they had nothing interesting to tell me. They would explain that nothing was significant about their work lives or themselves and that they were in no way significantly different from the other women I had interviewed. I had to convince them that each and every worker I interviewed had something slightly different to tell me. Usually, I had to explain that although my mother and her sisters-in-law were all garment workers, they had different experiences. For example, my mother eventually left the industry while the two sisters-in-law stayed. One had trouble learning basic sewing skills, and even with eight years in the industry, she still makes very little and stays only for the health insurance. The other likes her sewing job and feels productive, even though she makes what she considers a low wage. Moreover, I told my informants that if they were all to tell me exactly the same thing, they would be confirming a widespread assessment of their jobs.

They were not just being modest: they could not understand how their experiences could contribute to a scholarly work. The workers could not comprehend why I was interested in asking them about their experiences, but they spoke freely and confided their situations to me. I believe that they were open because this was the first time that anyone had interviewed them about their experiences. A few were embarrassed to discuss their personal situation because they thought that I would judge how far or little they had advanced economically since they arrived in the United States.

Two Chinese women did comprehend the relevance of speaking to me and became key contacts. Ann and Pen Ho (both are pseudonyms to protect their privacy) helped me gain entry to the sewing shops I visited. They were very popular and respected workers in their shops. Because they befriended me, other workers took me and my study more seriously. Moreover, workers and owners also felt more relaxed because Ann and Pen Ho had befriended me.

These two workers were more educated than the rest. In Guangdong, China, Ann had been an elementary school teacher and Pen Ho a medical assistant. Both understood what I meant by the study of people in their environment and sociology. Moreover, both were excellent sewers and frequently gave sewing tips to other workers who needed help. As a result of their strong personalities and their willingness to assist others, I easily met and recruited interviewees in their shops. Ann and Pen Ho also helped by answering the workers' and owners' questions about my study. They encouraged people to interact with me. I spent time in their shops making observations and inquiring about the work process.

I met Ann at an ESL class sponsored by the union. After I had interviewed her, I asked her to give me additional names and telephone numbers of workers who might want to be interviewed. Instead of just giving me names, she offered to take me to her garment shop so that I could visit on a regular basis and she could personally introduce me to other workers. When I first arrived at her shop, she had already told the owner and workers about my study. Workers were extremely friendly, and Ann apparently had also told them about my background. In the end, I interviewed six workers from this shop.

Pen Ho was a friend of a relative of mine. She had worked in the garment industry since the 1980s, and when I met her, she was working in a well-established shop that had been in business for more than twenty years. She was enthusiastic about the interview and participating in the study. After my interview with her, she was even more comfortable and offered to let me come visit the shop. I specifically asked her to help me gain an interview with her shop owner. She introduced me to the owner right away, but the owner would not agree to an interview. He did agree to let me visit his shop because I was a friend of Pen Ho's. During the next two weeks, Pen Ho introduced me to most other workers in the shop. I visited almost everyday and interviewed five workers, all friends of Pen Ho's. The owner finally approached me and volunteered to be interviewed. He saw how well I got along with his workers and wanted me to hear his side as well.

On the other hand, I was not as confident about gaining the trust of the Hispanic workers. They were mostly undocumented, could not speak English, and were newcomers to New York. I could not speak Spanish, and, worse, I resembled their Korean employers. To try to overcome some of these disadvantages, I hired a translator who would accompany me on my fieldwork and interviews.[10] I worked briefly with a native Ecuadorian translator who was also a doctoral student in sociology. And I was extremely fortunate in being able to hire two translators, both of Dominican descent, who grew up in New York City and whose parents were former garment workers. Moreover, these two translators also had experience in interviewing for qualitative studies. The ability to offer $10 to each of the workers also helped to generate interest among the potential interviewees.

While I recognized that there might have been differences in the Spanish spoken by my translators and the interviewees, and that their different ethnicities could hamper the openness of the workers, I found that the translators' background as daughters of garment workers usually overcame the interviewees' hesitation. The translators' experience with garment workers and "garment" language, as used in the shops, was more important in the interviews than the differences in ethnicity and spoken Spanish. Workers were more comfortable with them than with me.

The translators and I figured out that after they introduced themselves and the study, they should introduce me as the daughter of a Chinese garment worker doing comparative research. Some workers were satisfied with this information. A few found it hard to imagine that I was not Korean.[11] With reassurance and a thorough explanation of the ethnic structure of the current garment industry, they usually became more open. We also exchanged information during our interviews with Hispanic workers. They were very curious about why I would want to study them. Moreover, they were curious to learn about the Chinese in the industry and the differences in the shops. My translators were extremely helpful in obtaining the trust of the Hispanic workers.

As I began my research with the Hispanic workers, I was lucky to gain the confidence of one Mexican woman (Natividad) and one Ecuadorian man (Cesar; both are pseudonyms). Cesar became a key informant and helped me gain entry to and permission to stay and observe both at his shop and at another shop where he previously worked. He was a foreman and had the confidence of the Korean owners. He had stayed friendly with his previous employers and worked extra hours for them on weekends when they needed him. He was highly regarded by both sets of employers. His current employer had recruited him by offering him higher wages than he had been making. Natividad became a key informant by going out of her way to help recruit others for my interviews. When she did recruit, she would recite my entry script to the potential informers and would ask them to contact me or my translator. She found two other interviewees for this project.

Gaining Access to Workers Through the ESL Classes

I recruited other workers to interview through the union, the ESL classes sponsored by the Garment Industry Development Corporation, other garment shops, and the "for hire" corners. To gain entry to the union-sponsored ESL classes, I renewed my relationship with union representatives and officials whom I had met in 1992 and made a bargain with them to gain access. First, I explained that I wanted to recruit workers who worked for the Koreans and the Chinese for interviews for a sociological project. At the same time the union officials were eager to learn about the undocumented Mexican and Ecuadorian workers. Many Ecuadorian workers were attending union English classes; however, the union officials had not had the chance to speak to many of the Ecuadorians or Mexicans in depth. They liked my project, but they also wanted to ensure that they would have access to information that I learned.

Initially, the union officials wanted to be present at some of the interviews to listen and to learn about the workers. They felt that it was a perfect opportunity for them to learn about my project as well as the workers. I agreed to conduct one interview in their presence, and I quickly realized that the situation was not appropriate. The worker did not feel comfortable with the union officials sitting in. Although we spoke at a restaurant, the worker associated me with the union. I met with the union officials the next day and explained the situation. Instead of allowing them to be present at the interviews, I offered to meet with union officials after the completion of my fieldwork. I would present my findings to them, and I would allow them a chance to ask questions. This "bargain" satisfied the union officials.

Although the coordinator of the union ESL classes and others in the central office were party to this agreement, other union representatives at the ESL class sites were apprehensive about what workers might say and what researchers would write about the union, and I had to assure these representatives that I understood their concerns. They told me that they have had bad experiences with journalists and other student researchers who insisted on writing about only the abuses in the union and not about how the union has made a positive difference in these workers' lives.[12] Workers who have had bad experiences with interviewers have complained to the union in the past. And the union representatives feared that the workers would spend too much time with me. Although the union officials could not stop me from recruiting the workers, I felt that I needed to gain the union officials' trust in order to be able to interview the workers. These representatives met with the workers often, and I felt that if they did not trust my work, they would convey their fears to the workers, thus tainting the interviews.

I soon learned that the union had layers of bureaucracy and that I would have to gain the trust of each layer in order to gain access to the union members I wanted to interview. I reassured these union representatives that the study was not only about the union but about the workers themselves, and I offered them a similar bargain. They too wanted to learn more about the workers, especially about the workings of the Korean shops. Although these union people were experts on the abuses in these shops, based on the complaints of the workers, they knew little about the organization of the workplace and how Koreans found workers. Thus, while they were apprehensive, they also wanted access to information that I would be gathering. From these encounters I learned that there are many layers of authority in the union, with each group trying to protect its own domain. People in each layer acted as gatekeepers. Thus I had no single access point to the workers through the union.

I also recruited workers at the Garment Industry Development Corporation's ESL classes. I was able to recruit ten Chinese workers through the GIDC programs but was able to recruit only two Ecuadorians this way. The majority of the Hispanics who attended the GIDC's ESL classes did not work for Koreans. These workers were documented immigrants hired by Jewish and Dominican owners in all kinds of capacities. There were belt makers and knitting factory workers, among others. GIDC recruited workers to the ESL classes by advertising in unionized shops, unlike the union's workers' center, which advertised by handing out leaflets on the street. Thus I was unlikely to find workers who had any experience with Korean owners in the GIDC's ESL classes.

I had gained entry into the GIDC's ESL classes by meeting with the corporation's director and the coordinator of its training programs. They were much less guarded than the union officials because they were mainly in the business of researching the garment industry or developing training and ESL programs. They did not have a problem with my approach. Their only stipulation was that I could not interfere with class time. Therefore, I would visit their classes a few minutes before the break time to make an announcement, and I would talk to interested individuals during their break and lunchtimes.

Gaining Access at the Garment Shops

Another large recruitment area for workers for the study was through the garment shops. At certain garment shops key contacts led me to other shops to meet with workers whom they had already contacted for me. In these cases I did not have to gain entry through the garment shop owners; I just used my own entry script with the workers. In other shops I had an introduction from the Chinese or Korean business association, business owners whom I already had interviewed, or through worker contacts in the shop. I recruited workers either by making announcements or by talking individually with workers. I recruited the rest of the workers from shops I had visited and where I had established rapport with the owners and workers.

Workers at "For Hire" Corners

I recruited the majority of the Hispanic informants either through the union ESL classes or at the "for hire" corners in the garment district. I recruited six workers at the shops I visited (see table A.1). I would make announcements in ESL classes asking for volunteers. The workers who were enrolled in ESL classes were the most open and seemed the most comfortable with the idea of an interview. My translators and I used a different approach at the "for hire" corners.

The translator and I would approach the population at the "for hire" corner carefully. We wanted to recruit workers quickly, yet we did not want to be so aggressive that we would frighten them. We did not want to be confused with some government-sponsored study, for some workers had initially asked if we were with the government or, worse, the Immigration and Naturalization Service (INS). We thought that they would be suspicious of the money that we had to pay them. We wanted to convey the seriousness of our work. After going to the corner every other day for a couple of weeks, we were able to make headway. The Hispanic workers came to recognize us as regulars who were trying to recruit informants. At the end of the first week (1994), we had interviewed only two workers, but word spread quickly that we were willing to pay $10 per interview and that we were not associated with the INS, the state department of labor, or the Korean employers. What also helped to alleviate fears was that sometimes we would interview our informants right on the corner. Other potential informants overheard our questions and became much more relaxed about this study. Thus as time passed, it grew easier and easier to recruit informants at the corner. They came to recognize us as university students who were doing a project.

GARMENT SHOP OWNERS

I interviewed a total of thirty garment shop owners—fifteen Chinese and fifteen Koreans. I recruited the Chinese owners from the two shops I visited, through contacts in the business association, and garment owners' friends. Gaining interviews through the business association seemed by far the simplest approach, but it turned out not to be. After I met with officials from the organization and explained my project, they agreed to give me only a couple of names of owners to interview. I was hopeful that the two would lead to a larger sample through referrals. After calling and mentioning that the association had given me their names, they seemed more than happy to oblige. In the end, I interviewed only one Chinese owner through the association, and he did not give me any other leads. The rest of the owners I found through contacts I made through owners or workers.

Although I gained entry to two Chinese garment shops through worker contacts, it was hard for me to speak with the owners initially. Even though they allowed me to witness illicit activity at their shops—such as allowing children in the shops, paying workers in cash, and paying workers late—the owners were not ready to be interviewed. In the beginning they were somewhat skeptical of what I was doing, even though they trusted the workers who brought me in. After I had become a semiregular figure in their shop, where I often offered advice about particular high schools for their children, helped with their children's homework, provided translation services, and ran occasional errands, they began to trust me. I located the other owners I interviewed through friends of friends of these initial four.

The Chinese owners of the shops I visited did not complain to me about my visits. I think my being Chinese and an insider helped allay any distrust they had of me. The owners assumed that I had seen or knew everything that happened in a garment shop because my mother was a garment worker. I tried not to interfere with any of their regular operations. I was just an observer, and the slow approach that I took to gain their confidence helped me win interviews that were more thorough than they might have been.

I had a somewhat different experience with the Korean owners. The owners to whom the foreman introduced me proved to be reluctant interviewees. Although I did interview these owners, both were hesitant to introduce me to others.

These reluctant owner-interviewees told me that they did not want others to know that they had an outside visitor in their shops observing their work, and they especially did not want others to know that they were interviewed for a study. One reason that I believe they felt this way is that their foreman, not the owners, had given me permission to observe the shop. Because of the excellent relationship the foreman had with the owners and the extra favors he had done for them, he had convinced them that it was all right for me to observe. Also, I witnessed many violations of federal wage and hours laws that they thought were completely new to me.[13] These shop owners were uncomfortable with my presence. They did not ask me to leave, but I believe they felt as if they had lost control. They did not want to appear to their peers to be opening the secrets of their trade to an outsider, or a Chinese, or someone who could report their labor violations. All these issues were conflated.

The owners who were introduced to me by the Korean Contractors' Association were very friendly and forthcoming. They were more willing to speak and were willing to find others for me to interview. I interviewed three owners who were friends of officers of the association. I visited the shops of these owners briefly, and they participated only because the association had asked them to. I believe that these owners were as open as they were because the contractors' association had basically validated my study. I found the last ten owner-interviewees through various garment manufacturers. I interviewed manufacturers whom I knew were contracting work in New York City and through them I got the names of their contractors—some of whom were Korean. Everyone in this group was extremely open and friendly.

My sample of Korean owners may have been skewed toward those who spoke English well. Although all fifteen interviewees, as well as people who worked in the Korean Contractors' Association, were bilingual in English and Korean, they may not be representative of all Korean owners.

ANALYSIS

I began analyzing the data long before I completed all the interviews and visits. I constantly assessed my data with regard to new information, often developing and redeveloping themes. I often asked myself, "Was what I found today consistent with what I heard yesterday—why and how? Do I need to focus on one aspect rather than on another? What is everybody most concerned with?" I also refined and focused my questions so that I could gain better insight during my interviews. According to Schatzman and Strauss (1973:110), such analysis allows a researcher to "adjust his observational strategies, shifting some emphases towards those experiences which bear upon the development of his understanding, and generally, to exercise control over his emerging ideas by virtually simultaneous 'checking' or 'testing' of these ideas."

For example, when I was interviewing the Hispanic workers, I initially assumed that they got their jobs through personal recommendations like the Chinese did (this was also the model depicted in much of the literature). Thus I was interested in learning how the Korean owners thanked those who brought in good workers, what types of exchanges took place, and whether Korean owners or Hispanic workers initiated this chain of events. When I asked the workers about how they got jobs, they said friends and relatives told them about these positions. However, I also had gathered much contradictory evidence. Why was there a "for hire" corner? Why did Korean owners also tell me about workers who come knocking on the door looking for jobs? The Chinese did not have a "for hire" corner, and very few Chinese workers were hired because jobs had been posted or because they happened to knock on the door when the shop had an opening. After ten or so interviews with Hispanics, I realized that I had to probe much deeper to get at the exact process they used to find a job. Yes, some had friends who told them to go to certain shops, but their friends hardly ever came with them, and their friends also hardly ever introduced them to the owners. The majority had friends who told them about the general area and the "for hire" corner. Very few friends actually helped them in a personal manner.

I evaluated my data by first cross-checking information that I had received from different sources and by using the information to test and build my hypotheses. I also examined data for inconsistencies, contradictions, and incongruities. At first, I found many disparities. Because the focus of my data gathering was on the workers, I frequently found that their understanding of the employment process (workers were consistent with each other) was different from that of the owners, union representatives, and the New York State Department of Labor. At first, I found myself constantly trying to verify what they said because it was not similar to what union representatives and others told me. Only when I heard the same thing several times did I realize, for example, that the workers had their own interpretation of what it means to join the union. According to union representatives, any worker is eligible to become a member of the union so long as the contractor for whom they work has a collective bargaining agreement with the union.

Workers in these shops can join the union and pay membership dues of only $18 a month, in return for which they receive vacation days and other benefits. However, when I asked Chinese workers about joining the union and how they joined, they told me about a wage minimum of $3,500 that they had to earn in the first six months of work to qualify for union-sponsored health benefits. Health insurance cost $225 for every three months. Not one worker mentioned the $18 union membership fee that is assessed after the worker has collected four paychecks.[14] Thus in the workers' mind, becoming a member of the union and having health benefits are the same thing. They could not answer the question about union membership without explaining their health insurance benefits.

When I had completed three-quarters of my interviews, I started creating folders or documents in my computer word processor as well as paper files that I arranged according to themes I had found in my data. I did the majority of the sorting in my word-processing program. For example, I labeled some of my folders "how to be boss?" "men sewing," "migration patterns," "finding a job," "why NY?" "workers preferred," "child care," "transnationalism." Eventually, I found that I did not have enough data for some of these themes, such as students. Within these documents I started cutting and pasting relevant data into the appropriate themed folder, just as I would physically handle the cut-up pieces of paper. When it seemed that I could organize data into subthemes, I started grouping data accordingly. For example, in my migration patterns folder/document, I started grouping the data into the four emigration patterns that I had found: family, staged, transnational, and single emigration. When I found these themes, I went back to the field armed with questions to probe in these areas. I continued doing this throughout the rest of data gathering and stopped doing major reorganizing only right before I started writing. Thus my analysis took shape while I was sorting through the data. The analysis was informed by my ideas and concepts, and developing theories guided my data collection, in turn.

I should note that a few factors interfered with my ability to convey the subtle shades of meaning that were conveyed by the interviewees. The majority of the interviews were not conducted in English, so the data may have lost some of their nuanced meanings in translation. Because of the nature of the study and the study population, recording the interviews was impossible. Overall, I believe the information gathered from the interviewees is incredibly rich. What I have presented in this study is just a synthesis of what I learned. While this kind of in-depth qualitative study is very time consuming, hearing stories from people who rarely get to tell them to researchers is worth all the energy it requires.

Chapter 1. Legacies: New York City Garment Industry

1. According to the census of 1850, women outnumbered men in the ready-to-wear clothing industry (Seidman 1942:32).

2. Workers were often paid piecework wages for work done at home, but either piecework or time-based pay may have existed in the factories. According to Lorwin (1924), workers struck in 1894 to demand that payment be made weekly instead of by piecework. By the Depression, hourly wages had given way to piecework once more (Green 1997). However, payment in the shops continued to fluctuate between piecework and time-based wages. Employers interviewed by Odencrantz (1919/77) said that employers paid both piecework and time-based wages. For example, one paid his more skilled workers by the piece, another paid by the week.

3. The Tenement House Act of 1892 forbade contractors to carry on production in homes.

4. In Odencrantz's study, of the 94 percent of Italian women surveyed who were in manufacturing, nearly half were in garment work. Those in manufacturing made leather and fur goods, foodstuffs, candy, and tobacco. Very few Italian women were employed in professional or domestic services (Odencrantz 1919/77).

5. The section work, or team system, is based on the task system. After the seams are broken down into specific sewing movements, workers assigned to complete those tasks may be grouped together, either by task, so that a section or team of workers is all doing the same task. If they are grouped by section of the garment, each person working on a section is doing a different task, all of which add up to a completed garment. Employees can be paid per task completed or for each whole garment or piece that they complete.

6. The Dillingham Commission Report on Immigration in 1911 found that southern Italian women were more likely to be gainfully employed than Jewish women (Kessner 1977).

7. Green (1997) does not specify who the "American" women were. Perhaps she just means American-born women of various ethnicities.

8. The membership of Local 25 was comprised of 35 percent Italian women and 7 percent native-born Americans (Lorwin 1924:149).

9. This policy would be the crux of subsequent organizing by other minority workers in the union. Many had hoped to establish their own ethnic locals within the union.

10. According to Northrup (1944), the ILGWU sanctioned separate locals for Italian garment workers, who could not understand the Yiddish that was used to conduct business in the mainly Jewish locals.

11. During the prewar period speed was less important because most production was located in New York, which meant the factories had no need to schedule transportation time for their completed goods, and there was less competition. After the war improvements in transportation and communications made it easier for factory owners to move production outside New York City. These conditions remain much the same today. New York City maintains its competitiveness by providing quick and easy access to labor and the materials that the garment industry requires.

12. In 1950, blacks held 11 percent and Hispanics held 7 percent of the 213,840 jobs in the New York City garment industry. In 1970 African Americans held 11.5 percent and Hispanics 23 percent of the 113,700 jobs in the garment industry. These numbers show that even while the industry was shrinking, more Puerto Ricans than blacks were replacing second-generation Italian and Jewish workers.

13. In 1940 the garment industry had 145,500 white workers and 5,100 black workers. In 1950 it had 175,560 white workers and 23,430 black workers. By 1970 the industry had 69,800 white workers and 13,150 black workers (Waldinger 1996:142).

In 1962, the ILGWU became the subject of a congressional investigation led by Rep. Adam Clayton Powell, D-N.Y. (Laurentz 1980; Green 1997). This investigation found discrimination and antagonism in certain locals, and racial imbalances between leadership and members (Green 1997). Although the findings were revealing, the investigation offered no real solution for the racial problems in the union (Laurentz 1980).

14. Cutters usually were male workers who managed large machines with blades to cut the cloth into pieces that fit a pattern for a piece of clothing. Cutting requires not only strength but the ability to make accurate calculations and a good eye to minimize waste.

15. For example, in April 1961 Ernest Holmes and the NAACP filed a formal complaint of discrimination against ILGWU Cutters' Local 10. Originally hired as a general helper, Holmes started assisting the cutters. He learned the craft while still doing his general aid job and sought to become a full-fledged cutter. Because his shop was a closed shop, he applied several times to Local 10 to become a member but had no success. The complaint was dropped, but the New York State Commission for Human Rights found that "the evidence raises serious doubt as [to the ILGWU's] good faith to comply with the state law against discrimination" (Laurentz 1980; Green 1997).

16. Training was also an important issue for Puerto Ricans (Helfgott 1959b; Laurentz 1980). The ILGWU was interested in restricting the number of apprentices and helpers, especially those positions held by blacks and Puerto Ricans. The result was a smaller pool

of experienced and highly trained workers who could command higher wages (Wrong 1974; Ortiz 1996).

17. Many Chinese American veterans went to China after World War II to find a bride, married, and applied for immigration visas for their wives. The majority of these veterans met their wives in this way.

18. The Chinese owners were English speakers who had the ability to establish relationships with garment manufacturers that were similar to those enjoyed by their predecessors, the Jewish garment shop owners.

19. By 1997 the number of employees in the apparel and textile manufacturing sectors in New York City had actually increased to 84,000 from 82,500 in 1996 (Foderaro 1998).

Chapter 2. Doing Ethnic Business

1. See Bonacich and Appelbaum (2000:27) for a detailed discussion of this process, including the changing role of the manufacturer.

2. When I was doing my fieldwork in 1994–96 and 1999–2000, Chinese-owned garment factories were just beginning to emerge in the Chinese community of Sunset Park, Brooklyn. The shops in Sunset Park were much smaller than the Chinese shops in Manhattan, averaged about ten Chinese employees, and were not unionized.

3. The Chinese owners prefer to organize their employees by task and base their pay on completion of the whole garment. Task-based work is a form of de-skilling the garment sewing process. Each seam that has to be sewn in order to put a garment together becomes a separate task that is graded for difficulty, or "priced." The total price for all the seams is the price paid to the worker for a completed garment.

Korean owners pay their workers by the hour. The employees may well be organized by task and section, but they are paid for their time on the job, not the amount of work that they complete.

4. According to the 1990 census, the thirteen census tracts of Chinatown had a population of 49,002 Asians.

5. The Chinese workers usually sew most seams in a whole garment and are paid a certain price for each whole garment completed.

6. Jeff Hermanson, ILGWU director of organizing, interview by author, 1993.

Chapter 3. Getting from There to Here

1. For example, opportunities for women immigrants, especially in lower-paying industries, have increased. Undocumented women are more likely to arrive with only their male partner, so I speculate that it is also more likely for them to have children here. Families that include American-born children and undocumented parents are likely to remain in the United States.

2. For example, specialized Chinese chefs were in high demand during late 1970s and early 1980s.

3. Hispanics anticipate that they will earn enough money to support themselves as well as their whole family back home. The interviewees did not specifically state their plans in regard to helping other family members to emigrate. The Chinese, on the other hand, are saving for their future in the United States. Because their plan is for the entire family to reunite in the United States, they are saving to help other family members to emigrate.

4. Informants have told me that travel for a couple from Mexico may only cost $1,500, whereas from Ecuador it would be closer to $13,000. Travel from the Dominican Republic is usually less than $1,000.

5. One couple changed their family composition in the United States by bearing children here.

6. The only exception was a nineteen-year-old legal Mexican immigrant who was living with her grandparents. Her parents had emigrated with her but returned to Mexico. She was sending money home to support them.

7. One husband returned to the homeland after realizing that he could make more money there than in the United States. These seven women worked in the garment industry to support family back home.

8. Mary Corcoran's (1993) study of Irish illegals includes men who describe their visit to the United States in a similar manner.

9. According to the New York Department of City Planning, 59,798 legal Chinese immigrants (including people from Taiwan and Hong Kong) arrived in New York City between 1990 and 1994, whereas only 13,980 legal Ecuadorian and 3,449 legal Mexican immigrants entered the United States during that same period. (Dugger 1997).

10. Gendering in the two sectors of the garment industry—Korean and Chinese—is connected to work organization. In the Korean sector work is organized in sections, with individuals or groups of individuals assigned a specific task. One way of organizing section work is to divide workers into teams. Each team sews a whole garment. However, individual team or section members sew just a particular seam. The partially finished product is passed along to each team or section member until it is completed. Another method is to assign a whole team or section to only one task. When their task is finished, the partially sewn garments are passed to another team or section to sew their task. Teams or sections are often given quotas. Thus each group or individual depends on the work of the previous group or individual. In the Chinese sector the workers sew whole garments. Each worker takes bundles of clothing and sews almost all the parts together. In this organization workers are paid only for the pieces they complete. These workers have more freedom to come and go so long as the work is completed.

11. The men were referring to the garment shops in New York City as large factories, where work is more masculine than in a small garment shop.

12. She was referring to jobs that she had babysitting Mexican children in the United States whose mothers were working and could afford to pay her only $30 a week for each child.

13. In the early 1990s garment jobs were also plentiful for men in Mexico and Ecuador (Salzinger 2003).

CHAPTER 4. THE ATTRACTIONS OF CLOTH

1. The term *1.5 generation* is used to describe people who emigrated as children because they are first-generation immigrants but share characteristics of the second generation, those who were born in the United States.

2. Although I brought an interpreter with me, all the Korean owners refused to be interviewed in Korean. They were all comfortable speaking in English. It may have been a coincidence that I interviewed Chinese and Korean garment contractors who spoke English. On the other hand, it may be self-selection—that only those who spoke English well wanted to be interviewed.

3. I separated out members of the 1.5 generation because their entrance into the industry is different from that of immigrants. According to the 1.5 generation owners, they were trained in U.S. schools and are more qualified for jobs in the United States than the new immigrants who trained back home. The immigrants faced different conditions in the job market. They did not label it racism, but they said they found it difficult to get the jobs and the pay that they thought they deserved.

4. Park (1997) suggests that Korean immigrants' notion of achievement is a combination of financial success and the educational attainment of their children.

5. Between 1968 (when the Immigration Act of 1965 took effect) and 1975 most Koreans who came to the United States were professionals. After 1975 Koreans made greater use of the family reunification quotas. Thus many more Koreans who were not professionals emigrated. Furthermore, since 1978 Korea has allowed massive amounts of cash (up to $300,000) to be taken out of the country. Immigrants who arrive after 1978 are more heterogeneous, and some are very wealthy.

6. I have changed the names of factories and manufacturers.

7. Two Chinese owners were members of either the second or 1.5 generation. I interviewed only one Korean who classified himself as a member of the "knee-high generation," otherwise known as the 1.5 generation. I put him in that category because he classified himself in that way even though he emigrated when he was sixteen.

8. The three partners got their money from savings or by borrowing from parents and friends.

9. Some owners told me that they would use their share of the profits to pay off the loans they had received from their silent partners.

10. In many immigrant communities rotating credit associations or similar groups—both formal and informal—arise to pool money to make loan to individual members. Once the first loan is repaid, the sum is lent to another member. Thus the money pool becomes a form of rotating credit.

11. Only ninety-eight workers gave me information about their educational background. Percentages are based on the ninety-eight who answered.

12. A total of 106 workers interviewed gave answers about previous work experience. Percentages are based on the 106 who answered the question about the jobs they held in their home country.

13. Whole-garment piecework means that workers are paid according to how many whole garments they have sewn. Thus a brand new worker may sew only a few pieces, whereas a career garment worker can sew a hundred.

14. They are often given smaller-sized items to sew, so they can sew more pieces faster.

15. The Latinos who work in the delis and restaurants usually encourage male friends to seek jobs there.

16. Respectable Latinas are not supposed to be standing on the street. What I call the "for hire" corners are located at Eighth Avenue and 37th Street. At one point in 1994, the Fashion Industry–Business Industry Development District organized a "help wanted" bulletin board that was located on the southwest side of the street. This was discontinued after storeowners on the corner complained. However, the corners on the west side of the street, both north and south, became known to prospective Hispanic garment workers and the Korean shop owners. Hispanic workers continued to gather there (men on the south side and women on the north side—it is not considered proper for Latinas to stand on the same corner as the men to look for jobs), waiting for Korean owners to recruit them for work. Before this system began, workers would solicit work by going door to door.

17. According to the interviewees who discussed this aspect, getting a job at a grocery store or a restaurant is difficult for two reasons. First, groceries and restaurants hire fewer people than garment shops. The average restaurant or grocery store has ten or fewer employees, whereas a garment shop can hire forty or more. Second, restaurants and groceries mainly hire through personal recommendation. If a new immigrant knows only few people and has a small network of kin and friends, getting a job in food service is all the more difficult.

CHAPTER 5. WHAT EMPLOYERS WANT

1. *Immigrant incorporation* refers to how immigrants integrate culturally and economically. This chapter focuses on the ways that immigrants adapt economically in the New York City garment industry. The term *middleman minority economies* refers to the types of businesses minority entrepreneurs might have and where they might be located. In particular, middleman minorities are employers who hire employees of a different racial or ethnic group. Moreover, their businesses are situated in neighborhoods where the majority of people are of a different racial or ethnic group. Thus the employees or the community sometimes views the entrepreneur as an exploiter.

2. Koreans prefer to hire Mexicans and Ecuadorians, the two groups that have the most undocumented laborers in New York during the study period. Koreans also hire a few Dominicans and Central Americans. According to the Korean owners, many Dominican workers are documented and prefer to be paid by check, so that they have official documentation of their income. As a result, many choose not to work for Korean employers.

3. See Holzer (1996), Neckerman and Kirschenman (1991), and Wilson (1987).

4. This supports findings by Cheng and Espiritu (1989).

5. Workers probably feared that they would be fired or that they could handle the problem by discussing it directly with their coethnic employer.

6. As I will explain in a later chapter, Hispanic workers feel vulnerable when they personally recommend someone for a job. These workers also do not get any bonus or other incentive for bringing in friends and family as coworkers. Thus Hispanic workers will encourage others to join but do not want to be recognized as the "recommender" because of complications this new association might cause.

7. This makes sense because more Ecuadorians emigrated with a "visitor" visa, and those with higher socioeconomic status can get those visas more easily than the Mexicans can.

8. The Garment Workers' Justice Center was a UNITE-sponsored program with English and basic worker education classes.

9. If the workers are good and fast, owners sometimes (depending on the job market and season) retain these workers. This is when they offer the workers raises in their hourly rates.

Chapter 6. Landing Work

1. My interviewees were mostly Cantonese women, new immigrants in New York City.

2. See Granovetter's *Getting a Job* (1974) and Waldinger's *Still a Promised City* (1996).

3. The owner of the building where the posting site was located protested this use of his building wall. Eventually this location, the west side of 37th Street and Eighth Avenue, just evolved into the "for hire" corner, which workers and owners frequented to look for work and workers.

Chapter 7. The Bottom Line

1. A state labor department survey shows that 63 percent of companies in New York City's garment industry violate overtime or minimum wage laws (Greenhouse 1997).

2. The legal minimum wage in 1995, when I did my interviews, was $4.25 an hour.

3. Moreover, for those workers from rural China, the sewing shop wages are more than they received in China.

4. Chinese employers sometimes pay their employees with cash although at the same rate as the work that is paid by check.

5. See Michael Spence's 1973 work on job market signaling.

6. Sewers with various skills need to be placed on an assembly line according to the kinds of skilled work the factory has to sew. A more skilled person would sew elastic or fabrics that stretch or are slippery. Sewing armholes or other parts of a garment where the seam is curved also requires a skilled worker. A less skilled person would be assigned to sew a simple straight stitch on a piece of nonstretch cloth.

7. Piecework is an individualistic pay system. Individuals work as fast as they can to earn more money. Very often, the pay schedule is a problem of low rates for piecework, not a problem with uneven sewing paces.

8. Eight of the workers whom I interviewed owned their own homes, which had an average value of about $100,000. I did not ask when they bought their homes. These homes were located in Brooklyn and Queens.

9. Three undocumented Hispanic workers told me that they had gone to the Labor Department to complain of wage abuses after learning about wage regulations at classes and seminars held at the union's Garment Workers' Justice Center.

10. Moreover, according to a Labor Department official, the agency does not have enough inspectors to cover all the garment shops. So if it receives no complaints about a shop, the agency is unlikely to even inspect it.

APPENDIX. RESEARCH DESIGN AND METHODOLOGY

1. See chapters 1 and 2 for the ethnic breakdowns.

2. Some manufacturers want a "Made in the USA" label because customers value it. Customers pay more for U.S.-made goods because they believe that the workmanship is of higher quality than items made in certain foreign locations.

3. The Korean Contractors' Association is a voluntary membership organization of all the Korean-owned garment shops in the New York metropolitan area. Its membership lists more than four hundred Korean-owned concerns and, according to the organization, that list is 99 percent complete. The organization sponsors meetings with officials of and disseminates information from the Immigration and Naturalization Service, the New York State Department of Labor, the Occupational Safety and Health Administration, and the garment workers' union, among others, and holds a yearly banquet for the members. The organization also tries to represent Korean garment shop owners' concerns to city and local government.

4. The Korean owners that he contacted for me quizzed me on what I did in elementary school, middle school, and high school. They wanted to gain some insight or find a formula that would help their children follow my educational path. These Korean owners expressed an interest in sending their children to an Ivy League school. The Chinese were also impressed by my educational background but seemed much more interested in the U.S. educational process as a whole. They were less concerned than the Koreans were with the process of getting into an Ivy League school.

5. In New York the interviewees' socioeconomic statuses were fairly similar because the interviewees lived in neighborhoods with similar socioeconomic status.

6. Sometimes, when my translator and I arrived at the "for hire" corners at 7:30 or 8 A.M., Korean owners were already there, recruiting workers.

7. Only two of the Ecuadorian interviewees (from the ESL classes) said that they wanted to stay permanently in the United States. Although they had no one in mind during the interview, both said that they would try to legalize their status by marrying Puerto Ricans.

8. It is very hard for any of them to contemplate staying permanently because of their undocumented status. I think some will eventually stay here permanently, but they leave their status open (see Karparthakis 1993 on sojourners).

9. The entry script is the introduction I used to succinctly describe my study to all potential interviewees. The script was basically the same for all participants. Most agreed to be interviewed after they heard why I wanted to speak to them, and the money I used to compensate indicated that I was serious. I paid them at the end of the interview.

10. The National Science Foundation funding provided money for a Spanish translator as well as the $10 gratuities for the interviewees.

11. These few workers were newcomers, and Koreans were the only Asian ethnics they had met in New York City.

12. Some journalists and students have insisted on writing that the union is not critical of rates paid for piecework and therefore supports "sweatshops." Moreover, some are critical of the union and its assistance to undocumented workers.

13. For example, workers were required to punch the time clock at 8:30 A.M. and punch out at 5 P.M., but workers started work at 8 A.M. and left work at 6 P.M. The workers were paid $5 an hour from 8 A.M. 6 P.M. (minus 30 minutes for lunch) and were not given overtime, as the law requires.

14. The fees they were discussing were health insurance premiums of about $225 per quarter to ensure the worker, spouse, and children and $65 per quarter to insure the worker alone. At $900 a year, this was relatively expensive health insurance, but it pays for couples with children because uninsured medical appointments can cost $100–200 each. These costs can quickly become prohibitive when a worker has more than one child, and each healthy child averages three or four visits a year.

Abeles, Schwartz, Hacckel, and Silverblatt, Inc. 1983. *The Chinatown Garment Industry Study*. New York: Local 23-25, International Ladies' Garment Workers' Union and the New York Skirt and Sportswear Association.

Abelman, Nancy and John Lie. 1995. *Blue Dreams: Korean Americans and the Los Angeles Riots*. Cambridge, Mass.: Harvard University Press.

Asian American Federation of New York. 2002a. "Chinatown After September 11: An Economic Impact Study—An Interim Report." New York, April.

———. 2002b. "Chinatown One Year After September 11: An Economic Impact Study. New York, November.

Bailey, Thomas and Roger Waldinger. 1991. "Primary, Secondary, and Enclave Labor Markets: A Training Systems Approach." *American Sociological Review* 56:432–45.

Bao, Xiaolan. 2001. *"Holding Up More Than Half the Sky": Chinese Women Garment Workers in New York City, 1948–1992*. Urbana: University of Illinois Press.

Bonacich, Edna. 1973. "A Theory of Middleman Minorities." *American Sociological Review* 38:583–94.

Bonacich, Edna and Richard P. Appelbaum. 2000. *Behind the Label*. Berkeley: University of California Press.

Bonacich, Edna and John Modell. 1980. *The Economic Basis of Ethnic Solidarity*. Berkeley: University of California Press.

Bonacich, Edna et al. 1994. "The Garment Industry in the Restructuring Economy." In Bonacich et al., *Global Production: The Apparel Industry in the Pacific Rim*. Philadelphia: Temple University Press.

Bowles, Jonathan. 2000. "The Empire Has No Clothes." Report for the Center for an Urban Future, New York, February 19.

Cheng, Lucie and Yen Espiritu. 1989. "Korean Businesses in Black and Hispanic Neighborhoods: A Study of Intergroup Relations." *Sociological Perspectives* 32 (4): 521–34.

Chin, Margaret M. Forthcoming. "Moving On: Garment Workers After 9/11." In Foner, *Wounded City*.

Chinatown Study Group. 1970. "Chinatown Report: 1969." Columbia University East Asian Studies Center, New York.

Corcoran, Mary P. 1993. *Irish Illegals: Transients Between two Societies*. Westport, Conn.: Greenwood.

Dugger, Celia W. 1997. "For Half a Million: This Is Still the New World." *New York Times*, January 12, 1997. p. 27.

Foderaro, Lisa W. 1998. "'Made in New York' Is Coming Back into Fashion." *New York Times*, January 13, p. B7.

Foner, Nancy. 1986. "Sex Roles and Sensibilities: Jamaican Women in New York and London." In Rita James Simon and Caroline B. Brettell, eds., *International Migration: The Female Experience*. Totowa, N.J.: Rowman and Allanheld.

———. 2000. *From Ellis Island to JFK: New York's Two Great Waves of Immigration*. New York: Russell Sage Foundation and Yale University Press.

———, ed. Forthcoming. *Wounded City: The Social Effects of the World Trade Center Attack on New York City*. New York: Russell Sage Foundation Press.

Friedman, Tami J. 1992. "From Peking to Pell Street." Master's thesis, Columbia University.

Gamber, Wendy. 1997. *The Female Economy: The Millinery and Dressmaking Trades, 1860–1930*. Urbana: University of Illinois Press.

Glenn, Evelyn Nakano. 1983. "Split Household, Small Producer, and Dual Wage Earner: An Analysis of Chinese-American Family Strategies." *Journal of Marriage and Family* 45 (February): 35–46.

Glenn, Susan Anita. 1990. *Daughters of the Shtetl: Life and Labor in the Immigrant Generation*. Ithaca, N.Y.: Cornell University.

Gold, Steven J. 1992. *Refugee Communities*. Newbury Park, Calif.: Sage.

Granovetter, Mark. 1974. *Getting a Job*. Cambridge, Mass.: Harvard University Press.

———. 1985. "Economic Action and Social Structure: The Problem of Embeddedness." *American Journal of Sociology* 91, no. 3 (November 1985): 481–510.

Grasmuck, Sherri and Patricia R. Pessar. 1991. *Between Two Islands: Dominican International Migration*. Berkeley: University of California Press.

Green, Nancy L. 1997. *Ready to Wear and Ready to Work: A Century of Industry and Immigrants in Paris and New York*. Durham, N.C.: Duke University Press.

Greenhouse, Steven. 1997. "Garment Shops Found to Break Wage Laws." *New York Times*, October 17, p. B1.

Grieco, Margaret. 1987. *Keeping It in the Family: Social Networks and Employment Chance*. New York: Tavistock.

Hall, Max, ed. 1959. *Made in New York: Case Studies in Metropolitan Manufacturing*. Cambridge, Mass.: Harvard University Press.

Helfgott, Roy. 1959a. "Puerto Rican Integration in the Skirt Industry in New York City." In Aaron Antonovsky and Lewis Lorwin, eds., *Discrimination and Low Incomes*. New York: New York Interdepartmental Committee on Low Incomes.

———. 1959b. "Women's and Children's Apparel," pp. 21–134. In Hall, *Made in New York*.

Hendricks, Glenn. 1974. *The Dominican Diaspora*. New York: Teachers College Press.

Holzer, Harry J. 1996. *What Employers Want: Job Prospects for Less Educated Workers*. New York: Russell Sage Foundation.

Hondagneu-Sotelo, Pierrette. 1994. *Gendered Transitions: Mexican Experiences of Immigration*. Berkeley: University of California Press.

Howe, Irving. 1976. *World of Our Fathers*. New York: Harcourt Brace Jovanovich.

Hum, Tarry. 2003. "Mapping Global Production in New York City's Garment Industry: The Role of Sunset Park, Brooklyn's Immigrant Economy." *Economic Development Quarterly* 17, no. 3 (August): 294–309.

Jacoby, Sanford M. 1985. *Employing Bureaucracy: Managers, Unions, and the Transformation of Work in American Industry, 1900–1945*. New York: Columbia University Press.

Jensen, Lief and Alejandro Portes. 1992. "Correction." *American Sociological Review* 57:411–14.

Kang, Miliann. 1997. "Manicuring Race, Gender and Class: Service Interactions in New York City Korean owned Nail Salons." *Race, Gender and Class* 4 (3): 142–64.

Karpathakis, Anna. 1993. "Greek Sojourners." Ph.D. diss., Columbia University.

Kasinitz, Philip, Gregory Smithsimon, and Binh Pok. Forthcoming. "Disaster at the Doorstep: Battery Park City and Tribeca Respond to the Events of 9/11." In Foner, *Wounded City*.

Kessner, Thomas. 1977. *The Golden Door: Italian and Jewish Immigrant Mobility in New York City 1880–1915*. New York: Oxford University Press.

Kim, Dae Young. 1999. "Beyond Co-ethnic Solidarity: Mexican and Ecuadorian Employment in Korean-owned business in New York City." *Ethnic and Racial Studies* 22 (May): 581–605.

Kim, Illsoo. 1981. *New Urban Immigrants: The Korean Community in New York*. Princeton, N.J.: Princeton University Press.

Kinkead, Gwen. 1992. *Chinatown: A Portrait of a Closed Society*. New York: Harper Collins.

Kurt Salmon Associates, Inc. 1992. "Keeping New York in Fashion." Report prepared for the Garment Industry Development Corporation, New York.

Kwong, Peter. 1987. *The New Chinatown*. New York: Noonday Press.

Laurentz, Robert. 1980. "Racial/Ethnic Conflict in the New York City Garment Industry, 1933–1980." Ph.D. diss., State University of New York, Binghamton.

Lee, Jennifer. 1998. "Cultural Brokers: Race-based Hiring in Inner City Neighborhoods." *American Behavior Scientist* 41:927–37.

———. 1999. "Retail Niche Domination Among African American, Jewish, Korean Entrepreneurs." *American Behavior Scientist* 42:1398–1416.

Levitan, Mark. 1998. *Opportunity at Work: The New York City Garment Industry*. New York: Community Service Society.

Lieberson, Stanley. 1980. *A Piece of the Pie: Blacks and White Immigrants Since 1880*. Berkeley: University of California Press.

Light, Ivan. 1972. *Ethnic Enterprise in America*. Berkeley: University of California Press.

Light, Ivan and Edna Bonacich. 1988. *Immigrant Entrepreneurs*. Berkeley: University of California Press.

Lorwin, Louis. 1924. *The Women's Garment Workers*. New York: Huebsch.

Massey, Douglas et al. 1987–90. *Return to Aztlan: The Social Process of International Migration from Western Mexico.* Berkeley: University of California Press.

Min, Pyong Gap. 1996. *Caught in the Middle: Korean Communities in New York and Los Angeles.* Berkeley: University of California Press.

Neckerman, Kathryn and Joleen Kirschenman. 1991. "Hiring Strategies, Racial Bias, and Inner-City Workers." *Social Problems* 38:433–47.

Northrup, Herbert R. 1944. *Organized Labor and the Negro.* New York: Harper.

Odencrantz, Louise C. 1919/1977. *Italian Women in Industry.* New York: Arno.

Ortiz, Altagracia. 1996. "'En la aguja y el pedal eche la hiel': Puerto Rican Women in the Garment Industry of New York City, 1920–80." In Altagracia Ortiz, ed., *Puerto Rican Women and Work: Bridges in Transnational labor.* Philadelphia: Temple University Press.

Park, Kyeyoung. 1997. *The Korean American Dream: Immigrants and Small Business in New York City.* Ithaca, N.Y.: Cornell University Press.

Pessar, Patricia R. 1989. "The Linkage Between the Household and Workplace of Dominican Women in the U.S." *International Migration Review* 18 (4): 1188–1211

Polanyi, Karl. [1944] 1957. *The Great Transformation.* Boston: Beacon.

Pope, Jesse Eliphalet. 1905. *The Clothing Industry in New York.* Columbia: University of Missouri.

Portes, Alejandro, ed. 1995. *The Economic Sociology of Immigration: Essays on Networks, Ethnicity, and Entrepreneurship.* New York: Russell Sage Foundation.

Portes, Alejandro and Robert L. Bach. 1985. *The Latin Journey: Cuban and Mexican Immigrants in the United States.* Berkeley: University of California Press.

Portes, Alejandro and Leif Jensen. 1989. "The Enclave and the Entrants: Patterns of Ethnic Enterprise in Miami Before and After Mariel." *American Sociological Review* 54:929–49.

Portes, Alejandro and Ruben G. Rumbaut. 1990. *Immigrant America: A Portrait.* Berkeley: University of California Press.

Ragin, Charles C. 1987. *The Comparative Method: Moving Beyond Qualitative and Quantitative Strategies.* Berkeley: University of California Press.

Rischin, Moses. 1962. *The Promised City: New York's Jews, 1870–1914.* Cambridge, Mass.: Harvard University Press.

Salzinger, Leslie. 2003. *Genders in Production: Making Workers in Mexico's Global Factories.* Berkeley: University of California Press.

Sanders, Jimy and Victor Nee. 1987. "Limits of Ethnic Solidarity in the Ethnic Economy." *American Sociological Review* 52:745–67.

———. 1992. "Comment." *American Sociological Review* 57:415–17.

Sassen-Koob, Saskia. 1983. "Labor Migration and the New Industrial Division of Labor." In June Nash and Maria Patricia Fernandez-Kelly, eds., *Women, Men and the International Division of Labor.* Albany: State University of New York Press.

Schatzman, Leonard and Anselm L. Strauss. 1973. *Field Research: Strategies for a Natural Sociology.* Englewood Cliffs, N.J.: Prentice-Hall.

Seidman, Joel. 1942. *The Needle Trades.* New York: Farrar and Rinehart.

Smith, Robert C. 1994. "'Doubly Bounded' Solidarity: Race and Social Location in the Incorporation of Mexicans into New York City." Paper presented at Social Science

Research Council's Conference of Fellows: Program of Research on the Urban Underclass, University of Michigan, June.

———. 1996. "Mexicans in New York: Membership and Incorporation in a New Immigrant Community." In Gabriel Haslip-Viera and Sherrie L. Baver, eds., *Latinos in New York*. Notre Dame, Ind.: University of Notre Dame Press.

———. 1997. "Racial and Ethnic Hierarchies and the Incorporation of Mexicans in New York City: Transnational Communities and Labor Market Niches." Paper presented at the Transnational Communities and the Political Economy of New York City in the 1990s Conference.

Spence, Michael. 1973. "Job Market Signaling." *Quarterly Journal of Economics* 87:355–74.

Spero, Sterling D. and Abram L. Harris. 1931. *The Black Worker*. New York: Columbia University Press.

Tilly, Charles. 1997. "Chain Migration and Opportunity Hoarding." In Janina Dacyl, ed., *The Management of Cultural Pluralism*. Paris: UNESCO.

U.S. Bureau of the Census. 1992. *Immigration to Selected Metropolitan Areas in 1990*. 1992 Statistical Abstract of the United States. Washington, D.C.: U.S. Department of Commerce.

Waldinger, Roger. 1986. *Through the Eye of the Needle: Immigrants and Enterprise in New York's Garment Trades*. New York: New York University Press.

———. 1995. "The 'Other Side' of Embeddedness: A Case Study of the Interplay of Economy and Ethnicity." *Ethnic and Racial Studies* 18 (July): 555–80.

———. 1996. *Still the Promised City: African Americans and New Immigrants in Postindustrial New York*. Cambridge, Mass.: Harvard University Press.

Waldinger, Roger and Howard E. Aldrich. 1990. "Ethnicity and Entrepreneurship." *Annual Review of Sociology* 16:111–135.

Waldinger, Roger and Michael I. Lichter. 2003. *How the Other Half Works: Immigration and the Social Organization of Labor*. Berkeley: University of California Press.

Waldinger, Roger et al. 1990. *Ethnic Entrepreneurs: Immigrant Business in Industrial Societies*. Vol. 1. Sage Series on Race and Ethnic Relations. Newbury Park, Calif.: Sage.

Waters, Mary. 1999. *Black Identities: West Indian Immigrant Dreams and American Realities*. New York: Russell Sage Foundation and Harvard University Press.

Wilson, Kenneth L. and Alejandro Portes. 1980. "Immigrant Enclaves: An Analysis of the Labor Market Experiences of Cubans in Miami." *American Journal of Sociology* 86 (2): 135–60.

Wilson, William Julius. 1987. *The Truly Disadvantaged*. Chicago: University of Chicago Press.

Wong, Bernard. 1987. "The Chinese: New Immigrants in New York's Chinatown," pp. 243–72. In Nancy Fong, ed., *New Immigrants in New York*. New York: Columbia University Press.

———. 1988. *Patronage, Brokerage, Entrepreneurship in the Chinese Community of NY*. New York: AMS Press.

Wrong, Elaine Gale. 1974. *The Negro in the Apparel Industry*. Philadelphia: Industrial Research Unit, Wharton School, University of Pennsylvania.

Yoon, In-Jin. 1997. *On My Own: Korean Businesses and Race Relations in America.* Chicago: University of Chicago Press.

Zhou, Min. 1992. *Chinatown: The Socioeconomic Potential of an Urban Enclave.* Philadelphia: Temple University Press.

Zhou, Min and John Logan. 1989. "Returns on Human Capital in Ethnic Enclaves: New York City's Chinatown." *American Sociological Review* 54:809–20.